SUMTER

By the same author

American Talk
The Dictionary of Eponyms (originally *Human Words*)
More Cunning than Man
The Great American Chewing Gum Book: A Social History
The Grand Emporiums
The Literary Life

SUMTER

The First Day of
The Civil War

ROBERT HENDRICKSON

PROMONTORY
PRESS

First published by Promontory Press in 1996.

Promontory Press
A division of Budget Book Service, Inc.
386 Park Avenue South
New York, NY 10016

Promontory Press is a registered trademark of Budget Book Service, Inc.

Published by arrangement with Scarborough House/Publishers.

Library of Congress Catalog Card Number: 96-67468

ISBN: 0-88394-095-7

Printed in the United States of America.

For my grandson, Chris

War! An arm'd race is advancing! The welcome for battle, no turning away; War! Be it weeks, months, or years, an arm'd race is advancing to welcome it.

—Walt Whitman

CONTENTS

ILLUSTRATIONS

Fort Sumter on the eve of war
President James Buchanan
Secretary of War John B. Floyd
General Winfield Scott
President Abraham Lincoln
Gustavus Vasa Fox
Secretary of State Seward
All of Sumter's officers
Major Anderson with wife and son
South Carolina Governor Francis W. Pickens
Old Fire-eater Edmund Ruffin
Robert Barnwell Rhett, Sr.
Robert Barnwell Rhett, Jr.
Judge James Louis Petigru
Virginia Congressman Roger Pryor
Texas Senator Lewis T. Wigfall
Confederate President Jefferson Davis
Confederate Secretary of State Robert Toombs
General Beauregard
Fort Sumter
South Carolina flag and motto
South Carolina Secession Convention banner
Secession Hall in Charleston
Secessionists rallying in Charleston
Fort Moultrie
Evacuation of Fort Moultrie
Union troops landing at Fort Sumter
Gun carriages burning at Fort Moultrie
Families of the Sumter defenders
Carolinians at the U.S. Arsenal
The U.S. Custom House, Charleston
Castle Pinckney
The *Star of the West*

The reader should be aware that some of the old prints reproduced are not accurate in all respects. These prints, published in contemporary newspapers, magazines, and books noted in each picture caption, were often done by artists who never saw Sumter, although most did visit the scene of the battle shortly after it ended. The *Harper's Weekly* drawings by Theodore R. Davis, for example, were made by the 21-year-old artist two days after Sumter fell, when he traveled to Charleston with William Howard Russell of the *London Times*. Davis told Southerners he was from the *Illustrated London News* rather than have doors slammed in his face as a representative of the hated Yankee *Harper's*.

PREFACE

In writing of the first battle of the Civil War, I have tried to be as objective as possible and report the courage and cowardice, the profundity and folly on both sides, if there can be any real profundity in any battle or any war on any side. Much research over many years has gone into this work, and it is my belief, based on numerous sources North and South, that the persistent popular notion of the glorious siege of Sumter is far from true. I should note that I have included these sources in the text whenever necessary, rather than annoy the reader with distracting footnotes. As John Barrymore said, "A footnote is like running downstairs to answer the doorbell during the first night of marriage."

Many people assisted me in writing *Sumter,* but space limits me to only a heartfelt general thank-you to all the librarians, archivists, and scholars who were of so much help. I would, however, especially like to thank my distinguished teacher Dr. Robert Ernst, whose integrity as a scholar has long inspired me. Thanks also to my editors Benton Arnovitz, who has worked closely with me on many projects in the past, Bill Fryer, and Patricia Day, who guided this book to press and made many valuable suggestions. To my wife, Marilyn, as always, my deepest love and gratitude for everything.

—Robert Hendrickson
Far Rockaway, NY
July 22, 1989

SUMTER

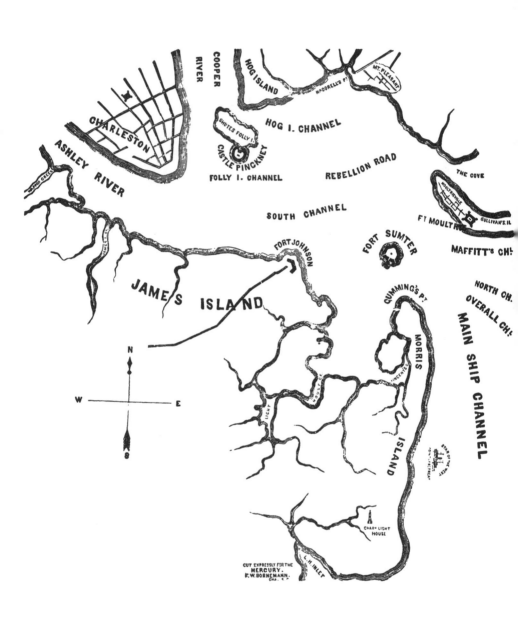

COOPER RIVER

CHARLESTON

HOG ISLAND

MT. PLEASANT

MADDRELL'S P?

SHUTES FOLLY I.

HOG I. CHANNEL

CASTLE PINCKNEY

ASHLEY RIVER

WAPPO CREEK

FOLLY I. CHANNEL

REBELLION ROAD

THE COVE

MOULTRIEVILLE

SOUTH CHANNEL

SULLIVAN'S I.

FT MOULTRIE

FORT JOHNSON

FORT SUMTER

MAFFITT's CH?

JAMES ISLAND

CUMMING'S P?

NORTH CH.

VINCENT'S

OVERALL CH?

N

MORRIS

MAIN SHIP CHANNEL

W ——— E

LIGHT

FOLLY CK.

ISLAND

STAR OF THE WEST

S

CHAR? LIGHT HOUSE

CUT EXPRESSLY FOR THE
MERCURY.
F. W. BORNEMANN.
CHA. S?

L. H. INLET

The Fire-eaters

Breathes there the man with soul so dead,
    Who never to himself hath said,
      "This is my own, my native land!" . . .
If such there breathe . . .
The wretch . . .
. . . doubly dying, shall go down
To the vile dust from whence he sprung,
Unwept, unhonour'd, and unsung.
               —Sir Walter Scott,
                  "Patriotism"

THE Civil War, in which brothers would kill 700,000 brothers, one out of every four soldiers involved, one out of every fifty Americans, ranks second only to the Napoleonic Wars in bloodletting, inflicting wounds that still haven't healed. But the opening battle of that war, exciting as it would be, was in fact a preposterous prelude to the tragedy that followed. Fort Sumter might be called the last romantic battle of the old wars, although it ushered in the first of the new or total wars involving conscripted unprofessional soldiers, bombardment of civilian populations, prison pens as vile as concentration camps, and other cloacae of modern history. Though it did contain many of the seeds for future horrors, Sumter was as absurdly romantic as any battle could be.

The events leading up to the battle and the siege itself are especially notable for the often inane, usually vain, and always colorful characters on both sides. This spectacular two-ring circus included—to spotlight but a few—a President with a broken heart and broken will who rarely looked any man or issue in the eye; a U.S. senator dressed like a pirate who plotted to kidnap the President; a secretary of war who acted as if he were employed by the enemy; a gouty, waddling, three-hundred-pound general; acned schoolboys and doddering old men firing cannon at each other; chivalry who dined and danced at balls and picnics while watching the shells exploding overhead; and even a babe-in-arms rumored to have fired the first shot. Dickens himself could or would not have assembled in one place such an improbable cast of curiosities; it was a task better suited to P. T. Barnum.

Though Fort Sumter's roots reach back to the beginnings of the slave trade and beyond (see Appendix I), the battle for the "impregnable fortress" three miles out in Charleston Harbor, and the prelude to it, probably began in earnest with the delegates flocking toward the South Carolina Secessionist Convention early on December 17, 1860, a little over a month after Abraham Lincoln won the presidency. Foremost among these delegates, or perhaps the most ludicrous among them, was that old Lochinvar from out of Virginia, Edmund P. Ruffin, a phenomenon beyond compare who, tradition holds (wrongly), fired the first shot at Fort Sumter early in the morning of April 12, 1861.

"So faithful in love, and so dauntless in war, / There never was knight like the young Lochinvar!" Ruffin did love his Sir Walter Scott, like all the Southern lads, but this lad, a veteran of the War of 1812, was pushing sixty-seven years old. Partially deaf, Ruffin never could clearly hear what people were telling him and rarely cared anyway. This archsecessionist with hardened political arteries even had a good word for his fellow fanatic John Brown. The terrorist with a "face like a meat axe" may have slaughtered people in Bloody Kansas for disagreeing with his antislavery views, believing that God had ordained him to "break the jaws of the wicked," but Ruffin could understand that. "It is impossible for me not to respect his thorough devotion to his bad cause," Ruffin once testified, "and the undaunted courage with which he has sustained it, through all losses and hazards." However, his admiration for the paranoid abolitionist (nine relatives on Brown's mother's side, six of his first cousins, two of his children, and his wife died insane) hadn't stopped him from journeying to Charles Town, Virginia (later West Virginia), on December 2, 1859, to watch Brown of Osawatomie, who had been captured by a contingent of marines led by a colonel named Robert E. Lee, swing from the gallows for multiple murders and treason at Harpers Ferry. The boy actor John Wilkes Booth, then in the ranks of the Virginia Militia, stood salivating in the crowd only a few feet away. As Herman Melville described it, "weird John Brown hung there, white muslin hood over his eyes, slippers on his feet, his streaming beard the meteor of the war."

Charles Town wasn't all that far from Ruffin's plantation on the Pamunkey River in Virginia's Prince George County. Here the old man had made his considerable fortune pioneering in soil chemistry and improving a starving land worn out by the tobacco cash crop by adding to it marl, a soil that contains calcium carbonate. Against much opposition Ruffin proved the value of this practice. His *An Essay on Calcerous Manures* (1832) became the classic work on the subject, and his periodical *The Farmer's Register,* which he founded and edited until 1842, was regarded as an essential publication by agriculturists and dirt farmers alike. Along with fame came riches, including a huge plantation and over two hundred slaves, but while sweetening up "sour" land, he himself seemed to have soured on life a bit. Like many eccentric geniuses, Ruffin became discontented in the winter of his life with what he thought was his narrow lot, no matter how many thousands of acres he owned, and looked to expand his holdings. The all-knowing specialist became the mile-wide-inch-deep generalist with all the answers. If he had saved the soil with marl, he reasoned, he could surely save the land with his philosophy. Actually, he would live to see that philosophy bring the land back full circle to starvation again.

The Farmer's Register eventually failed because of its vicious editorials against banks, and thereafter Ruffin devoted himself exclusively to the cause of states' rights and secession. He joined the ranks of the Southern fire-eaters, those proslavery extremists who included William Lowndes Yancey, author of the 1848 Alabama Platform, which demanded that Congress protect slavery in the territories and soon became the creed of the whole South, and the redoubtable Robert Barnwell Rhett, a U.S. senator, Charleston newspaper publisher, and incendiary secessionist who even favored restoration of the slave trade. It was Rhett's idea for America to conquer all the warmer regions of the world with the South's black slaves. As he reasoned in an 1859 Independence Day speech: "Let the North colonize the colder regions, where the white man can labor advantageously in the fields for the productions of nature. We with the African, will possess the rest." In the same speech he remarked that "all governments have their bigots and fanatics," never thinking that he referred to himself.

Of the major radicals or fire-eaters perhaps only Ruffin and Yancey might be called Southern nationalists, the others caring more for their individual states than for a united South, which to them held value mostly as an alliance against the North. The vice-president-to-be of the Confederacy, boyish-looking Alexander H. Stephens, for example, wrote in prison after the war: "My native land, my country, the only one that is country to me, is Georgia." Ruffin and Yancey, on the other hand, envisioned a South united by shared distinctive qualities, and they cared for the whole more than any of its parts. After Lincoln's election Ruffin had written, "If Virginia remains in the Union under the domination of this infamous, low, vulgar tyranny of Black Republicanism, and there is one other state in the Union that has bravely thrown off the yoke, I will seek domicile in that state and abandon Virginia forever."

In any case, the fire-eaters, Southern nationalists or not, had urged secession upon the South as early as their Nashville convention of 1850, but Henry Clay's compromise of that year (allowing California to enter the Union as a free state yet leaving other new territories the freedom to determine whether they would permit slavery) had postponed the matter for almost a decade.

Ruffin was a sort of grand old man among the "Southrons," as Southern patriots, or "statriots," often called themselves. Like most of the Southrons, he believed that the election of "Black Republican" Abraham Lincoln had come as a divine answer to his prayers. Though he had voted for John C. Breckinridge, the prophet of secession, he had actually prayed for Lincoln's victory on his knees at night, hoping that with the election of this "vulgar mobocrat and Southern hater," as Rhett's vitriolic *Charleston Mercury* called him, South Carolina and the rest of the South would be more likely to secede from the Union. Ruffin believed, as another down-home newspaper put it, that before the South accepted Lincoln as President she would "see the Potomac crimsoned in human gore, and Pennsylvania Avenue paved ten fathoms deep with mangled bodies," a prediction that would certainly have come true if all the future Civil War dead, all the hundreds of thousands, could have been carted to Washington and dumped in the streets.

But prayers to God weren't nearly enough to occupy Edmund P. Ruffin, "the Virginia Volcano." Neither were the Ladies' Shooting Clubs Ruffin organized to teach Southern womanhood self-defense, nor his street-corner harangues, nor the inflamatory pamphlets he wrote and handed out. Ruffin had even gotten hold of some of the one thousand long pikes John Brown commissioned to be made (no one knows exactly why) for his tiny band of followers, obviously expecting its ranks would swell by the hundreds. These Ruffin brought home from the Charles Town hanging, reserving one to carry with him on his travels and sending one to the governor of every Southern state along with a request that it be prominently displayed in the capitol. He demanded that each pike be labeled: "Sample of the Favors Designed for Us by Our Northern Brethren."

Ruffin wanted action and, tired of too-genteel Virginia, headed toward South Carolina to get it. The old man wasn't as bloody-minded and callous as Old Osawatomie, who had answered his son's painful death cries at Harpers Ferry with a curt, "If you must die, die like a man," but not even his darling daughter Elizabeth's recent death in childbirth could keep him from the hotbed of secession in South Carolina. He did grieve for Elizabeth, but he was strangely happy, glad to put his head in the lion's mouth. Later he would say of his days in Charleston participating in the attack on Fort Sumter, "The time I have been here has been the happiest of my life."

Plowing through nine inches of snow a heavy storm had deposited on his plantation that early December in 1860, a John Brown pike in hand, Ruffin made his way by carriage, steamboat, and train toward Columbia, South Carolina, to join the secessionists. Greeted there by friends and fellow "Seceshes," he gave a brief speech in the Congaree House lobby, declaring that secession, not marl, had been the one great idea of his life. He firmly believed that "the first drop of blood spilled on the soil of South Carolina" would unite the South. "The defense of the South, I verily believe," he attested, "can only be secured through the lead of South Carolina. As old as I am, I have come here to join in that lead." But he soon learned that the secessionist convention had been forced to move from Columbia to Charleston due to an epidemic of smallpox, and quickly caught a train to the new site, arriving just in time.

No place in America could have been more appropriate for a secessionist convention than Charleston, South Carolina, with her long tradition of resistance to the Federal government and blind, fanatic support of the South's "peculiar institution." "Secession is the fashion here," an English newspaper correspondent would write of the state and Charleston in particular. "Young ladies sing for it; old ladies pray for it; young men are dying to fight for it; old men are ready to demonstrate it."

Even to Southerners, South Carolinians seemed outspoken and hotheaded on the questions of secession and slavery, and Northerners regarded South Carolinians as "factious, querulous, headstrong and loud-mouthed," according to a history of the day. As far back as Nat Turner's Virginia slave rebellion in 1831, when fifty-five whites were killed and seventeen blacks hanged for their murders, South Carolinians had burned abolitionist tracts in the U.S. Post Office in Charleston. Of the more than 250 rebellions by slaves over the previous two centuries, many had been put down in the area around Charleston, notably the aborted 1822 revolt of Denmark Vesey, which resulted in the hanging of thirty-five slaves and inspired "slave codes" restricting slaves throughout the South. In 1827 a protective tariff that crippled the South's cotton trade with England inspired Thomas Cooper, president of South Carolina College, to question whether "it is worthwhile to continue the Union of States, where the North demands to be our masters and we are required to be their tributaries."

The following year came what South Carolinians called the Tariff of Abominations, which the South Carolina legislature condemned, appending to its formal resolution an unsigned essay by Vice-President John C. Calhoun, a former senator from South Carolina. The essay argued that a state convention could nullify any Federal law it considered unconstitutional. This led to an 1832 state ordinance nullifying two Federal tariff acts and adopting military measures to enforce the ordinance, even calling for secession if the Federal government resorted to force. President Jackson reinforced all the Federal forts in Charleston Harbor at the time, personally dispatching General Winfield Scott to control the nullifiers, and issued a proclamation that no state can secede from the Union. Confrontation seemed inevitable, but the "Great Compromiser," Henry Clay, saved the Union by working out a bill including a gradual cutback in tariffs, leading South Carolina to suspend its nullification ordinance. The state, however, had shown King Jackson that she would resort to civil war to defend what she considered her inalienable rights, even raising a volunteer unit to repel any Federal invasion Old Hickory might order. As for Jackson, he remained as tough as ever, telling the governor of Virginia, who had vowed that Federal troops would pass through Virginia to South Carolina only over his dead body, that as commander-in-chief he would not only lead Federal troops through Virginia over the governor's body, if necessary—he would also cut both ears off that dead body before he passed.

The delegates to the December 1860 South Carolina Secessionist Convention, like the aged Ruffin himself, would never call the bloody war on the horizon the Civil War. Yankee terms weren't for them; many of these hard-core secessionists, like Ruffin, considered *Webster's Dictionary* "Yankee trash." Like the Virginia Volcano, they, too, were already talking about the War of Secession, or the War for Southern Independence, or the Second War of Independence (to their minds it was an extension of the Revolutionary War), or the War for Constitutional Liberty, or Mr. Lincoln's War, or even the War to Suppress Yankee Arrogance. No one had yet called it the Lost Cause.

Present at the convention were the entire South Carolina state government, Charlestonian statriots and secessionists from all over the South, including four past U.S. senators, the governor of Florida, a former U.S. attorney general, and official representatives sent by Mississippi and Alabama. Ruffin counted 169 delegates in all, each man, no matter where he hailed from, at home in this haven of secessionists.

Convivial Charleston was the largest seaport south of Baltimore, which gave an international flavor to the beautiful, graceful town where America's closest counterpart to a landed aristocracy had built a charming vista of red brick and white marble, the quaint houses standing with their verandas facing the ocean to catch the sea breeze. Here planters from the up-country came to their town houses for the winter social season. The walled gardens with rows of orange trees and bountiful flowers were unexcelled in America, and Mary Boykin Chesnut, wife of U.S. Senator James Chesnut, exulted in her famous Civil War diary that Charleston's roses were unrivaled in all the world. On this little peninsula bounded by the Ashley and Cooper rivers were imposing churches; the College of Charleston, which in the 1850s counted Louis Agassiz among its faculty; and the Bond Street Theatre, where the world-famous diva, Adelina Patti, had appeared just a few weeks before.

The low, narrow peninsula of Charleston jutted into the water where her two great rivers met and flowed out to sea. Long regarded as a kind of Venice on the Atlantic, the city was built on mud filled with ballast and protected against tide and storm by huge walls of crushed oyster shell called tabby. An old joke, told not without pride, had it that "the Ashley and Cooper rivers come together to form the Atlantic Ocean here." Since the days of its chief lord proprietor, Lord Anthony Ashley Cooper, eponym of both rivers embracing it, the city had been a proud, aristocratic one, especially unique in a land founded on the principle that all men are created equal. For Lord Ashley at the very beginning planned the settlement to be a bastion of the aristocratic form of government, a miniature England in the New World where gentlemen would rule, and he went so far as to hire philosopher John Locke to devise Fundamental Constitutions for it that eschewed "a too numerous democracy."

The high-toned Charlestonian "aristocracy," however, would always be one of wealth and excellence rather than heredity. It started with people like the enterprising Manigaults— Huguenots in a city offering religious freedom to all—who escaped persecution in France and worked the land here, building great plantations that made them one of the three wealthiest families in America by the time of the Revolution. Planters like the Manigaults made their fortunes in rice, a packet of which Captain John Thurber, a Yankee shipmaster, had presented to one of the early settlers on putting into Charleston harbor late in the 1680s. The settler planted this Madagascar rice rather than dining on it, and after it sprouted, he gave seed to his friends, who in turn raised rice on their fertile land. Charleston and the Carolina Low Country soon became the "Rice Coast," rice fortunes building Charleston and marking the beginning of a plantocracy considered by many, especially itself, the New World aristocracy. The only crops that rivaled rice in the region were cotton and indigo, a dye plant introduced in the early eighteenth century that did more to enrich South Carolinians than New World gold did for the Spaniards.

The Fire-eaters

Rice, along with cotton and indigo, made possible a small oligarchy. Its members were often educated in England in order "to mix with their equals," and they lived the good life in Charleston, building their distinctive tall mansions with long piazzas and making the city a fragrant garden of camellias, gardenias, jasmine, oleanders, and other flowering shrubs imported from all over the world. The beautiful blush noisette rose variety was crossed in Charleston by plantsman Philip Noisette in 1816, and while serving as the first American minister to Mexico in 1825, Joel Roberts Poinsett, a distinguished Charlestonian, sent home specimens of the gorgeously colored poinsettias that bear his name. Since 1741 the city had boasted Middleton Gardens, built by one hundred slaves over ten years and filled with live oaks, camellias, and a world of colorful flowers. Property along the Battery, one of America's most majestic avenues, was so valuable that the houses were designed with narrow fronts so as to conserve expensive waterfront footage.

Charlestonians even then were developing their own southern accent, consisting of a smattering of Old English, a sea-island lilt, and soft southern tones, although they were often taken for Britons or Scots. The Battery in their dialect was pronounced *bottry*; a virgin was a *version*; the heart, the *hot*; a fence, a *faints*; and the mayor, the *mare*. One persistent old joke even has the Civil War itself resulting from the Carolinian dialect. It seems that three high-ranking Northern generals stomped into a Washington, D.C., bar and shouted, "We want a bottle right away!" A Carolinian spy, and there were many of them, overheard and telegraphed Jefferson Davis: "Top Union generals want a battle right away." Chivalrous Davis obliged, sending General Beauregard to Charleston, where he gave them the bottle, or battle, of Fort Sumter.

Since the early eighteenth century, Charleston had been a rich, cultivated, international city, unrivaled in these respects by any city in the South save New Orleans. Its first theater was built on Dock Street in 1736, and London players frequently crossed the Atlantic to present the latest dramas. There were Philharmonic concerts, balls, and innumerable elegant dinners. Renowned authors like William Gilmore Simms and Henry Timrod, the tubercular "laureate of the Confederacy" whose most famous work would be his "Ode" to the Confederate dead, called the city

27

home; Robert Mills and other brilliant architects designed her buildings, famous for their distinctive doorways and decorative ironwork. With their beautiful homes, splendid formal gardens, fine private libraries, racehorses, and grand cotillions, dressed in all the latest fashions of the day, the planters of Charleston were noted for their "refinement, intelligence and hospitality." In the minds of most of Charleston's white inhabitants, planter was an honorable term that was almost a title and indicated a versatile Renaissance man.

But, like a huge open sewer running through and defacing the charming landscape, the enslavement of other men, women, and children made the planters' elegant lifestyle possible and made all the chivalry false. South Carolina at the time had a population of 301,271 whites served by 402,441 slaves; in Charleston itself there were 29,000 whites and 37,000 slaves. Slaves were needed to sow and harvest the crops, to fell the enormous forests of cypress and clear the swamps and erect the miles of dikes and tidal gates necessary in the cultivation of rice. Prosperous Charleston was built upon their blood, brains, and bones as much as it was upon ballast, even though most Charlestonians and Carolinians did not own slaves. It was much the same as in the South as a whole, where of 6 million whites some 385,000 were slave owners, about one out of four families. According to a recent scholarly study, "Of these, 77,000 owned only one slave, and 110,000 owned between two and five. Many of these Negroes were house servants, and those who worked on farms would occupy the place of hired hands, in either case bringing their owners into no practical relation to the slave-labor system. As 90,000 owners had more than five slaves but less than ten, roughly three-fourths even of slaveholders belonged to the small planter class. As 61,000 had more than ten but less than twenty, then nearly 90 percent were still outside the class of the grandees—the Old Massas of the symbol. . . . The real Bourbons, the true plantation system masters with over one hundred slaves, numbered only 2,300 in thirteen Southern states—less than one-twentieth of 1 percent of the population." However, this small minority of slave owners constituted the most vocal group in the South, and their strong, often shrill voices demanding the eternal existence of slavery, combined with the equally loud voices of Northern abolitionists who wanted the immediate death of the abomination, were the major cause of secession and the war that came hand in hand with it.

Slave owners or not, most Charlestonians supported slavery and secession. "I have taken pains to ascertain the prevailing sentiment of all classes," wrote J. W. Claxton, a visitor to the city at the time, "and have yet to find a single Southerner who does not prefer disunion before submission to the incoming [Lincoln] administration. The young men ardently desire disunion. So do old men and wise men. The tradespeople wish it, entertaining a consciousness of its disastrous entailment upon their business. The clergy add their counsels on the same side."

He might have added that the old and wealthy, the slave owners and their white minions, had throughout the South attracted the young and poor to their radical banner with lies. As William John Grayson later bitterly recalled in his biography of the Carolina Unionist Judge James Louis Petigru: "To induce the simple people to plunge into the volcanic fires of revolution and war, they were told that the act of dissolution [secession] would produce no opposition of a serious nature; that not a drop of blood could be spilled; that no man's flocks, or herds, or negroes, or houses or lands would be plundered or destroyed; that unbroken prosperity would follow the ordinance of secession; that cotton would control all Europe, and secure open ports and boundless commerce with the whole world for the Southern States."

These radicals had little respect for those they persuaded. Carolinian politician Alfred Aldrich said it best in a letter to a friend: "I do not believe the common people understand it [our cause]; in fact, I know that they do not understand it; but whoever waited for the common people when a great move was to be made? We must make the move and force them to follow. This is the way of all revolutions and all great achievements, and he who waits until the mind of everybody is made up will wait forever and never do anything."

Or as William Lowndes Yancey, "half thrush, half alligator," had put it in a letter, more positively: "We shall fire the Southern heart—instruct the Southern mind—give courage to each other, and at the proper moment, by one organized concerted action, we can precipitate the cotton states into a revolution."

Of course Yancey's rationale for his fire was the same as his

Northern counterpart's; this rebel extremist, like Ruffin, would have eagerly agreed with abolitionist William Lloyd Garrison: "I have the need to be on fire, for I have icebergs around me to melt!"

In any case, Yancey's "proper moment," secession and Sumter, was coming. Most Carolinians knew it, though not the consequences, and even relished the idea. Ruffin and his fellow fire-eating delegates to the convention (there were no women in attendance) enjoyed the city of Charleston as much as they did the unequivocal support they received from almost each and every Charlestonian, ranging from planter aristocrats to the mounted police of Irish descent who enforced law and order on the streets outside. That the city was under martial law at night, and no blacks were permitted out after nine o'clock, bothered them no more than the local slave auctions in the center of the town. They liked the huge, ominous banner reading "The South Alone Shall Govern the South" that stretched across Broad Street from the headquarters of the radical 1860 Association. They would not have considered the flocks of turkey buzzards in the public marketplace an ill omen, as did some blacks, nor did they consider that they might have run from one pox in Columbia smack into another that would compare with the black death.

Well, perhaps one or two might have. Cranky old Judge James Louis Petigru, revered by his fellow South Carolinians and regarded as the South's greatest living lawyer by many, remained firm for Union. Judge Petigru is said to have been asked the way to the Charleston lunatic asylum. The judge pointed to a church where the secession delegates had assembled and replied: "It *looks* like a church, sir, but it is now a lunatic asylum; go right there and you will find one hundred and sixty-nine maniacs within." It doesn't ruin a good story to give another version in which Petigru answered by pointing south and saying, "There it is. And there," pointing north. "You can't go wrong, stranger. The country is a lunatic asylum and the people all lunatics." Petigru is only known, certainly, to have answered someone who asked him if he would join the secessionists: "I should think not! South Carolina is too small for a republic and too large for a lunatic asylum."

If any Southerner sharing Petigru's sentiments was present at the convention in the small auditorium at St. Andrews Hall, he must have been hiding somewhere behind the altar. Flags and buntings were everywhere, one bunting showing a gangly clown of an Abe Lincoln vainly trying to split a palmetto log—South Carolina was too much for the Rail-splitter. Union officer Captain Samuel Wylie Crawford, the surgeon serving at Fort Moultrie, who was observing the convention, noted in his diary "cockades of palmetto . . . in every hat; flags of all descriptions, except the national colors . . . everywhere displayed," even "the business streets . . . gay with buntings and flags." But anonymous doggerel of the day best described the fire-eaters themselves.

> Down in a small Palmetto State the curious ones may find
> A ripping, tearing gentleman, of an uncommon kind,
> A staggering, swaggering sort of chap who takes his whiskey straight,
> And frequently condemns his eyes to that ultimate vengeance which a clergyman of high standing has assured must be a sinner's fate;
> This South Carolina gentleman, one of the present time.

2

The Vile Yankee Race
Out in the Harbor

New York merchant to a Charleston planter ordering flour
early in 1861: "Eat your *cotton*, God damn ye!"

S TROLLING along the majestic Battery and surveying the harbor before the South Carolina Secessionist Convention began, Ruffin and his fellow fire-eaters remarked that the damn Yankees out at the chief Federal fortification were led by a Southerner now, Kentuckian Major Robert Anderson, who commanded the garrison at Fort Moultrie on Sullivan's Island across the harbor from Charleston. Recently U.S. Secretary of War John B. Floyd, a Virginian and friend of the South almost to the point of treason, had come to feel uncomfortable with Brevet Colonel John L. Gardner, a War of 1812 veteran usually too enamored of Charleston's social whirl. Colonel Gardner had had the colossal Yankee gall to demand weapons from the Federal arsenal for his Federal troops, and Floyd—who was later charged with trying to ship army guns South so that secessionists could seize them—didn't at all like that. Gardner, a loyal and brave New Englander, was ordered to "repair without delay" to San Antonio, Texas, on November 15, and Floyd, probably searching his list for someone with Southern sympathies, chose Kentucky-born Major Anderson of the First Artillery to replace him.

How wrong Floyd proved to be if he expected Anderson to favor his homeland over the Union! Major Anderson, a sturdy, medium-sized man, about 5 feet 9 inches in height, with dark eyes, swarthy complexion, thinning steel-gray hair, and military carriage, but with a warm smile and impeccable manners, was first and foremost a loyal army officer, a gentle person yet much respected for having learned mastery in the world of men. Twice brevetted, or promoted for gallantry in action, fifty-five-year-old Anderson had fought in the Black Hawk, Seminole, and Mexican wars, three bullets badly wounding him at Molino del Rey in the latter conflict. During the Black Hawk War, in which he contracted cholera, Anderson served with Jefferson Davis, the future president of the Confederacy (who greatly admired him, facilitat-

35

president of the Confederacy (who greatly admired him, facilitating his promotion to major), and had sworn in a young recruit named Abraham Lincoln. In the Mexican War he had served with Grant, Lee, Meade, Johnson, Beauregard, Longstreet and Pickett—all soon to be generals on one side or the other in the war to come.

Major Anderson could have boasted (though he never did) of a brilliant military record without blemish, but promotions were hard to come by in the peacetime army, even if one were a West Pointer. Anderson's invalid wife, Eliza, was the daughter of the late General Duncan Clinch, a Georgian, and the major himself had owned slaves in Georgia up until he sold them a year or so before. (The buyer later refused to pay Anderson because he had fought for the Union and helped make the slaves free and valueless.) Anderson had many friends who would fight for the South in a cruel war that would set brother against brother and even father against son, a war in which historian D. W. Brogan reminds us: "Thousands of Northerners served in the ranks of the Confederate Army ... thousands of Southerners served in the ranks of the Union Army ... Mrs. Lincoln's brothers fought for the South ... two Crittenden brothers became generals in opposing armies ... [and] the son of the commander of the Confederate Navy served in the Union Navy."

Major Anderson could sympathize with professional army officers from the South and may have agreed with Confederate naval hero Raphael Semmes, who later defended those who went with the South when they had no stake in slavery or planter politics. "It must be admitted indeed that there was some little nerve required for an officer ... to go with his state," Semmes argued. "His profession was his own fortune; he depended on it for the means of subsisting himself and family. If he remained where he was, a competency for life, and promotion, and honor, probably awaited him: if he went with the South, a dark, uncertain future was before him; he could not possibly better his condition, and, if the South failed, he would have thrown away the labor of a lifetime."

This was the practical reason most Southern regular army officers of field and general ranks stayed with the Union rather than resigning, while most junior Southern officers went with their states, having less to lose. But Anderson's reasons for staying were by no means practical. A deeply religious, patriotic man, despite his proslavery sentiments, he would never have seriously considered placing state above country. According to his half-brother, Richard Anderson, "the Ten Commandments, the Constitution of the United States, and the Army Regulations were his guides in life."

Ruffin was old enough to know that Anderson had learned his love of country from his father, Major Richard Clough Anderson, a hero at Fort Moultrie during the Revolutionary War. Indeed, loyalty to the Union seemed to run in the family, for the Major's brother, Colonel Charles Anderson, would barely escape with his life when he refused to join the Confederacy and was captured and imprisoned after General David E. Twiggs surrendered to state authorities all the Federal forts in Texas on February 18, 1861. Anderson could remember President Monroe and Andy Jackson, among a number of renowned visitors, calling upon his highly regarded father. Duty, honor, and country were stressed from his earliest days to the years at West Point, where he was a thorough, solid student, finishing fifteenth in his class of thirty-seven, and where he later served a tour of duty as an artillery instructor, writing the standard army textbook *Instruction for Field Artillery*.

One of Anderson's favorite pupils at West Point had been Pierre G. T. Beauregard—"Old Bory" or "Peter," as his soldiers would call him when he became commander in chief of the Confederate forces in Charleston and Major Anderson's nemesis in early March 1861. This vain, dashing, quick-on-the-trigger soldier and social lion offered a striking contrast to the plain, pious Major Anderson, who preferred to keep to himself and constantly worried about his actions. Anderson's whole life had been devoted to the army, except for the year and a half after his graduation from the Point when his half-brother, Richard, U.S. minister to Colombia, employed him as his secretary and he learned lessons in diplomacy that would serve him well in Charleston.

Among the score of garrisons at which Major Anderson had been stationed over his career was this same Fort Moultrie, where he had served for a year in 1845. He had accepted the post again with some misgivings. Before saying his farewells to his wife and four children in New York, he sought help from his mentor, General Winfield Scott, the army's ranking officer, at Scott's home in the city. Scott was a bit miffed at Secretary Floyd for appointing Anderson, who had been Scott's aide-de-camp in Mexico, without consulting him. Although he sincerely liked his former aide, Scott stubbornly refused to be of much assistance, though he did advise Anderson that Fort Moultrie's indefensible position might make it necessary for him to move his men to Fort Sumter out in the harbor and command Charleston from there, an idea that stuck in Anderson's mind. The major also consulted with Captain George Cullum, an engineer who had spent several years at Fort Sumter recently and who advised him that it was the sole place in the harbor suitable for U.S. troops to be stationed, under the right conditions. On his way to Charleston, Anderson made it his business to stop off for a parlay with Secretary Floyd, but Floyd told him little except that great discretion would be needed at his new post. The secretary did not even commit himself to sending reinforcements should they be needed.

"On the 21st our new commander arrived and assumed command," Captain Abner Doubleday, second in command at Fort Moultrie, wrote, remembering his first impression of Anderson. "He felt as if he had a hereditary right to be there, for his father had distinguished himself in the Revolutionary War in defense of old Fort Moultrie. . . . We had long known Anderson as a gentleman; courteous, honest, intelligent, and thoroughly versed in his profession. . . . In politics he was a strong pro-slavery man. Nevertheless, he was opposed to secession and Southern extremists."

Doubleday, in a distinct minority among his fellow officers, always felt that on balance Anderson's Southern heritage made him unfit for the position he held, and he criticized him for this throughout his memoirs. Though Anderson's loyalty cannot be questioned, there is no doubt that his heart wasn't in his job, especially when the Southern states began to secede one by one after South Carolina did so. He would launch repairs of all Charleston Harbor fortifications and restore military discipline, including daily gun drills, to the sloppy garrison Colonel Gardner had commanded at Moultrie, but he was a man torn between his duty and his beloved South. He often prayed for divine guidance, yet never fully resolved this conflict. "Major Anderson was neither timid nor irresolute, and he was fully aware of his duties and responsibilities," Doubleday wrote. "Unfortunately, he desired not only to save the Union, but to save slavery with it. Without this, he considered the contest as hopeless. In this spirit he submitted to everything, and delayed all action in the expectation that Congress would make some new and more binding compromise which would restore peace to the country. He could not read the signs of the times, and see that the progress of civilization had already doomed slavery to destruction."

Anderson seemed more "an arbiter between two contending nations than a simple soldier engaged in carrying out the instructions of his superiors," Doubleday thought. Certainly, as the major himself wrote to South Carolina's Governor Francis Pickens and others, his "heart was never in this war." And his death at an early age would be due largely to his tearing himself apart in his command. "The difficulties he experienced in his unavailing attempts to defuse hostilities seriously impaired his health and spirits," Doubleday observed, "and ultimately brought on the disease which kept him almost entirely out of the service during the remainder of the war, and in all probability hastened his death."

Captain Doubleday had been at Fort Moultrie since the summer of 1860 and his strong abolitionist views made him to Ruffin and other fire-eaters the most hated man in the garrison, "the only Black Republican in the fort," the worst of the vile Yankee race out in the harbor. A tall, stocky, slow-moving man of forty-one with a thick black mustache and the enthusiasm if not the celerity of an early, bully Teddy Roosevelt, Doubleday was a West Pointer who had served as a second lieutenant in the Mexican War, distinguishing himself at Monterey and Buena Vista. Doubleday's grandfather had seen the whites of redcoat eyes at Bunker Hill, and his father had served in Congress. The captain of Company E, First United States Artillery, possessed a logical inventive mind, but he did not invent the game of baseball at Cooperstown, New York, in 1839, as so many biographies claim. This is a durable myth created by baseball owners at the beginning of the century to disassociate the all-American game from any connection with rounders, the English game that is clearly its direct ancestor. As Harold Peterson's *The Man Who*

Invented Baseball shows, one Alexander Cartwright was most likely the inventor of baseball. In any event, Doubleday wasn't even at Cooperstown in 1839, and nowhere in any of his writings or speeches is there a single reference to baseball, much less the claim that he invented it. Doubleday probably never played or saw the game, but since he died in 1893, eleven years before baseball's Mills Commission declared that he invented the national pastime, he never had a chance to repudiate the myth.

Unlike most of his fellow officers, Doubleday hadn't much enjoyed Charleston's country-club atmosphere before Major Anderson arrived at Fort Moultrie. Shunned by Charlestonians for his outspoken abolitionist, pro-Lincoln opinions, he looked upon them in turn as traitors who were waiting to seize all the U.S. fortifications in the harbor only until the government had spent hundreds of thousands of dollars improving those same positions. No one could accuse him of being a moderate, reasonable man willing to admit error on both sides. No gray nonsense for Doubleday, no subtlety at all; black was black, and white was white. Something of a self-styled spy for the Union, the captain even devised a secret code to smuggle out information. "Fearing that in the course of events our correspondence [from the fort] might be tampered with," he wrote in his reminiscences, "I invented a cipher which afterward proved to be very useful. It enabled me to communicate, through my brother [Ulysses] in New York, much valuable information to Mr. Lincoln at Springfield . . . and other leaders of public opinion, in relation to our strength and resources. My brother and myself each owned copies of the same dictionary. Instead of using a word in my correspondence, I simply referred to its place in the book, by giving the number of the page, number of the column, and number of the word from the top of the page."

All along Doubleday did what he could to strengthen the decaying, undermanned Fort Moultrie. Under Colonel Gardner he experimented with the canister and hand-grenade supplies. "With a view to intimidate those who were planning an attack, I occasionally fired toward the sea an eight-inch howitzer loaded with double canister," he recalled after the war. "The spattering of so many balls in the water looked very destructive, and startled and amazed the gaping crowds around. I also amused myself by making some small mines, which would throw a shell a few feet out of the ground whenever any person accidentally trod upon a concealed plank: of course the shell did not have a bursting charge in it. These experiments had a cooling effect upon the ardor of the [South Carolina] militia, who did not fancy storming the fort over a line of torpedoes."

After Major Anderson arrived and Moultrie was strengthened somewhat, each officer was given a certain portion of the wall to defend. Captain Doubleday erected a peculiar structure on his portion: "I caused a sloping picket fence, technically called a *fraise,* to be projected over the parapet on my side of the work, as an obstacle against an escalading party. I understood that this puzzled the military men and newspapers in Charleston exceedingly. They could not imagine what object I could have in view. One of the editors said in reference to it, 'Make ready your sharpened stakes, but you will not intimidate freemen!'"

Doubleday's wife, Mary, was also an ardent Unionist who had indeed appeared in the columns of the *New York Evening Post* with a letter criticizing the apathy of the U.S. government regarding fortifications in Charleston Harbor. Both husband and wife regarded the Carolinians as "rebel rabble" and were regarded in turn as representatives of "the vile Yankee race."

Most prominent among the rest of Moultrie's garrison was Surgeon Samuel Wylie Crawford, a medical doctor who aspired to military glory. Captain Crawford, also a competent artilleryman, had joined the army after the Mexican War. He was, in Doubleday's phrase, "a genial companion, studious, and full of varied information . . . his ambition to win a name as a soldier soon induced him to quit the ranks of the medical profession." The thin, thirty-year-old Pennsylvanian had served in New Mexico, Texas, and Kansas, never seeing action in his nine years' duty. Sporting a mustache and bushy side whiskers, he was something of an adventurer, having climbed and explored an active volcano, among his other exploits.

Crawford's fellow senior officers under Anderson included Captain Truman Seymour, commander of Company H, First Artillery. Breveted for gallantry at Cerro Gordo and Cherubusco in the Mexican War, this strong Union man was in Doubleday's opinion "an excellent artillery officer, full of invention and resource, a lover of poetry, and an adept at music and painting." Brevet Captain John G. Foster, the engineer assigned to repair

Fort Moultrie and all fortifications in Charleston Harbor, was a thirty-seven-year-old New Hampshire soldier considered "one of the most fearless and reliable men in the service." Limping still from a severe wound at Molino del Rey in the Mexican War, the tall, bearded West Pointer ranked with the best engineering minds in the army, but he was responsible to the Department of Army Engineers in Washington rather than Major Anderson, and this caused conflicts and resentment between the two men, though both managed to contain their anger without ever letting it explode.

Major Anderson's junior officers were as capable as his captains, if not as seasoned in war. Only First Lieutenant Jefferson C. Davis, who was much kidded about his rebel name but was no relation to the future president of the Confederacy, had seen any action. The "boy-sergeant of Buena Vista," as he was called, had served as an enlisted man in the Mexican War; "brave, generous and impetuous," he won his commission by gallantry in battle. Second Lieutenant Norman Hall, a West Pointer, was under his beard and sideburns the youngest and greenest of the officers, serving as quartermaster and adjutant, while First Lieutenant George W. Snyder, a New Yorker and first in his class at West Point, served in the Corps of Engineers under Captain Foster. Doubleday thought that another engineer, Second Lieutenant R. K. Meade, a Virginian who graduated second in his West Point class, was "full of zeal, intelligence and energy," although the southerner with magnificent mustache, whose father had been U.S. minister to Brazil, did find it difficult taking sides against the South.

Smallest in size but not spirit was First Lieutenant Theodore Talbot, a Kentuckian whose bad lungs kept his health in a precarious state. "Talbot when very young had shared in the dangers, privations and sufferings of Fremont's party in their explorations to open a pathway across the continent," wrote Doubleday. "He was a cultivated man, and a representative of the chivalry of Kentucky, equally ready to meet his friend at the festive board, or his enemy at ten paces." Though Talbot played an important role in the preliminaries, he would later be promoted to captain and transferred to another post, being the only one of the officers who would not fight at Fort Sumter in the first battle of the Civil War.

We have it on the authority of Captain Doubleday that "the habits of all the Union officers at Moultrie were good, and there was no drunkenness or dissipation in the garrison." He also found the majority of enlisted men "old soldiers, who could be thoroughly relied upon under all circumstances." All in all, nine Moultrie officers (all except Talbot), seventy-three enlisted men, and forty laborers would be present at the siege of Sumter, as the complete roster in Appendix II indicates.

From their vantage point on the Battery, the secessionists could clearly make out Fort Moultrie and the three other Federal fortifications that so irritated almost every Charlestonian, although they took up a total of no more than fifteen acres of good Southern ground. The most distant but most imposing of these Federal strongholds was Fort Sumter, four times bigger than Moultrie and some 3.3 miles from the Battery. Fort Sumter, located on a shoal commanding the sea approach to the city, although incomplete, was menacing, occupying a prominent place in the odd configuration of the harbor. "A map of Charleston Harbor is perhaps as close as cartographers can come to sensual expression," writes E. M. Thomas in *The Confederate Nation* (1979). "The city of Charleston occupies a V shaped peninsula formed by the confluence of the Ashley and Cooper Rivers. Because the south Atlantic coastline is geologically advancing into the ocean, a torso-shaped body of water separates the city from the sea. Charleston Harbor is enclosed by low-lying mainland, marsh-covered islands, and sandy spits. At the 'neck' of the harbor, Charleston's channel to the Atlantic, Sullivan Island to the north and Morris Island to the south arch toward each other like collarbones and define irregular curves in the harbor shoreline behind them. Rising from the water, between the tips of Sullivan and Morris Islands, lies a man-made blemish on the harbor body. At roughly the position of a geographical sternum is Fort Sumter."

Sumter took its name from Revolutionary War hero General Thomas Sumter, the plucky "Gamecock" who, like the more famous "Swamp Fox," Francis Marion, had led a guerrilla band that harassed the British in the Carolinas, and at the time of his death in 1832, aged eighty-eight, was the last surviving general officer of the Revolution. Fort Sumter had been planned as one of a number of coastal forts built after the War of 1812, a war that proved U.S. coastal defenses grossly inadequate and in late 1815 had inspired President Monroe to beg Congress for money to improve them. The fortress belonged to what came to be known as the third American system of coastal defense, embodying "structural durability, a high concentration of armament, and enormous overall firepower." Its site was surveyed along with the entire U.S. coastline beginning in 1817 under the direction of Brigadier General Simon Bernard (former military engineer to Emperor Napoleon I), who unofficially led the U.S. Military Board of Engineers for Seacoast Fortifications.

Plans for Fort Sumter weren't drawn up until 1827 and work began on the fort in 1829, honoring General Sumter while he still lived. Ironically, the 2.4-acre island it was built upon might be said to be Northern as well as Southern territory, for though it rose up out of Charleston Harbor it was made from ten thousand tons of granite rubble shipped from Yankee New England and dumped into the water along with sixty thousand tons of other rock. It took ten years and over a half million dollars to complete the island made from the leavings of New England quarries and another ten years and half a million dollars to build on it the large five-sided brick fort, which was still only about 80 percent complete in 1860. More than politics, the delay had been mainly due to Congress appropriating money in dribs and drabs over the years—there had been no urgent need for the fort in times of peace. But delays were also caused by legal trouble involving a vague land grant of 870 acres of land in the harbor supposedly given to Charlestonian William Laval (the state's attorney general eventually decided against him), questions as to whether the fort would interfere with commerce in the harbor, the excessive heat of Charleston summers, and outbreaks of yellow fever.

In 1846 Jefferson Davis, then a young congressman, had proposed that local militia replace all U.S. troops manning coastal fortifications like Fort Sumter. There would have been no trouble at all at Sumter had his motion carried, but Davis was voted down. Few Charlestonians didn't fear or respect Sumter's guns, which could level the city. Fort Sumter was designed to be among the greatest forts in America, a stronghold commanding Charleston Harbor that could garrison over 650 men and hold 146 or more guns of different caliber. Its pentagon-shaped brick masonry walls, surrounded by water, stood 50 feet high and varied in thickness from 12 feet at the granite base to over 8 feet at the top. But although the fort itself was virtually complete, only fifteen of the planned guns were mounted, and the interior left much to be desired. According to one Union officer, the inside "was filled with building materials, guns, carriages, shot, shell, derricks, timber, blocks and tackle, and coils of rope in great confusion. Few guns were mounted, and these few were chiefly on the lowest tiers."

Captain Doubleday thought that the dark brick structure of Fort Sumter "had a gloomy, prison-like appearance." In 1859, he noted, "it had been used by us as a temporary place of confinement and security for some negroes that had been brought over from Africa in a slaver captured by one of our naval vessels. The inevitable conflict was very near breaking out at that time; for there was an eager desire on the part of all the people around us to seize these negroes and distribute them among the plantations; and if the Government had not acted promptly in sending them back to Africa, I think an attempt would have been made to take them from us by force."

After the blacks left Sumter, the fort was manned only by an ordnance sergeant who lived there with his wife and two children. "Supplies were sent to him regularly," Doubleday relates, but in case of emergency he could communicate with Moultrie only by means of a small boat. "One wild stormy day when the wind was blowing a gale, he was suddenly struck down with yellow fever. His wife saw that if he did not have immediate medical assistance he would die. She herself could not go, as he required constant attention, and the children were too young to be of any service. A day passed and it became evident that he was growing worse. In a frantic state of mind, she rushed up to the top of the fort waving a sheet backward and forward, and raised and lowered the garrison flag repeatedly, in hopes of attracting the attention of some passing vessel; but although several went by, no one seemed to notice the signals, or, if they did, they would not stop, on account of the tempest which still continued. She then took the desperate resolution of putting her two little children in

45

the small boat, and trusting to the flood tide to drift them somewhere in the vicinity of Charleston. She placed a letter in the hand of one of them to be given to the first person they met, imploring that a physician might be sent to her at once. It was a terrible experiment, for the children might easily have been swept out to sea by the ebb tide before they could make a landing. They succeeded, however, in reaching the shore near Mount Pleasant. A doctor finally arrived, but too late to be of service." Thus the ordnance sergeant might be called the first casualty of Fort Sumter, and his family the first survivors.

About six weeks before Major Anderson took command in Charleston Harbor, army engineer Captain John Gray Foster had been ordered to get both Fort Sumter and Fort Moultrie in shape. The tall, splendidly bearded Foster inspired a grudging respect among Ruffin and his fellow fire-eaters. Captain Foster hadn't been able to hire enough skilled workers locally for the job so he imported a gang of stonemasons, carpenters, and laborers from Baltimore, an experienced crew that he had supervised in repairing Fort Carroll, Maryland. Foster sent one hundred laborers out to Sumter, but most of his work thus far had been in repairing Fort Moultrie, where the sand had drifted so high against the 16-foot brick walls in places that cattle frequently wandered at will into the fort. By the most conservative estimates, there were months of work ahead for him in both places.

Fort Moultrie, a sacred spot in the hearts of all South Carolinians, was the fortress on Sullivan's Island in the harbor about a mile north of Sumter and dominated by her guns. Here, Major Anderson's father, Major Richard Clough Anderson, defended Charleston when the British attacked in 1780. The Virginia-born Kentuckian had fought the British valiantly but unsuccessfully. Captured by the redcoats, he was thrown into jail for nine months, which could hardly have been considered a good omen by his son if he reflected upon it.

Edgar Allan Poe had served as a soldier at Moultrie and later set his tale "The Gold Bug" on Sullivan's Island. Fort Moultrie was also the garrison where the imprisoned Seminole leader Osceola, seized while carrying a flag of truce, literally died of a broken heart and was buried. Walt Whitman, told the story by a marine stationed at Moultrie at the time, later wrote a little-known poem about it:

When his hour for death had come,
He slowly rais'd himself from the bed on the floor,
Drew on his war-dress, shirt, leggings, and girdled his
    belt around his waist,
Call'd for vermilion paint (his looking-glass was held
    before him),

Painted half his face and neck, his wrists, and back-hands,
Put the scalp-knife in his belt—then lying down, rested
    a moment,
Rose again, half sitting, smiled, gave in silence his
    extended hand to each and all,
Sank faintly low to the floor (tightly grasping the
    tomahawk handle),
Fix'd his look on wife and little children—the last:
(And here a line in memory of his name and death.)

    Sullivan's Island had long been a favorite summer resort of Charlestonians, and Fort Moultrie was considered "a rather pleasant station" by the soldiers Major Anderson commanded there. "Many of the wealthy citizens of Charleston had their summer residences there," Union artillery Sergeant James Chester wrote, "and indeed some of them lived there all the year round. There was a large summer hotel on the beach half-way up the island, and a horse railway connected the steamboat wharf and the hotel. The military reservation stretched across the island from the front to the back beach, like a waistbelt of moderate width, and the fort looked like a big buckle at the front end. It was a brick structure, or rather an earthen structure revetted with brick. It was bastioned on the land side, and had a scarp wall perhaps fifteen feet high; but the sand had drifted against it at some points so as to almost bury its masonry."
    During the Revolution Colonel William Moultrie had repulsed the British from a hastily constructed palmetto-log fort on Sullivan's Island. He earned the sobriquet "the hero of Sullivan's Island," and after he was elected governor of South Carolina, the fort on the island was named for him. But Moultrie had seen its

days of glory. Captain Doubleday wrote that its walls were "so full of cracks that it was quite common to see soldiers climb to the top by means of the support these crevices afforded to their hands and feet."

In this wreck of a fort the two skeleton companies and the regimental band of the First Artillery had been garrisoned since 1857. Sergeant Chester points out that even before Major Anderson took command, the men, a number of them Southerners, had been wooed by the Carolinians—not only the officers, who were always treated with respect in the South, but the enlisted men, who were traditionally social outcasts everywhere they went in America. "The secessionists," wrote Chester, "were determined to have the fort, and they wanted to get it without bloodshed." They tried every blandishment. At a political barbecue on Sullivan's Island "everything eatable had been devoured except a remnant of ham which rested on a platter in front of the chairman—who perhaps was also the candidate—at one end of the long table. The chairman was speaking, and the audience was enthusiastic. A storm of applause had just broken out at something the speaker had said, when a soldier, who had had his eye on the fragment of ham for some time, deliberately mounted the table at the lower end, and carefully picking his way among the dishes, walked to the chairman's end, picked up the coveted fragment, and started on the return trip. The audacity of the man stunned the audience for a moment, but indignation soon got the better of astonishment, and the soldier was in some danger of rough treatment. But the chairman had his revolver out in a second, and holding it aloft proclaimed: 'I'll shoot the first man who interferes with that soldier!' Of course . . . [the soldier] was drunk; but he could not have done the same thing without a drubbing [the year before] in 1859. This indicates the policy and perhaps the expectations of the secessionists in connection with the soldiers of Fort Moultrie."

Both Moultrie's enlisted men and officers, even the Southerners among them, resisted all temptation, remaining loyal to the Union. But this didn't change the fact that Fort Moultrie was almost indefensible. Even with the full complement of 1,050 men within its cracked walls, the post-Revolutionary War fortress was vulnerable from the land side. It had been built solely to protect Charleston Harbor from a sea invasion, and it was over-looked on the land side by high sand dunes and buildings from which marksmen could slaughter the garrison—consisting of not 1,050 but merely sixty-five men. Most Carolinians thought that if it were attacked Major Anderson's only choice would be to abandon it, and this was the opinion of its garrison, too.

No American flag flew over Fort Johnson, directly across from Moultrie on James Island to the north of Fort Sumter, for this small, abandoned pre-Revolutionary fort was not only unarmed but literally in ruins. The Stars and Stripes did wave above Castle Pinckney, situated in the harbor on marshy Shute's Folly Island, less than three-quarters of a mile from Charleston. Only the foundation of this masonry fort remains today. Named for Charles Pinckney, South Carolina patriot, statesman, and framer of the Constitution (at least thirty-two of the Constitution's eighty-four provisions are said to derive from a draft he made and presented to the Constitutional Convention), the half-moon-shaped fortress seemed only a long stone's throw from the city's docks. Built between 1809 and 1811, it had replaced a 1798 earth and timber structure on wood pilings destroyed by the great hurricane of 1804. Its menacing guns—consisting of four 42-pounders, fourteen 24-pounders, four 8-inch seacoast howitzers, one 10-inch mortar, and four light artillery pieces—could have inflicted great damage on nearby Charleston, so close were they to the Battery. The secessionists were well aware, however, that it was permanently occupied only by U.S. Ordnance Sergeant Jake Skillen and his fifteen-year-old daughter, Kate. Skillen's official duties were to act as caretaker, to trim the lamp serving as a harbor navigation light, to oil the guns, and to keep the lacquer bright on the cannon and solid shot. But he had grander ambitions. Writes Doubleday: "The brave ordnance sergeant . . . begged hard that we would send him a few artillerists. He could not bear the thought of surrendering the work to the enemies of the Government without a struggle, and would have made a determined resistance if he could have found any one to stand by him. We talked the matter over, and Captain Foster thought he could reinforce Skillen by selecting a few reliable men from his masons to assist in defending the place. He accordingly sent a body of picked workmen there, under his assistant, Lieutenant

49

R. K. Meade, with orders to make certain repairs. The moment, however, Meade attempted to teach these men the drill at the heavy guns, they drew back in great alarm, and it was soon seen that no dependence could be placed upon them. So Castle Pinckney was left to its fate." From then on the party of thirty-four laborers headed by Meade was not expected to fight. It was no wonder that Ruffin and his fellow secessionists looked at Castle Pinckney as a plum to be plucked at will.

Fort Sumter, Fort Moultrie, and Castle Pinckney were theoretically meant to be supplied by the Federal Arsenal in Charleston. The arsenal, its flag proudly displayed at the end of a tree-lined street, stood to the west of the city. The building edged the marshes of the Ashley River and occupied a full city block. Here U.S. military storekeeper Captain F. C. Humphreys, nine enlisted men, and six hired hands protected ammunition, supplies, and 22,430 pieces of ordnance ranging from cannon to pistols and valued at about half a million dollars. There had already been trouble at the arsenal, and more was expected. In November, before Major Anderson had replaced him, Colonel Gardner, goaded into action by his officers but fearing local interference, had detailed Captain Seymour to sneak into the building with a squad of soldiers and obtain badly needed ammunition and hand grenades for Fort Moultrie. Seymour and his detail, all disguised as civilian laborers, left after dark on November 8, sailed a small schooner up the Ashley River, and moored at a wharf behind the arsenal. Stealing into the building, the troops began carrying out two or three cartloads of cartridges and routinely loading the boxes aboard the schooner for transport to Moultrie. They were startled when a stranger stepped out of the dark and told them that he was the owner of the wharf and wouldn't permit it to be used to help Yankees in any way. This fire-eater was soon backed by a large crowd that materialized from nowhere (some observer had probably spread the word), jeering and threatening the soldiers. Captain Seymour chose not to confront the crowd and ordered his men to return all the ammunition they had taken from the arsenal. He and his soldiers in mufti sailed back to Fort Moultrie empty-handed.

Captain Seymour got an apology from Mayor Charles Macbeth the next day at Charleston's city hall, and the promise that he could take all the arms he needed from the arsenal without interference. But this particular farce within a farce continued when Colonel Gardner learned of the incident. Who was the mayor of Charleston to tell the U.S. government whether or not it could use its own ammunition and weapons, demanded the usually placid Gardner, who had ordered a secret mission in the first place. The thought may have occurred to Colonel Gardner that he was spiting himself, but he stubbornly refused to accept Mayor Macbeth's permission, with the result that he still had no ammunition at all! Meanwhile, Secretary of War Floyd, pressed by the South Carolina statriots, advised that he had given no orders for guns to be issued to Federal soldiers through the arsenal and never would. Never mind that Floyd misunderstood and thought guns, not ammunition, were the issue here. For some time this U.S. secretary of war had been trying to arrange for the sale of several thousand surplus government rifles to the state of South Carolina, which was already on the verge of secession, and now he was forbidding U.S. forces to arm themselves. No wonder several U.S. officers at Moultrie grew suspicious of their own government. It was at this time that Captain Doubleday began using his secret code in writing to his brother Ulysses in New York.

Just a day after the secessionist convention convened, rumors buzzed among Ruffin and the other delegates about new trouble that had broken out at the arsenal. Major Anderson, in command of Fort Moultrie and all other Federal fortifications for a month now, had on December 17 determined that it was necessary for the unarmed ordnance sergeants at Fort Sumter and Castle Pinckney to have muskets with which to protect the premises. Anderson had been refused one hundred muskets two weeks earlier, thanks to Secretary of War Floyd's order, but he decided to send Captain Foster to try again. Arsenal storekeeper Humphreys wouldn't part with the two muskets, but Foster produced an old requisition for *forty* muskets that Floyd had unwittingly approved on October 31, but which Moultrie's former commander had for some reason declined to use. Captain Humphreys gladly gave Foster the forty muskets, advising him, however, that he could not give him the two!

At the time the U.S. Arsenal was ringed with a twenty-man

guard of South Carolinian militia, which Governor Pickens, a portly man with flabby features, an oversized head, and an inflated opinion of himself, had convinced Humphreys was necessary to protect it from "any insurrectionary movement on the part of the servile population." This guard of course constituted no more than an effective watchdog for the Carolinians, and when Captain Foster victoriously left with his forty muskets, his departure and all the particulars were quickly reported to state militia commander Major General John Schnierle. General Schnierle hastened to the arsenal, warning Captain Humphreys that there was sure to be a violent reaction in Charleston if the forty muskets weren't immediately returned. His threat worked, for Humphreys quickly wrote a letter to Foster at Fort Moultrie practically pleading with him to return the muskets. Foster justifiably felt that the Carolinians had no right whatsoever to meddle in Federal affairs and was determined not to relinquish the firearms. "To give them up," he explained in a letter to Washington, "would place the two forts under my charge at the mercy of a mob." He added that "neither of the ordnance sergeants at Fort Sumter and Castle Pinckney had muskets until I got these, and Lieutenants Snyder and Meade were likewise totally destitute of arms."

The Carolinians, however, were just as determined and soon got word of their plight to Secretary of War Floyd in Washington. Floyd, still acting as if he was on the secessionist side, promptly wired Foster at Fort Moultrie: "I have just received a telegraphic dispatch informing me that you have removed forty muskets from Charleston Arsenal to Fort Moultrie. If you have removed any arms, return them instantly."

An obedient Foster gave back the muskets early the next day, but his anger was apparent in his report to Washington: "The order of the Secretary of War of last night I must consider decisive upon the question of any efforts on my part to defend Fort Sumter and Castle Pinckney. The defense now can only extend to keeping the gates closed and shutters fastened, and must cease when these are forced."

Major Anderson doubtless concurred, and when the news spread of the affair of the forty muskets, all the Union men in Moultrie were bitterly disillusioned and about equally divided as to whether Secretary of War Floyd was a traitor or an incompetent fool. As for the Carolinians, they were certain now that the arsenal, like Moultrie and Pinckney, was theirs any time they wanted it. Floyd would resign from office on December 29 at the request of lame-duck President James Buchanan, after discovery of the secretary's involvement in a scandal that included the embezzlement of over $870,000 in Indian bonds, but he had already done infinite damage. The Carolinians had much to be cheerful about, while the Federal troops felt deserted by their own government. Wrote Captain Doubleday: "So we were left to our own scanty resources, with every probability that the affair would end in a massacre."

3

Secession! Secession! Secession!

Where's the coward that would not
    dare
To fight for such a land?
            —Sir Walter Scott,
                "Marmion"

Then comes Sir Walter Scott with his enchantment, and by his
single might checks the wave of progress . . . sets the world in
love with the . . . silliness and emptinesses, sham grandeurs,
sham gauds and sham chivalries of a brainless and worthless
long-vanished society. . . . He did measureless harm; more real
and lasting harm, perhaps, than anyone who ever wrote. . . . It
was Sir Walter that made every gentleman in the South a major
or a colonel . . . it was he that created rank and caste down
there. . . . Sir Walter had so large a hand in making Southern
character . . . that he is in great measure responsible for the
war. . . ."

                    —Mark Twain,
                Life on the Mississippi

AFTER leaving the Battery with its clear view of the Federal fortifications and arriving back on December 19 at the secessionist convention, where he had been accorded a seat of honor, old Ruffin found to his delight that the convention was chaired by David Flavel Jamison, a man who was something of a scholar but first and foremost a Barnwell plantation owner with two thousand acres and some seventy slaves to work them. Ruffin liked Jamison's unique gavel. Only Captain Crawford, dashing in his Yankee dress uniform and luxuriant muttonchop whiskers, seems to have been offended by the gavel, which had the word *Secession* carved deep into it. Ruffin, joyous among his friends in their colorful gold-braided uniforms of various militia —clergymen, bankers, judges, and publishers among these Southern gentry—gave not a thought to the tiny, drafty room he was lucky to have found in the Charleston Hotel. He roared with the crowd when Chairman Jamison called the convention to order—Jamison, who in Columbia had urged the delegates, in the words of Danton, "To dare! and again to dare! and without end to dare!"

Although Seceshes gave out rebel "yales" and the hall went wild on occasion as the convention proceeded, Crawford reported that the delegates were for the most part quiet: "There was no visible sign that the Commonwealth of South Carolina was about to take a step more momentous for weal or woe than had yet been known in her history." A committee had been appointed to study and report on U.S. installations within the state of South Carolina, especially the three forts held or occupied by the Yankees in Charleston Harbor—Castle Pinckney, Fort Moultrie, and Fort Sumter. Hearing its report, the delegates resolved that the convention's Committee on Foreign Relations, as it was termed, send three commissioners to Washington to demand the transfer of these forts and all similar U.S. holdings to the new republic of South Carolina. From this wording alone it was obvious before any vote that there was no question that South Carolina would secede. Wrote the peppery Ruffin in his diary for the day: "Heard several interesting discussions on subjects incidental and preliminary to the act of secession."

In fact, Robert Barnwell Rhett, master of 190 on his two plantations, and foremost of the fire-eaters, was already working on "An Ordinance to dissolve the Union between the State of South Carolina and other States united with her under the Compact entitled the Constitution of the United States of America," as the Ordinance of Secession of South Carolina was ponderously entitled. Rhett had been drafting such an ordinance of disunion in his overheated head for years. More than any other man he had ushered South Carolina to the doors of secession. In addition to his public and editorial duties at the *Charleston Mercury* and responsibilities as the father of twelve, Rhett was a prominent churchman active in the Charleston Bible Society and the Young Men's Temperance Society, among other religious organizations. A man of relentless energy, he was proud to hear Southerners applaud and cheer him as "the father of secession" and "the author of disunion" at the convention. Secession and a Confederacy built on the cornerstone of slavery seemed his very reason for being, the driving force of his life over the past decade, and he spent every spare minute organizing for it, even buttonholing delegates at the convention to make sure secession had enough votes.

Rhett agreed with A. P. Aldrich about the common people being mere "followers" not to be waited for. This was an aristocratic view, and Rhett and his fellow fire-eaters considered themselves aristocrats no matter what their origins. Never mind that there had been no time for a real aristocracy to develop in a country settled only two centuries before (even the famous Lee family of Virginia went back only to 1664) and that in any event the very nature of a democracy prevented the formation of one. All too many Southerners imagined themselves the American aristocracy, relegating Northerners to serfdom. "We are not the brothers of the Yankees," the editor of the *Louisville Courier* was to write late in 1861, carrying this philosophy to its most ridiculous extreme, "and the slavery question is merely the pretext, not the cause of the war. The true irrepressible conflict lies fundamentally in the hereditary hostility, the sacred animosity, the eternal antagonism between the two races engaged. The Norman cavalier can not brook the vulgar familiarity of the Saxon Yankee, while the latter is continuously devising some plan to bring down his aristocratic neighbor to his own detested level. Thus was the contest waged in the old United States ... [and] when the Yankee hirelings placed one of their own spawn [Lincoln] over us, political connection became unendurable, and separation necessary to preserve our self-respect. As our Norman kinsmen in England, always a minority, have ruled their Saxon countrymen in political vassalage up to the present day, so have we, 'the slave oligarchs,' governed the Yankees till within a twelvemonth. We framed the Constitution, for seventy years moulded the policy of the government, and placed our own men, or 'Northern men with Southern principles' in power. On the 6th of November, 1860, the Puritans emancipated themselves, and are now in violent insurrection against their former overseers. This insane holiday freak will not last long, however, for, dastards in fight, and incapable of self-government, they will inevitably again fall under the control of the superior race. A few ... thrashings will bring them once more under the yoke as docile as the most loyal of our Ethiopian Chattels."

Such masterpieces of illogic were commonplace among the would-be aristocrats who, in the words of Bruce Catton, were mostly "self-made entrepreneurs with the instincts of an agrarian Jay Gould," who "had bulldozed the cotton frontier from Carolina to Texas within a single generation." But they clung to their vision of the South as some absurd combination of "a cultural feudal aristocracy based on landed estates" and "a pristine Greek democracy based on slavery." Even John C. Calhoun, a relative of Governor Pickens and the most highly regarded man in the South prior to the Civil War, had been born on the frontier to a struggling family and could hardly qualify as an aristocrat. Rhett himself was no aristocrat; his family did go back to colonial days,

59

but his original family name, Smith, had been changed to the more distinguished Rhett (after another ancestor) only in 1837, when Rhett, already a prominent man of thirty-seven, must have had a large say in the decision. Many more examples could be given, but no matter what the backgrounds of these men were, they believed in their hearts that they were young Lochinvars; weaned on Sir Walter Scott, they were sure they were the Norman knights, and the Yankees were the vulgar Saxon peasants. At bottom, their rationalization for secession was that the Yankees had in reality seceded from the South! No one seemed to remember that it was exactly this attitude of superiority toward "the Yankee rabble" that had lost America for the British.

The supercilious Rhett, tall, eyes blazing, shoulders held way back and head held high, was as we have seen capable of far wilder theories. He was even proud to be called a traitor: "The word has no terrors for me . . . I have been born of Traitors, but thank God, they have ever been Traitors in the great cause of liberty." The archangel of the Cause not yet Lost knew he was right always. Lincoln's running mate, the swarthy-complexioned Hannibal Hamlin, was a mulatto, he charged, and his incendiary *Mercury,* edited by his son Robert Barnwell Rhett, Jr., printed the lie. It had developed because Hannibal Hamlin's father had christened four of his other sons America, Europe, Asia, and Africa—and anyone with such a dark complexion and a brother named Africa to boot obviously must be black. A good number if not all of the *Mercury's* readers believed the canard—a "nigrah" just a heartbeat away from the presidency!

But then Rhett's *Mercury* printed anything that reflected favorably upon the South. New York diarist George Templeton Strong told of how he signed a letter to the newspaper "a friend of the Sunny South" and went on to praise cotton "as king in war as well as peace" because it could be used with several chemicals added as a gunpowder substitute. "I didn't dream that any newspaper (unless it might be one published for the delectation of a lunatic asylum) would print this palpable gas and bosh . . . until . . . the *Mercury* accepted and published this as the bona fide suggestion of a friend."

Later, in February 1861, when six Southern states formed the

Confederate government at Montgomery, Alabama, Rhett and fellow fire-eaters like Yancey and Ruffin would be almost eliminated from the ranks of Southern leaders. Rhett, Yancey's choice for President, would be passed over entirely and given no office in the new government. Needing respectability in the eyes of foreign governments, the new nation not only made it clear that Rhett was too much of a monomaniac and hothead by not employing him, but struck out at the father of secession and all other advocates of the African slave trade by outlawing it in their newly adopted constitution. Yet here at the convention in December Rhett was the torch of revolution, and he was enjoying his moment of glory, savoring every cheer and hurrah.

While there is little doubt that the majority of white South Carolinians favored secession, neither is there much doubt that Rhett, Yancey, Ruffin, Judge James D. B. De Bow of Louisiana, and other fire-eaters were the major leaders in the secession movement and had guided South Carolina to the door of secession over the past twenty years. And these fire-eating leaders were for the most part old men. (At the convention, the otherwise representative delegates were on the average much older than the members of the legislature who had created it.) "There never was such a resurrection of the dead and forgotten," Mary Chesnut wrote in her diary of the delegates at the convention. They were ancients in revolt, unwittingly leading the lambs to the slaughter, a minority of hardheaded old fools making a war for young men to die in. Of course this was not a unique phenomenon in the history of America or the world. Neither was the fact that they were a minority leading a revolution. As one writer put it: "Secession has been castigated as a usurpation because a majority did not support it wholeheartedly; yet these same historians applaud the glories of the American Revolution when all agree that barely one-third favored independence."

On December 20, 1861, a day after Ruffin's far more moderate home state of Virginia had passed resolutions in its General Assembly to send commissioners to Washington to adjust the sectional differences of the nation, Rhett's Ordinance of Secession was read by Chancellor John A. Inglis of Chesterfield to the South Carolina Secession Convention, which listened in respectful silence. The ordinance, although a mere 134 words, was among the most momentous proclamations in American history. Wrote "the father of secession, the author of disunion":

An ordinance to dissolve the Union between the State of South Carolina and other States united with her under the Compact entitled the Constitution of the United States of America

We, the people of the State of South Carolina, in convention assembled, do declare and ordain, and it is hereby declared and ordained, that the ordinance adopted by us in convention, on the 23d day of May, in the year of our Lord 1788, whereby the Constitution of the United States of America was ratified, and also all acts and parts of acts of the General Assembly of this State ratifying amendments of said Constitution, are hereby repealed; and that the Union now subsisting between South Carolina and other States, under the name of the United States of America, is hereby dissolved.

Hereby dissolved. South Carolina had come a long way since Carolinian Henry Laurens, president of the Second Continental Congress, offered thirteen toasts to the United States of America during the first Fourth of July celebration in 1778—including, "May the Union of the United States be perpetual!" Declared South Carolinian delegate John Andrew Calhoun, a kinsman of the great statesman: "We have pulled the temple down that has been built three-quarters of a century. We must now clear the rubbish away and reconstruct another. We are now houseless and homeless—we must secure ourselves against storms."

But the debate on the resolution in St. Andrews Hall was mostly unemotional, quiet, and orderly. One would not have thought, again in Mrs. Chesnut's words, that "nobody could live in this state unless he was a fire-eater." The "old fossils . . . ages ago laid on the shelf" were temporarily quite proper and pious. They even saw to it that a Declaration of Causes giving South Carolina's reasons for leaving the Union (see Appendix IV) would be issued to the world immediately upon the passage of the Ordinance of Secession. This much longer, legalistic document in essence tried to prove that South Carolina was a "free, sovereign, independent state," and could do as she wished; since the Northern states hadn't upheld their obligations under the Constitution, especially as regarded slavery and returning fugitive slaves to their owners, South Carolina wanted no part of them, and "appealed to the Supreme Judge of the world for the rectitude of our intentions."

For over an hour the delegates discussed the Ordinance of Secession almost dispassionately. In the alphabetical roll call John H. Adams of Richmond District was the first to vote "Yea" on the question. When the voice vote was counted, 169 Carolinians had voted to break from the Union, and none had voted to stay. The "Yea" of Henry C. Young of the Laurens District made the vote unanimous at exactly 1:15 P.M.

By a vote of 169 to nothing on that warm, bright, cloudless afternoon, the convention had severed the ties of Union, and when the tally was announced to the people crowding Broad Street outside the hall a "mighty shout arose"; according to one observer, "It rose higher and higher until it was as the roar of the tempest. . . . It spread from end to end of the city." The fire was fueled by Rhett's *Charleston Mercury,* which had an extra edition, prepared long ahead of time, out on the streets only fifteen minutes after the vote. "The Union Is Dissolved," read the printed sheets thrown out the windows of the *Mercury* office. Merchants closed their shops, taverns overflowed, people cheered, and cannon roared. Flags of every description save the Stars and Stripes flew from poles or were waved from windows, and grim banners were displayed reading: PREPARED IN MIND AND RE-SOURCES—READY TO GIVE LIFE AND PROPERTY!

This bedlam was just the beginning. To make the unanimous vote legally binding the delegates met again that evening at six-thirty to sign the Ordinance of Secession. President Buchanan's special envoy to Charleston, the Massachusetts Democrat Caleb Cushing, was invited to observe the signing as a foreign diplomat, and he left the city in a huff. But most traffic moved *toward* Charleston. Forming a solemn procession at St. Andrews Hall, the delegates marched over to the larger Institute Hall, which could accommodate the three thousand people who had gathered from far and wide to witness and cheer the signing.

After the convention was called to order, the eminent naturalist Reverend John Bachman delivered an opening prayer asking for divine blessing on this new Declaration of Independence. The delegates filed by the ordinance, spread out on a table, signing their names in alphabetical order by election district; and at the end of the two-hour ceremony, after the last man had signed, Chairman Jamison rose before a hushed audience to announce: "The Ordinance of Secession has been signed and ratified, and I proclaim the State of South Carolina an Independent Commonwealth."

At that moment a roar went up, men tossed their hats to the ceiling, ladies waved their handkerchiefs, and both delegates and spectators flowed out into the street. Remembered Ruffin, who had grabbed one of the pens used to sign the Ordinance of Secession as a memento: "In the streets there had been going on popular demonstrations of joy from early in the afternoon. Some military companies paraded, salutes were fired, and as night came on, bonfires, made of barrels of rosin, were lighted in the principal streets, rockets discharged, and innumerable crackers fired by the boys. . . . I heard the distant sounds of rejoicing, with music of a military band, as if there was no thought of ceasing." It was certainly, as Crawford put it, as if "the whole heart of the people had spoken." Men, women, and children snake-danced through the streets; Roman candles and rockets cut through the night sky, their glare silhouetting St. Phillip's spire and reflected in the gilded ball atop St. Michaels. Church bells rang out with "Auld Lang Syne," and the whole town was illuminated, including the liberty pole across from the tall-pillared Charleston Hotel where a party was in full swing. Colorful state militia units— there were forty-two in all through 1860 and 1861, composed of about seven thousand men—marched behind bands that played the "Marseillaise," moving on to the homes of prominent citizens who made speeches to them. Pealing church bells mingled with roaring cannon and shotgun salutes as, in Surgeon Crawford's words, "old men ran shouting down the street," and everyone entitled to wear a uniform put one on.

The news spread swiftly elsewhere. Representatives were dispatched to all parts of the South inviting other states to join the newly independent South Carolina, and it wasn't long before six states agreed to send delegates to a February 4 meeting at Montgomery, Alabama, to discuss proposals for a new confederacy. In the meantime there were great "demonstrations of joy" throughout the South, notably in Augusta, Georgia, where a one-hundred-gun salute was fired by the Washington Artillery, and in Mobile, Alabama, where "the wildest enthusiasm prevailed among all classes" in a "totally illuminated" city.

"We are divorced, North and South, because we have hated each other so," wrote Mary Boykin Chesnut in her diary. For the most part Northern reaction was as expected—vituperative, with vitriolic editorials directed at South Carolina in most of the Northern press. Unionists were already calling the seceded state a "cotton republic." Many Northerners must have been making diary entries like George Templeton Strong's calling Charleston a "damnable little hornet's nest of treason" that "deserves to be shelled" and "a political Sodom"; observing that "the madness of slaveholders" made slaveholding seem "doomed"; and lamenting that "it's a grave affair for any family when one of its members goes mad." On December 15, Strong had suggested that manning all the Federal forts in Charleston properly would control South Carolinian commerce, which would "bring that Bedlamite state to its senses, like a bucket of cold water on the head of a [mental] patient."

But there were Northern exceptions to those who thought South Carolina a Bedlam, even in New York, where some politicians had recently suggested that Brooklyn, Long Island, and Staten Island secede from the state and form an independent commonwealth! Then of course there were vultures like the salesman from Colt Revolvers of Hartford, Connecticut, who took orders for guns even as he watched the secession celebration from the portico of the Charleston Hotel, enriching his boss Samuel Colt who was even then building a kind of plantation of his own in the Nutmeg State. And certainly there were, as has ever been the case, plenty of politicians on both sides like that apocryphal fellow who, while making a speech to a group of farmers, stepped in a pile of horse manure, glanced down, and cried in alarm, "Oh, my God, I'm melting!"

In Washington, D.C., where enough such gathered, complete confusion reigned. President Buchanan was at a wedding reception when South Carolina Congressman Laurence Keitt came in with the news, crying, "Thank God! Oh, thank God!" little realizing how little there would finally be to be thankful for. When told the news, the President said nothing, but fell back stunned, grasping the arms of his chair.

In Charleston the celebrations continued in full force well past dawn. A *Washington Post* reporter filed his story about a procession of "several thousand Minute Men, citizens, strangers, firemen, and military," their line "brilliantly illuminated with large locomotive reflectors and presenting quite an imposing display" as they marched by brightly lighted private residences and public buildings, the huge crowd serenading Governor Pickens and Mayor Macbeth at their homes. The festivities actually lasted up until Christmas and two days after they began Mayor Macbeth was forced to issue a proclamation forbidding the shooting of fireworks within the city. Said Congressman Keitt: "We have carried the body of the Union to its last resting place, and now we will drop the flag over its grave."

Poet Paul Hamilton Hayne, known as "the last literary cavalier," who was too sickly to serve in the Confederate Army but would win fame for his martial lyrics, was so inspired on secession night that he couldn't sleep and sat at his desk composing his "Song of Deliverance":

O, glorious Mother Land!
In thy presence stern and grand,
Unnumbered fading hopes rebloom, and faltering hearts grow brave,
And a consentaneous shout
To the answering heavens rings out—
"Off with the livery of disgrace, the baldric of the Slave!"

In contrast, Oliver Wendall Holmes, who would be wounded three times in the war, was already formulating his "Brother Jonathan's Lament for Sister Caroline," which he would publish in March. It is notable mostly for its expression in poetry of the

conciliatory sentiments Lincoln later expressed in his first
inaugural address:

She has gone,—she has left us in passion and pride,—
Our stormy-browed sister, so long at our side!
She has torn her own star from our firmament's glow,
And turned on her brother the face of a foe!

O Caroline, Caroline, child of the sun,
We can never forget that our hearts have been one,—
Our foreheads both sprinkled in Liberty's name,
From the fountain of blood with the finger of flame!

You were always too ready to fire at a touch;
But we said, "She is hasty,—she does not mean much."
We have scowled, when you uttered some turbulent threat;
But Friendship still whispered, "Forgive and forget!"

Has our love all died out? Have its altars grown cold?
Has the curse come at last which the fathers foretold?
Then Nature must teach us the strength of the chain
That her petulant children would sever in vain.

They may fight till the buzzards are gorged with their spoil,
Till the harvest grows black as it rots in the soil,
Till the wolves and the catamounts troop from their caves
And the shark tracks the pirate, the lord of the waves:

In vain is the strife! When its fury is past,
Their fortunes must flow in one channel at last,
As the torrents that rush from the mountains of snow
Roll mingled in peace through the valleys below.

Our Union is river, lake, ocean, and sky:
Man breaks not the medal, when God cuts the die!
Though darkened with sulphur, though cloven with steel,
The blue arch will brighten, the waters will heal!

67

SUMTER

O Caroline, Caroline, child of the sun,
There are battles with Fate that can never be won!
The star-flowering banner must never be furled,
For its blossoms of light are the hope of the world!

Go then, our rash sister! afar and aloof,
Run wild in the sunshine away from our roof;
But when your heart aches and your feet have grown sore,
Remember the pathway that leads to our door!

For his part, red-bearded William Tecumseh Sherman, who
was to help fulfill his own prophecy in his march through the
South, predicted on hearing of South Carolina's secession, "The
country will be drenched in blood." To his daughter he wrote,
"Men are blind and crazy." But there were few Carolinians who
agreed with Holmes or Sherman, and almost all of those who did
kept their opinions to themselves. South Carolina merchant
Jacob Schirmer, for example, wrote in his secret diary: "This is
the commencement of the dissolution of the Union that has been
the Pride and Glory of the whole world, [and] after a few years
have rolled around we will find the beautiful Structure broke up
into as many pieces as there are now States, and Jealousy and
discord will be all over the land."

As one Southerner put it, "You might as well try to control a
tornado as to attempt to stop the Carolinians from secession."
About the only person who opened his mouth in dissent was the
respected Judge Petigru, and he was as right as when he earlier
compared South Carolina or the country to a lunatic asylum.

"Where's the fire?" Petigru demanded of a former law student
of his on hearing Charleston's church bells tolling from every
steeple.

"No fire," replied the student. "They're ringing bells in honor
of the Ordinance of Secession."

"I tell you there is a fire," Petigru insisted. "They have this day
set a blazing torch to the temple of constitutional liberty and,
please God, we shall have no more peace."

One man can see more than multitudes.

4

Escape to Sumter

As yet, behind their ramparts stern and proud,
    Her bolted thunders sleep—
Dark Sumter, like a battlemented cloud,
    Looms o'er the solemn deep.
                        —Henry Timrod,
                        "Charleston"

MAJOR Anderson had no intention of surrendering Fort Moultrie the way his father had before him—if he did have to leave, he was determined to salvage something from the situation. The wild, unrestrained secession celebrations that lasted up until Christmas in Charleston made him and his small band all the more aware of how dangerous their position was at the fort. Anderson, increasingly uneasy, began to formulate a secret plan, which he entrusted to no one.

On December 11, Assistant Adjutant General Major Don Carlos Buell, after inspecting the Charleston fortifications, had advised the major, "You are to hold possession of the forts in this harbor and, if attacked, you are to defend yourself to the last extremity. The smallness of your force will not permit you, perhaps, to occupy more than one of the three forts . . . and you may put your command into either of them which you may deem most proper to increase its power of resistance." Although ten days later President Buchanan objected to the phrase "defend yourself to the last extremity" and ordered young Buell to instruct Anderson "to yield to necessity and make the best terms in your power," Anderson had good reason to assume that he was expected to do his best in this perilous situation. Even Secretary of War Floyd had authorized him to move from Moultrie to one of the other Federal fortifications should there be "tangible evidence of a design to proceed to a hostile act" on the part of Carolinians, and he could ignore as irrelevant Floyd's confidential letter of December 23, which in effect ordered him to surrender Moultrie rather than "make a vain and useless sacrifice of your life and the lives of the men under your command, upon a mere point of honor."

Sergeant James Chester was putting it mildly when he said the

71

position of the Federal soldiers at Moultrie had become "anomalous" by Christmas week with its clear, crisp weather. Though Anderson had closed Moultrie's gates to the uniformed Carolinian militia officers who had actually prowled the fort making notes while old, lax Colonel Gardner was in command, a foraging stray cow or two still wandered in now and again over the sand dunes that had drifted against the walls. The fort's walls themselves were only as high as a parlor ceiling, and through the years Charlestonians had built seaside cottages close to them from which they could peek over at the soldiers, had built them so close in fact that sentries who weren't voyeurs had to avert their eyes when they walked the walls at night. Both the cottages and dunes were ideal places for sharpshooters to pick off soldiers at their leisure, Anderson must have thought, and he certainly knew that Moultrie was virtually defenseless from the rear, pitifully undermanned (with sixty or so men doing the work of three hundred, the wives of exhausted officers taking the shifts of their husbands on several occasions), and still in poor repair despite Captain Foster's best engineering efforts.

Bands of armed militia from Moultrieville patrolled the boundary of Fort Moultrie regularly, and hostile Carolinian cannon were aimed at the approach of any vessel that might attempt a relief mission from out at sea. Captain Doubleday had advised his commander that "lines of countervallation have been quietly marked out at night, with a view to attack the fort by regular approaches in case the first assault fails," while "two thousand of the best riflemen in the State" occupy nearby sand dunes and rooftops, "the intention being to shoot us down the moment we attempt to man our guns." Doubleday also noted that the Carolinians were building batteries at nearby Mount Pleasant and on the upper end of Sullivan's Island and that "ladders have been provided for parties to escalade us." Add to this the fact that Fort Moultrie had more historical significance to the Carolinians than any of the other forts, people in the streets crying that their shrine should be taken back from the damn Yankees, and it becomes clear that Major Anderson really had no choice but to get out. He surely had, as Floyd required, "evidence of hostile plans by the South Carolinians." In addition, he suspected that the secretary of war intended to betray the garrison to the secession-

ists. This was apparent in Floyd's orders to Captain Foster directing the engineer to have guns mounted on Sumter immediately;
plainly, the Carolinians could then seize the fort after the guns
were in place and turn them on Fort Moultrie. It was obvious that
Floyd had consistently undermined General Scott's plans to reinforce Moultrie. This was a man who had entertained the Southern spy Belle Boyd in his home. As he himself said in a speech
made to a group of Virginia secessionists when he left office a few
days later on December 29, "I undertook to dispose of the power in
my hands [as secretary of war] that when the terrific hour came,
you, and all of you, and each of you, should say, 'This man has
done his duty.'"

Anderson rejected a suggestion of Captain Foster's that he
place mines around Fort Moultrie and fit Fort Sumter's magazine
with an electric device that could be detonated from Moultrie
should the Carolinians seize the fort out in the harbor. Clearly he
planned to get to Sumter before the rebels did; certainly both
General Scott and Captain Cullum of the army engineers, among
others, had advised him that it would make his best defensible
position, and it didn't take a Clausewitz to see that they were
right. Anderson knew he had to act quickly, however. As recently
as the night of December 20, Lieutenant Snyder, the only Federal
officer out at Sumter, had spotted an unlighted steamer taking
soundings close to the fort. It then proceeded to Castle Pinckney
to do the same, and when the watchman there demanded it state
its business, a voice cried back, "You'll know in a week!"
Obviously the Carolinians had designs on Sumter, Pinckney, and
the other Federal installations, and they were surely expecting
Anderson to make a move. Governor Pickens had two guard
boats, the *Nina* and the *General Clinch*, patrolling the waters
between Sumter and Moultrie with detachments of troops
aboard.

Anderson did not even tell his wife about his plan, although he
did write her on Christmas day: "I am sorry I have no Christmas
gift to offer you. Never mind—the day may very soon come when I
shall do something which will gratify you enough to make
amends for all the anxiety you now feel on my account." Feeling
at Moultrie like "a sheep tied watching the butcher sharpening a
knife to cut his throat," believing that the improvements Captain

Foster kept making there would only be to the secessionists' advantage eventually, and getting no help or even replies to his questions from the by now disgraced Floyd, Anderson gave up completely on the war secretary and decided that he and his men would no longer be political pawns. He determined to move out to Fort Sumter a mile away on the evening of Christmas day, when all of Charleston would be sated and tired after a day of celebration. But he continued to mislead his own men, believing that his plan would work only if kept secret, that they might inadvertently alert the Carolinians. Anderson even requested Captain Foster to send him the screws and pintle bolts of Sumter's cannons so that he could be sure the rebels wouldn't turn the big guns against Moultrie. This convinced Foster and the other officers that he couldn't possibly be thinking of occupying Sumter. As a final ruse he ordered quartermaster Lieutenant Hall to provide transportation for the families of the enlisted men. He feared an attack here on Moultrie soon, he said, and the women and children were to be moved from the garrison to Fort Johnson on James Island for their own safety.

Only Doubleday suspected anything. "Without knowing positively that any movement had been projected, two circumstances excited my suspicions," he wrote. "Once, while I was walking with the major on the parapet, he turned to me abruptly, and asked me what would be the best course to take to render the gun carriages unserviceable. I told him there were several methods, but my plan would be to heap pitch-pine knots around them, and burn them up. The question was too suggestive to escape my attention. On the day previous to our departure [at a Christmas party at the cottage of Lieutenant and Mrs. Hall], I requested Anderson to allow me to purchase a large quantity of wire to make an entanglement in front of part of the work I was assigned to defend. He said with a quizzical look, 'Certainly; you shall have a mile of wire if you require it.' But when I proposed to send for it immediately, he smiled, and objected in such a peculiar way that I at once saw he was no longer interested in our efforts to strengthen Fort Moultrie."

Heavy rains and fog delayed Major Anderson's escape until noontime on December 26, when the wives and children, forty-five in all, boarded two engineer lighters also loaded with enough provisions, ostensibly for Captain Foster's laborers at Sumter, to feed the entire garrison for four months. Only now did Anderson let anyone in on his plan, advising Lieutenant Snyder, the officer in charge at Sumter, and Lieutenant Meade, officer in charge at Castle Pinckney, because the two lighters were normally used by the engineers at those fortifications. Anderson then placed Lieutenant Hall in charge of the two ships and told him the secret, giving Hall orders to head in the direction of Fort Sumter but to anchor nearby and await two signal shots from Fort Moultrie indicating that the government troops had landed safely at Sumter. He was then to head for the new base with the dependents and supplies.

Down at the wharf, Moultrieville residents were told that the women and children were headed for Fort Johnson and accepted this explanation without much suspicion. After the lighters left, Anderson let Captain Foster in on his secret and directed him to collect all available boats in the vicinity and have them ready to leave by dark. When Surgeon Crawford came back to Moultrie from his medical rounds out at Sumter, the Major explained the secret plan to him. The last officer to know was Captain Doubleday, who approached Anderson, Crawford, and a few other "silent and distrait" officers on the parapet late in the afternoon as the sun was setting and invited the major to take tea with Mrs. Doubleday and himself. "I have determined to evacuate this post immediately, for the purpose of occupying Fort Sumter," Anderson advised him. "I can only allow you twenty minutes to form your company and be in readiness to start."

Though surprised, the captain moved much faster than his nickname, Twenty-four Hours Doubleday, would indicate. "I made good use of the twenty minutes allowed me," he notes in his memoirs. "I went first to the barracks, formed my company, inspected it and saw that each man was properly armed and equipped. This left me ten minutes to spare. I dashed over to my quarters, told my wife to get ready to leave immediately and as the fighting would probably commence in a few minutes, I advised her to take refuge with some family outside, and get behind the sand-hills as soon as possible, to avoid the shot. She hastily threw her wearing-apparel into her trunks, and I called two men to put her baggage outside the main gate. I then accompanied her there, and we took a sad and hasty leave of each other, for neither knew when or where we would meet again. As soon as this was accomplished, I strapped on my revolver, tied a blanket across my shoulders, and reported to Major Anderson that my men were in readiness to move."

At about six o'clock Major Anderson, the garrison flag carefully folded under his arm, led Doubleday and twenty men of Company E out of Fort Moultrie and about a quarter of a mile down the beach, where three six-oared boats were hidden behind "an irregular pile of rocks" that had once formed a seawall. Luckily no one saw them marching by, since most of Moultrieville was taking supper at the time, and the troops filed into the boats, hiding their muskets at their feet. Soldier oarsmen commanded by Major Anderson and Lieutenant Snyder rowed the first boat, Lieutenant Meade commanded the second, and Captain Doubleday took charge of the last boat. The troopers were shocked. Private John Thompson later wrote in a letter home to his father in Ireland: "So completely did our Commander keep his own counsel that none in the garrison officer or soldier ever dreamed that he contemplated a move."

Left behind when Anderson pulled out into the dusk were Captain Seymour's Company H, waiting on the beach for the boats to return for them, and a rear guard at Fort Moultrie consisting of Surgeon Crawford, Captain Foster, Lieutenant Davis, and the rest of Doubleday's company. This rear guard was to fire on the guard boats or any ship that attempted to stop the crossing contingent and to fire the two signal shots advising the schooners that it was safe to land at Fort Sumter. Once they accomplished these tasks they were to destroy all the cannon in Fort Moultrie so that nothing of value would be left for the secessionists.

The full moon brightened as Anderson's three boats made their way into midstream. The troopers in their brass-buttoned greatcoats and big-brimmed black hats made an easy target, yet it hadn't occurred to Major Anderson, in his plumed hat, to have the men strip to their shirtsleeves. When one of the guard boats, the *Nina,* suddenly appeared farther up in the channel, Anderson and Meade directed their boats away from her and headed toward Fort Sumter in a wide circle, hugging the shore. Captain Doubleday thought it best to head for Sumter on a straight line, calculating that his boat could be out of sight before the *Nina* passed by. But he hadn't reckoned on the clumsy landlubbers at the oars, who moved at a crawl despite all Doubleday's urging. Captain Doubleday thought fast: "While the steamer was yet afar off, I took off my cap, and threw open my coat to conceal the buttons. I also made the men take off their coats, and use them to cover up their muskets, which were lying alongside the rowlocks. I hoped in this way that we might pass for a party of laborers returning to the fort. The paddle-wheels stopped within about a hundred yards of us; but, to our great relief, after a slight scrutiny, the steamer kept on its way."

The guard boat *Nina,* which was towing a barge, steamed off into the gathering darkness, and Doubleday's men picked up the stroke, reaching Fort Sumter's wharf first because of their more direct course. The crowd of workmen on hand weren't at all pleased when they realized what was happening. All but a few workers were Carolinians wearing the blue cockade of secession, and over the lusty cheers of several Union men they demanded to know, "What in hell's name are these soldiers doing here?"

Captain Doubleday responded with force, taking no chances with the unarmed but scowling laborers. Forming his men into ranks, he had them drive the 115 workers into the fort at bayonet point and hold them there until Major Anderson landed soon after. The boats were then sent back for Captain Seymour's Company H, and Captain Foster fired the two signal shots from Moultrie directing Lieutenant Hall to proceed to Fort Sumter with the lighters carrying the women, children, and provisions. So enraged was the secessionist captain of one of the lighters that he vowed to turn the ship back, putting up such a fight that he had to be overcome by several soldiers. Once the lighters reached Sumter and were unloaded, all of the workmen with secessionist leanings were put aboard them and shipped back to the mainland. Sergeant Chester later wrote that "those workers who remained to the end were excellent men" who should be considered the "first volunteers for the Union," though they never received Civil War veteran's benefits because they were not mustered in.

Major Anderson was as elated as he was capable of being. He had managed the move out of Moultrie to Fort Sumter without a single casualty and without the Carolinians knowing about it. Holding aloft a flask of brandy Lieutenant Davis broke out, he proposed a toast among the six officers "to the success of the garrison," and joked that he would be glad to serve as Davis's counsel if they were court-martialed for making the move. After securing Sumter as well as possible for the night, the God-fearing major said a prayer and sat down to write Secretary of War Floyd's adjutant general, Colonel Samuel Cooper, a report on the mission that would not reach Washington until December 29, three days later.

Colonel:

I have the honor to report that I have just completed by the blessing of God, the removal to this fort of all my garrison except the surgeon, four non-commissioned officers and seven men. We have one year's supply of hospital stores and about four months' supply of provisions for my command. I left orders to have all the guns at Fort Moultrie spiked, and the carriages of the 32-pounders, which are old, destroyed. I have sent orders to Captain Foster, who remains at Fort Moultrie, to destroy all the ammunition which he cannot send over. This step which I have taken was, in my opinion, necessary to prevent the effusion of blood.

Respectfully, your obedient servant,

Robert Anderson
Major, First Artillery, Commanding

While Major Anderson slept that night, Captain Foster and his men were busy spiking the guns and destroying any partly finished additions and alterations of work in Fort Moultrie. The flagstaff was cut down so that it couldn't be used to fly a secessionist flag, and by morning the gun carriages were set afire, a huge column of dense smoke rising above the fort. Even now the Carolinians suspected nothing. Mayor Macbeth, believing Moultrie had caught fire, ordered two fire companies to go to Anderson's aid. Actually, by an odd coincidence, old fire-eater Edmund Ruffin had been the first person to suspect something was wrong. On the night of the twenty-sixth, Ruffin, invited by Madison S. Perry to attend the Florida Secession Convention, was out at sea

78

on the upper deck of a steamboat bound for Fernandina when he heard the two signal shots fired from Fort Moultrie some four miles away. He commented that the shots "must have been a signal for something," but dismissed the incident when he heard no more firing.

Charleston didn't know what had transpired until the guard-boat *Nina,* making her rounds of the harbor, passed Fort Sumter early on December 27 and saw the entire garrison lining the ramparts examining its new quarters. The *Nina* hastily steamed back to town with the startling intelligence that the damn Yankees were established in full force out at Fort Sumter. Secessionist workmen back from the fort soon confirmed the story to the shocked Charlestonians, and messengers were dispatched all over the city to ring doorbells and alert the people. One rumor spread that Major Anderson had concealed his escape by drinking with secessionist authorities the night before and pretending to get stone drunk—papers like the *Washington Star* later printed the apocryphal tale. The Charlestonians were sheepfaced. No one was celebrating the Ordinance of Secession anymore.

Governor Pickens, who had acted with restraint despite public boasting that he was "born insensible to fear!" decided to send Colonel J. Johnson Pettigrew and Major Elison Capers of the state militia out to Sumter to demand "courteously but peremptorily" that Major Anderson leave the fort and go back to Moultrie. Had he not thought the fort impregnable, Pickens would no doubt have ordered an assault, but as it was, he gave Anderson time to strengthen the unfinished fortification, which Doubleday considered so weak that "four hundred men, with short ladders, could easily have taken it." Anderson's men were "hard at work mounting guns, preparing shells to be used as hand-grenades, stopping up surplus embrasures and removing debris" even as Pickens's emissaries presented their demand. Needless to say, Anderson rejected it out of hand. Colonel Pettigrew, a brilliant young lawyer who was to die a hero at Gettysburg, put it to the major that he had violated an unwritten agreement between former South Carolina Governor William H. Gist and President Buchanan that no reinforcements would be sent to Sumter. Anderson, a victim of both poor communications and an incompetent bureaucracy, advised that he'd never heard of the agreement and, besides, he hadn't *reinforced* Sumter—there had been no troops there—he had merely moved his men from Moultrie.

When asked why he felt threatened at Fort Moultrie, Anderson told the emissaries all his fears, adding that he had made the move to Fort Sumter to avoid bloodshed. "In this controversy between North and South," he told them, "my sympathies are entirely with the South." Yet, he quickly added, his sense of duty as an officer in the United States Army and U.S. commander in the harbor would always come first: "I cannot and will not go back!"

The emissaries returned to Pickens empty-handed, full of propaganda sly Doubleday had planted about "the great strength" of the fort and the fiendish shells all ready to be thrown "down on the heads of an attacking party." After the Carolinians left at noontime, Major Anderson had his men fall out on the parade grounds. Soldiers and laborers alike assembled around the flagstaff for a religious flag-raising ceremony. At parade rest, the men prayed with Chaplain Matthias Harris, giving thanks that God had delivered them safe and hoping that the country would soon be united. In the words of one man present, it was a prayer that was "such an appeal for support, encouragement, and mercy as one would make who felt that 'man's extremity is God's opportunity.'"

After the amens, Major Anderson, kneeling bareheaded with the halyards in his hand, hauled up the flag he had carefully carried from Fort Moultrie. The most hardened troopers cheered as the Stars and Stripes waved in the breeze and the band on the parapet played "Hail Columbia!" The rousing cheers, "repeated again and again and again," were almost as much for the quiet courageous Anderson as for the flag, Sergeant Chester observing that "If any of those who doubted the loyalty to the Union of Major Anderson could have had but one glimpse of that impressive scene, they would have doubted no longer." They were cheers of confidence and defiance, too, when the flag rose, "the men vowing in their hearts, that while in their hands, it should suffer no dishonor."

Historians of the day saw the results of Anderson's move more clearly than many historians today who go on at length about the major's motives. "Major Anderson's movement placed the Charlestonians in the attitude of open enemies of the national government, with whom intercourse was thereafter to be on a war footing," Alfred H. Guernsey, the editor of *Harpers Magazine,* wrote at the end of the war. "Unless what he had done was disavowed by the President (which it was not), and he was ordered to retire from Charleston Harbor, or at least to return to Fort Moultrie, his occupation of Fort Sumter was an official declaration to seceders that they could accomplish even the first of their purposes only by proving too strong in arms for the military forces of the United States. His movement but not himself, accomplished this. The rebels themselves were alone responsible for the grave significance of the fact; for, as commandant of the harbor, he might have his garrison in whichever of the forts he thought best, and no one, save the head of the War Department, had the right to ask a question. If the transfer of fourscore men from one fort to another meant war, it acquired that meaning only by reason of what had been done and planned in Charleston. So the cry of wrath which went up from the rebel city was answered by a voice of admiration, encouragement, and, above all, confidence from almost the entire country outside of South Carolina." The "almost," however, took in a lot of territory!

Major Anderson's move did indeed "touch the national honor and awaken national pride," in the words of another writer. "Exciting State of Affairs at Charleston," headlined one newspaper. It was the best news the North had enjoyed for months. Sketches of the Sumter flag raising appeared in many Northern newspapers, and "Major Anderson's name was on all lips which did not utter treason." From that day until New Year's Day, salvos of artillery resounded in Northern cities amid cheers for Major Anderson. The House of Representatives voted approval of Anderson's "bold and patriotic act" by a solid majority. Stocks on the New York Exchange went up significantly the next day, reflecting a new confidence in the government among investors. The *Washington Star,* noting the many South Carolina palmetto cockades seen in shop windows, instructed its readers how to make a *Union* cockade: "... a double rosette, the centre one being of red silk and the pendants of blue ... the gilt button that fastens the whole together showing the eagle of America surrounded by the stars of the United States." Many proud Unionists were wearing them now.

In the executive mansion, however, tall, white-haired President Buchanan showed the same indecisiveness that had led writers to brand him a "moral coward" and cry for his impeachment. At the time, three South Carolinian commissioners appointed by Governor Pickens were in the capital to negotiate the evacuation of all Federal forts in Charleston Harbor. Onstage came another comedy within the grand comedy. Commissioners Robert W. Barnwell, James L. Orr, and James H. Adams were in their hotel room when who burst in with the news of Anderson's Sumter coup but Senator Louis Trezevant Wigfall, a fire-eater quite as incendiary as Ruffin. Wigfall, born in South Carolina, had moved to Texas to improve his fortunes, but his heart had never left the home nursery. The burly, black-bearded adventurer, elegant and witty, "with the eye of a sea rover," had killed or wounded seven or eight men in duels over the years and was fond of telling Northern senators before packed galleries that the North never sent Christians or gentlemen to the Senate. He was to have a starring role in the chaos around Fort Sumter for the next few months.

The commissioners may not have believed Wigfall's news at first—after all, rumor had it that the senator had on Christmas day proposed to Secretary of War Floyd that they kidnap President Buchanan and hold him hostage until after Vice-President Breckinridge, a Southerner, succeeded to the presidency and did all the South wanted done. Fortunately, even Floyd rejected what would have been the only presidential kidnapping in American history, even though the hotheaded Wigfall, rarely deviating into sense, came close to challenging him to a duel over his opposition.

Whatever he may have thought of Wigfall, the urbane former Assistant Secretary of State William Trescot, a Carolinian who had resigned his position when his home state seceded and had been visiting the commissioners that morning, hastened to the White House with several Southern senators to confront Buchanan with the news of Sumter. The President, whose neck was so twisted that his left cheek always rested on his left shoulder, seemed even more off balance than usual. "My God!" he wailed. "Are calamities never to come singly!" He insisted that Major

Anderson had acted against his policy, whatever that was, but refused Floyd's demand that he withdraw all Federal troops from Charleston Harbor. As usual, the President vacillated, refusing to do anything until he consulted with his cabinet. He stood all the while leaning against the fireplace, squinting out of his bad eye, grinding out a live cigar in his calloused palm as was his nervous habit, no doubt wishing that it was March 4 and President-elect Lincoln were standing there in his place.

Buchanan, a compromise candidate and a minority President who hadn't won a majority of the popular vote in the 1856 election, was a melancholy man long before the Sumter crisis. In his youth his fiancée was found dead in a Philadelphia hotel room, apparently a suicide because she had heard his name linked with that of another young lady. The girl's father refused Buchanan permission to attend her funeral. "A grief not to be spoken of" ruled his life from then on, according to a friend. The only bachelor to serve a full term as president, his niece Harriet Lane served as his hostess. This golden-haired girl was immensely popular compared to her uncle—a gown, a racehorse, a flower, and even the warship *Harriet Lane* were named after her, and the song "Listen to the Mockingbird" dedicated to her. She had no real political clout, however. One wit observed, "There is no power *behind* the throne, either."

Buchanan was never a man much admired by strong decisive types. Old Andy Jackson, for instance, in 1845 asked President Polk why he had made Buchanan secretary of state. "Why, you yourself appointed him minister to Russia," said Polk defensively. Snapped back Old Hickory: "It was as far as I could send him out of my sight and where he could do the least harm. I would have sent him to the North Pole if we had kept a minister there!"

Even while Polk's secretary of state Buchanan vacillated. One time, it's said, he expressed an interest to meet Edgar Allan Poe and aides arranged to have Poe call upon him. But when the day came and Buchanan glimpsed the poet sitting in his outer office dressed in dirty wrinkled clothes, he changed his mind and cancelled the meeting.

Buchanan defined himself as an OPF, Old Public Functionary, but the public, knowing nothing of his broken heart, thought him icy and distant. He was a learned constitutional lawyer, perhaps

America's best, and while he thought that slavery was morally wrong, he believed that the Constitution protected it where it was established; similarly, he reasoned that no state had the right to secede, but that he as President had no power to coerce an erring state.

In his diary New Yorker George Templeton Strong insisted that OPF had come to mean "Old Pennsylvania Fossil." Strong, like many others, thought the "wretched old Chief Magistrate" stood lowest "in the dirty catalog of treasonable mischief-makers," for "without the excuse of bad Southern blood, without passion, without local prejudices, and in a great degree, by mere want of moral force to resist his confessedly treasonable advisers, he has somehow slid into the position of boss-traitor and master-devil of the gang. He seems to me the basest specimen of the human race ever raised on this continent." When the war came, Strong predicted the President would "have to emigrate below the Potomac and become a 'poor white' dirt-eater of the pine-barrens," and even then the South might "hang . . . and tar and feather him" for not being "a thorough-going [enough] Southerner."

At the cabinet meeting on December 27, the morning after Sumter became news, Secretary of War Floyd had new demands for the much-abused Buchanan. Floyd had already been asked to resign by the President for his part in the misappropriation of $870,000 of government funds and would do so on December 29, his guilt or innocence as hotly argued by the next day's newspapers as it is by historians today. Yet, tainted by scandal as he was, Floyd had the brass to insist that Major Anderson be ordered back to Fort Moultrie. The new attorney general, Edwin M. Stanton, an able, forceful man who brought some backbone to the administration, vehemently held that Anderson had only done as instructed and should remain at Fort Sumter. Adjusting his steel-rimmed spectacles, Stanton sneered at Floyd before he addressed Buchanan: "A President of the United States who would make such an order [sending Anderson back to Moultrie]," he asserted, "would be guilty of treason!"

Buchanan rolled his eyes and threw up his hands in the air. "Oh, no! not so bad as that, my friend!" he cried. "Not so bad as that!"

The cabinet meeting predictably ended without any decision,

and Buchanan, ever allergic to the definitive, was not any more resolute the next morning when the commissioners presented him with South Carolina's Ordinance of Secession and a written demand that all Federal troops be removed from Charleston Harbor. When they pressed for an immediate reply, the President again refused, this time putting the matter in God's hands. "You don't give me time to consider," he cried in dismay, "you don't give me time to say my prayers. I always say my prayers when required to act upon any great State affair."

It is hard to believe that Buchanan, as the shrewd Trescot observed, didn't have "a fixed purpose to be undecided," but whatever the case, no decision would be forthcoming until Washington received official word that same day of the Carolinian attack on all Federal installations in Charleston except Fort Sumter. Until then, Buchanan seems to have leaned toward giving all the concessions he could to the commissioners. But the secessionists' aggressive acts were something even he could not ignore. Buchanan could count on Stanton's and his entire cabinet's resigning if he did so, and he might never be able to retire to his farm in Pennsylvania, where ardent Union men had already offered to buy him out at a profit if he swore not to come back. "If I withdraw Anderson from Sumter, I can travel home to Wheatland by the light of my own burning effigies," he confided to a friend.

Perhaps Buchanan's desire to be liked was the most important reason for his backing Anderson ultimately, as well as for all his vacillation over the years. That, and an astounding obtuseness. When Robert Toombs of Georgia visited him the afternoon of December 28 and inquired about Fort Sumter, for example, the President wondered aloud why Georgia should have any interest in South Carolina.

"Sir," Toombs advised him, "the cause of Charleston is the cause of the South."

"Good God, Mr. Toombs," he continued incredulously, "do you mean that I am in the midst of a revolution?"

"Yes, sir—more than that," Toombs said dryly as he left the office, "you have been there for a year and have not yet found it out."

While hundred-gun salutes were being fired for Major Anderson and his brave band in New York City, Schenectady, Philadelphia, Boston, Chicago, and other Northern cities (many of the celebrations planned by the brilliant Unionist Stanton), Charlestonians were on the verge of striking out against the "damn thieving Yankees," or "foreigners," as the incendiary press had taken to identifying them. Robert Barnwell Rhett's *Charleston Mercury* called Anderson's escape "an outrageous breach of faith." All patriotic women should begin rolling bandages, a Rhett, Jr. editorial advised. A Charleston correspondent for *The New York Times* claimed that "Anderson has opened the ball." While this is debatable, the *Times* man was right in his observation that by moving to Fort Sumter, Anderson had created an impasse from which no graceful exit could be made—on the mainland he might have been able to withdraw with honor against overwhelming odds, but now he was on a defensible island and could hardly back down without a fight. A centuries-old cliché was increasingly heard North and South: Anderson had gone from the frying pan into the fire.

Outraged Charlestonians gathered in the streets, where military organizations paraded menacingly and "loud and violent were the expressions of feeling against Major Anderson and his action." Anderson would be comforted by letters from the North ("The Lord bless your noble soul!" one admirer wrote. "Oh, my dear sir," gushed another, "the whole country will triumphantly sustain you!"), but now he and his men were lepers on their little island 3.3 miles from the city. "Why did that green goose Anderson go into Fort Sumter," Mary Boykin Chesnut would later write in her diary. "Then everything began to go wrong." This was namby-pamby when compared with the *Charleston Courier*'s pronouncement: "Major Robert Anderson, U.S.A., has achieved the unenviable distinction of opening civil war between American citizens by an act of gross breach of faith."

But obviously Anderson hadn't opened the ball, or civil war, no matter how hard the Carolinians tried to convince themselves of it. Anderson had merely withdrawn to another fort, which was clearly U.S. government property. The first overt actions of the Civil War came the same day that he raised his flag on Fort Sumter—Thursday, December 27—and they were made by the Carolinians.

5

Damnation to the Yankees: South Carolina Attacks the United States of America

What if, both mad and blinded in their rage,
Our foes should fling us down their mortal gage,
And with a hostile step profane our sod!
We shall not shrink, my brothers, but go forth
To meet them, marshalled by the Lord of Hosts,
And overshadowed by the mighty ghosts
Of Moultrie . . .

—Henry Timrod,
"Ethnogenesis"

THE day after the Yankees moved out to Sumter, South Carolina received offers of military aid from Georgia and Alabama and expressions of sympathy from other Southern states. Perhaps her first overt act that day was the seizure of the U.S. revenue cutter *William Aiken* lying in Charleston Harbor—an action often ignored by historians. The *Aiken,* however, was merely a plum dropped in ready Carolinian hands. Her captain, N. L. Coste of the reserve service, had told his second in command, Lieutenant John Underwood, two weeks before, that he wouldn't serve under Lincoln, and if and when South Carolina seceded, he would resign and put the cutter in Underwood's command. On that Thursday afternoon he instead hauled down the U.S. flag, raised the palmetto flag of revolt and placed his ship and his services at the disposal of the insurgent Carolinians. Unlike him, his men honored their military oaths; they left South Carolina and reported for duty in Washington.

If the *William Aiken* incident fails to qualify as an act of war because of the captain's complicity, the taking of Castle Pinckney by the Carolinians on December 27 certainly does. After Colonel Pettigrew returned from Sumter with Anderson's negative reply, Governor Pickens, without the legally necessary concurrence of the state legislature, dispatched three companies of elite troops from the Washington Light Infantry to seize the castle. The troops, assembled on The Citadel green before boarding the *Nina,* could see old, deteriorating Castle Pinckney across Cooper River channel on the southwestern point of the island. Colonel Pettigrew gave instructions to the 150 men, who were dressed in winter uniform and carrying rifles, revolvers, knapsacks, and blankets. When they landed at the Pinckney wharf at about 4:00 P.M., they knew exactly what to do.

89

Just as many observers today regard the taking of Pinckney as the first overt action of the Civil War, involving the first seizure of U.S. property, most of the Carolinian troops believed it could be the first real fight of the impending war. They advanced with caution, then dashed down the wharf at Pettigrew's command of "Charge!", trying to get in the main gate before it was closed. But they were far too late; Lieutenant Meade had ordered the gates shut on sighting the *Nina* in the channel. Colonel Pettigrew, expecting stiff resistance inside, called for scaling ladders and carefully led his eager men up the castle wall. Much to his chagrin, when he climbed over the parapet he was met by Lieutenant Meade, Ordnance Sergeant Skillen and his family, and a party of civilian laborers who had been repairing the fort. This constituted the entire garrison, which offered no resistance at all. The first "battle" of the Civil War had proved to be one of the most ludicrous in American history.

As soon as the triumphant Pettigrew began reading his orders, Lieutenant Meade interrupted him and advised that he refused to acknowledge the authority of Governor Pickens to seize the fort, adding that he offered a *verbal* protest only because he had no means to offer a *fighting* protest. Meade further refused to accept receipts for U.S. property and declined to give his parole, as war hadn't been declared and he didn't consider himself a prisoner of war. He and four mechanics were allowed to leave for Fort Sumter, and Pettigrew promised that Sergeant Skillen and his family would be treated considerately. Colonel Pettigrew then lowered the U.S. flag and put up his own.

It was a fitting end to the little drama. A flag had to be borrowed from the *Nina,* as no one had thought to bring one from Charleston—thus a nautical flag with a white star against a red background, instead of the palmetto tree of South Carolina, was the first in the war to take the place of the Stars and Stripes. As for Castle Pinckney, its thirty or so guns would help complete the ring of fire around Fort Sumter, but it would play a very minor role in events to come, serving chiefly as a prison for Yankees captured at First Manassas in 1861 and further deteriorating over the years into the neglected ruins it is today.

When the Carolinians hoisted their makeshift flag, Ordnance Sergeant Skillen's pretty daughter Kate, age fifteen, began weeping bitterly at the foot of the ramparts. One of the rebel officers assured her she would not be harmed. "I am not crying because I am afraid," she replied.

"What is the matter then?" he asked.

"I am crying because you have put that miserable rag up there," she said, pointing to the new flag at the top of the staff. She was considerably braver than most of the workmen in the fort, many of whom, on seeing the Carolinians coming, hid weeping in closets and under beds.

Even as the *William Aiken* and Castle Pinckney were being seized, Major Anderson and Captain Doubleday stood side by side watching with spy glasses from the parapet at Fort Sumter. It was from this time that Doubleday began growing disenchanted with Anderson. "From his expressions of indignation," the captain later recalled, "I was in hopes he would take prompt measures to close the harbor against any further encroachments of the State troops, made with a view to occupy Fort Moultrie or Fort Johnson. It would have required but a short time to mount a few pieces; and when these were once in position, it would have been easy to cut off all direct communication by water between the different ports. In short, he could take possession of the harbor. He did threaten to put out the lights in the lighthouse with his artillery and close the port in that way; but his anger soon passed away, and he took no aggressive measures of any kind." Doubleday ventures that by now Anderson had already lost all interest in the Union because his wife's native state of Georgia seemed certain to secede along with South Carolina, and "he merely desired to be a spectator of the contest." But it seems more likely that the major believed his orders clearly instructed him not to take the offensive and that he wouldn't be the one to fire the first shots of the war, a philosophy he never abandoned. Probably the most prudent hero in America's pantheon, Anderson would not fire until he was fired upon.

While Colonel Pettigrew's troops were assaulting Castle Pinckney, Governor Pickens had assembled 225 more troops: detachments from the Washington, Lafayette, Marion, and German artilleries, under the command of Colonel Charles Allston and Lieutenant Colonel Wilmot G. DeSaussure. After the *Nina* returned from Castle Pinckney to her wharf, these troops

91

boarded her and the steamboat *General Clinch* and wheeled through the darkness for Fort Moultrie, where resistance was also expected. Docking at Sullivan's Island at about 7:30 P.M., the troops slowly advanced, fearful of mines Captain Foster was rumored to have concealed around the fort. Reaching Moultrie, Colonel Allston approached the gates and demanded the fort's surrender. But only an engineer sergeant and several laborers came out to meet him—they were Moultrie's sole occupants. The Carolinians planted their palmetto flag inside, yet they waited outside until morning before occupying the fort, afraid that there were mines all over the parade grounds.

Once inside, the secessionists searched in vain for someone empowered to surrender the fort to them. The situation wasn't without its humor. "They were greatly enraged to find the flag-staff cut down," Doubleday related, "for they had hoped to run up their own flag on the very spot where ours had formerly waved. They found, too, the gun carriages burned, and the guns, which had gradually settled down as the carriages gave way, resting with their breeches on the platforms, and the muzzles leaning against the walls. Out of the mouth of each gun hung a white string. As many of the guns had been kept loaded for a consider-able length of time, these strings had been tied by me to the cartridges, in order that the latter might be pulled out and sunned occasionally, as a precaution against dampness. The Carolinians imagined that these strings were arranged with a view to blow up the guns the moment anyone attempted to interfere with them, and each soldier, as he passed, avoided the supposed danger."

Captain Doubleday also looked back with amusement on the puzzlement of the South Carolina officers about the tar-coated cannonballs that the Yankees left behind. "All cannonballs used in the army, and exposed to the weather, are coated with a varnish of coal-tar, to protect them from rust," he explained. "Many of those we left behind were in piles near the guns, and when the carriages were burned, the tar melted, ran down in streams, and coagulated in lumps. It was immediately reported [by the Carolinians] that before leaving we had taken great pains to tar the balls, to render them useless. The problem which puzzled the military savants of Charleston was to determine in what way cannonballs were ruined by tar. Some months after-ward ... one of the officers ... took [Captain] Seymour aside, and asked him confidentially if he had any objection to telling him why we tarred our balls, assuring him most earnestly that they could scrape it off."

Although Anderson had spiked many of Moultrie's guns, burned many of the gun carriages, and shipped a boatload of supplies to Sumter, the Carolinians captured a total of fifty-six weapons, including nineteen 32-pounders and sixteen 24-pounders, in addition to large stores of ammunition. Work was immediately begun repairing the weapons and building new carriages. Work also started on a new battery across from Fort Moultrie on Morris Island at Cummings Point. Professor John McCrady, a physics professor at the College of Charleston, had stowed away on the *Nina,* hoping to join his two militiamen brothers in the assault on Moultrie. But he was instead field commissioned an engineer and sent over to construct the new battery. When news of this reached his college, the entire senior class took a leave of absence and joined him in building the latest addition to the ring of fire, these guns being less than a mile from Fort Sumter.

Soon after, Governor Pickens, anticipating that an attempt would be made to reinforce Fort Sumter, ordered still another battery built on Morris Island, this emplacement facing the sea beyond the reach of Sumter's guns. Manned by The Citadel cadets, the new installation would become famous as the Star of the West Battery that fired the first shots of the Civil War. Pickens also stationed Carolinian troops in dilapidated Fort Johnson on James Island, pulling the noose even tighter.

"Damnation to the Yankees!" was the favorite drinking toast in Charleston by now. War fever swept through the town, and on the next day, December 28, both the U.S. Post Office and Customhouse were seized by the secessionists. A far more important prize came two days later, on December 30, when the U.S. Arsenal fell in a bloodless coup. The arsenal had been encircled by South Carolinian troops since November 12, to see that no arms were transferred from there to the Federal troops in the harbor, and now Governor Pickens sent Colonel John Cunningham with a detachment of the Union Light Infantry to demand its surrender under the pretext of preventing "any destruction of public property that may occur in the present excited state of the public mind."

Captain F. C. Humphreys, the arsenal's military ordnance

storekeeper, was in charge at the time. A conscientious man who had insisted on traveling to Fort Moultrie with the secessionists to deliver a message from the War Department to Anderson—even though he knew the chances were that Anderson wasn't there—Humphreys surrendered under protest, stating that with only nine men he had insufficient strength to resist. He insisted on firing thirty-two shots upon lowering the U.S. flag, one for every state remaining in the Union.

The Carolinians took a rich prize in capturing the arsenal, seizing arms and ammunition valued at nearly half a million dollars, including 22,000 muskets, 3,400 rifles, 1,000 pistols and five 24-pound howitzers—enough arms to supply three divisions. Captain Foster's engineering office in Charleston was taken at the same time, the secessionists seizing maps and diagrams of all the Federal forts. As for Humphreys, he remained at his arsenal post awaiting orders from Washington. Very concerned about the careless way state troops were handling the ammunition, he expected to be blown sky-high at any moment.

Back in Washington, President Buchanan was having a change of heart. Even he could not ignore Governor Pickens's seizure of the *Aiken,* Castle Pinckney, Fort Moultrie, the arsenal, and the U.S. Post Office and Customhouse without violating his presidential oath of office—not with headlines like the *Washington Star*'s "Overt Act Committed" staring him and all the country in the face. But far more important, his good friend Secretary of State Jeremiah Sullivan Black threatened to resign if he ignored this Southern aggression, and he would probably take Stanton and Holt with him. In fact, Buchanan had already framed a weak-kneed reply to the Southern commissioners—a reply unfortunately lost to history—which Black read and threatened to quit over. "You don't intend to desert me, do you?" Buchanan asked him.

"I promised as long as there was a button to the coat I would cling to it," the tall, ungainly Black said. "But your action has taken every button off, and driven me away from you. I would not leave you for any earthly consideration so long as I could stay by you with self-respect, but I cannot do it, if the paper you have prepared is sent to the gentlemen from South Carolina."

As a result, Buchanan let the scholarly, strong-minded lawyer revise his letter. Buchanan's long reply to the commissioners, running three thousand words or so, became an eloquent defense of the Federal government's position that did not yield a millimeter to the Carolinians' demands. Referring to South Carolina's "armed action" against U.S. property, the Buchanan-Black letter vowed: "It is under . . . these circumstances that I am urged immediately to withdraw the troops from the harbor of Charleston, and am informed that without this, negotiation is impossible. This I cannot do; this I will not do." Buchanan-Black added that Fort Sumter would be defended and that he did not "perceive how such a defense can be construed into a menace of the city of Charleston."

South Carolina commissioners Barnwell, Adams, and Orr replied in an even lengthier letter written on New Year's Day that "by your course you have probably rendered Civil War inevitable." But Buchanan had frequently heard such sentiments. Just the day before he had listened to Louisiana Senator Benjamin predicting that within a week Mississippi, Alabama, and Florida would leave the Union (they did in fact leave within two weeks), and that Georgia, Louisiana, and Arkansas would soon follow. (Actually, Georgia, Louisiana, and Texas would secede by February 1, Virginia taking until April 17, and Arkansas until May 6). Benjamin, too, felt Civil War was inevitable, and vowed that the South would never surrender: "You may carry desolation into our peaceful land, and with torch and firebrand may set our cities in flames; you may even emulate the atrocities of those who in the days of our Revolution hounded on the bloodthirsty savage; you may give the protection of your advancing armies to the furious fanatics who desire nothing more than to add the horrors of servile insurrection to civil war; you may do this and more, but you can never subjugate us; you can never degrade us into a servile and inferior race—never never never!"

This was bombastic enough to scare a less timid man, yet Buchanan was swayed more by Black and his cabinet, and the equally bombastic pro-Union sentiment in the North where he lived and where the real political power lay now—power that he could not help knowing might arrange his impeachment. On the same day that he wrote to the commissioners, Buchanan finally approved a plan to reinforce Fort Sumter by sea proposed earlier by General Scott. This plan would prove an undertaking fraught with difficulties and danger but did reflect a turn in the tide of public opinion. Both a reluctant Buchanan and his administration, as well as most of the people in the North, were squarely behind Major Anderson and the boys at Sumter now. "It is indeed refreshing in these sad days of demagogues, traitors, fanatics, idiots and rascals in high places, to see one true man, who, occupying a most important and serious position, knows his duty, and most determinedly fills it," Leverett Saltonstall wrote Anderson from Boston. "Your name is a watchword for Patriots, and while you hold Fort Sumter, I shall not dispair of our noble, our glorious Union."

Ironically, Anderson—who wanted peace just as badly as did Buchanan and who had also taken every action he could to avoid confrontation—found himself hailed as an aggressive warrior. Moreover, despite his Southern sympathies, he became a hero of the Union. Both he and Buchanan were caught in the strong, swift current of events. In the streets and barrooms of the North they were singing:

> Bob Anderson, my brave, Bob, when we were first aquent,
> You were in Mex-i-co, Bob, because by order sent;
> But now you are in Sumter, Bob, because you chose to go,
> And blessings on you anyhow, Bob Anderson, my beau.

6

The First Firing on the Flag

And down the dunes a thousand guns lie couched,
    Unseen, beside the flood—
Like tigers in some Orient jungle crouched
    That wait and watch for blood.
              —Henry Timrod,
            "Charleston," 1861

V ERY soon she would be racing down the royal red carpet the rising sun unrolled upon the sea, the Carolinian guns welcoming her, rebel balls and shells coming much too close for comfort as she tried relieving beleaguered Fort Sumter. But now the *Star of the West* rested in her peaceful Manhattan slip, the flood tide lapping gently against the jetties, and no one on board was even sure that she would go to war. After all, she was a graceless, unglamorous vessel with her conglomeration of side-wheels, smokestack, and sail masts, hardly a ship fit to be paddling into history.

From shore, no one could see whether Federal troops were aboard her, but the smell of war hung in the air like gunpowder, and rumors persisted that this sidewheel steamer was in reality a U.S. Navy vessel. "Say, sailor, what you hiding on there?" an onlooker shouted from the Warren Street dock where the *Star* was being loaded. "Headed down for Fort Sumter, are ye?" another man cried. But the crew and longshoremen remained tight-lipped, if indeed they did know anything about what, thanks to the teredos of secession riddling the ship of state in Washington, was to be one of the worst-kept secrets in the history of naval operations. Ostensibly, the *Star of the West* was bound for New Orleans and Havana, her usual ports of call. All through the afternoon of January 5, 1861, she took on cargo until, at 5:00 P.M., while the ghost of daylight remained, she set off on the first leg of her secret mission. Her destination was Fort Sumter.

The sidewheeler chugged away from her slip and out of New York Harbor, cutting her engines off Robin's Reef lighthouse and drifting without lights in the dark cloudy night. For almost two hours there was silence. Then, at about seven o'clock, engines

99

were heard chugging closer from the east. Another steamer, her lights also extinguished, came alongside the *Star*. She was the *Lockwood,* carrying a secret cargo of two hundred Federal troops from Governors Island, where the soldiers, all but fifty of them green recruits, had been stationed for weeks without leave, waiting to play their part in a clandestine mission of which they knew nothing except that it was secret. The troops, under the command of First Lieutenant Charles R. Wood of the Ninth Infantry, filed onto the *Star of the West* in the dark, holding their voices to a whisper. "I don't care where we're going or what we do, just so long as we're off that damn island," one soldier said. Countered another trooper: "Well, I still say they could've told us something."

William Conant Church, a reporter for the *New York Evening Post,* heard many such remarks as the troops filed below decks, where he had been hidden since the *Star* left her Warren Street berth. This stowaway reporter was to be the first war correspondent of the Civil War. In fact, the term *war correspondent* was coined only in 1861, when the first writer to use it noted: "Since the opening gun discharged at Fort Sumter awoke the American world to arms, War Correspondence on this side of the Atlantic has been as much an avocation as practicing law or selling dry goods.... *The War Correspondent is the outgrowth of a very modern civilization.*"

Though war correspondent Church cultivated good sources like most reporters, neither he nor most of the men aboard had much more than vague hunches about the *Star*'s mission. Captain John McGowan, skipper of the paddle-wheel freighter, may have been the only person aboard with complete knowledge of the secret plan, and he wasn't talking. Yet the rough-and-ready McGowan himself added fuel to the rumors about the *Star*. A veteran of the U.S. Revenue Service, his years at sea had been spent aboard cutters patrolling the coast for smugglers. What business had such a man commanding a civilian sidewheel freighter?

The *Star of the West,* famous recently for carrying that one-hundred-pound phenomenon of Manifest Destiny, William Walker, and his filibusters on their mission to "colonize" Nicaragua, had been chartered by the U.S. government from the M. O.

Roberts Shipping Line. Its owner, Marshall O. Roberts, hardly acted out of patriotic motives, demanding $1,500 a day and the cost of three hundred tons of coal for the voyage—though he may have rationalized that he gave the government a break when he finally agreed to accept $1,250 a day and no fuel costs. This was the payment proposed by the secret military commission headed by General Scott's Assistant Adjutant, General Lorenzo Thomas, who called upon him privately, acting outside of normal government channels. In any case, the *Star of the West* was ill-equipped for a military mission, being unarmed except for a small brass cannon long without ammunition, which was just as well, for in the expert opinion of Captain McGowan, the antique piece was more likely to kill the gunners firing it than those at whom it was aimed.

The only "weapon" the *Star* carried was a 20 x 40-foot American flag that McGowan had been ordered to hoist to the masthead if and when the first shot was fired at her by the South Carolinians—this a signal to Sumter's commander that the Union guns there should protect the *Star* by returning fire. In fact, the operation's planners had no good reason for selecting the *Star*. General Scott had originally chosen the mighty warship U.S.S. *Brooklyn* for this relief expedition, but had changed his orders. The tall-masted steam sloop *Brooklyn,* a first-class fighting ship of about two thousand tons burden with twenty-four big guns, now waited at Hampton Roads, Virginia, much closer to Fort Sumter than the *Star*. She could make nine knots on smooth water, and had been loaded with four companies of seasoned, fully armed regulars from Fort Monroe, along with three month's supplies, but thanks to General Scott's change of heart she would see no action.

Though so vain and pompous he was known as Old Fuss and Feathers, General Winfield Scott had been a genuine American hero and a general since the War of 1812, when he was captured by the British. He was said to love himself, food, and wine—in that order. Six-feet five-inches tall, over three hundred pounds, suffering from gout, old bullets from old battles aching in his body, he still dressed to the nines in his splendid self-designed gold-braided uniform and plumed hat. He was "almost a parade by himself" when he waddled down the street; or, as a contem-

101

porary put it: "What a wonderful mixture of gasconade, ostenta-
tion, fuss, feathers, bluster and genuine soldierly talent and
courage is this same Winfield Scott! A great smoking mass of
flesh and blood!"

Scott may be the eponym behind the still-common expression
Great Scott!, a euphemism for *Great God!* that has been traced to
his day, and his troops during the Mexican War were the first
Yankees to be called *gringos,* possibly, the old story goes, because
they often sang the Robert Burns song that begins *Green grow* the
rushes O . . ." A Virginian by birth, the bejowled, red-faced
war-horse ardently opposed secession, and his loyalty to the
Union was beyond question. Widely regarded as a bold fighter
known for his daring, but never foolhardy, strategy (he would
later be one of the few Union generals to oppose the disastrous
first battle of Bull Run), this forthright mountain of a man was
respected, if not loved, both by enlisted men and officers for his
firm-minded and just discipline. He is generally regarded as the
greatest American general between Washington and Lee. No one
really knows why Scott abandoned his plan for reinforcing Fort
Sumter with the *Brooklyn*—a bold overt operation that would
have proudly displayed the full force of Union arms—in favor of
the *Star.* Scott probably did believe that the deep-draft *Brooklyn*
would run aground on the shoals in Charleston Harbor (though
this is debatable, and she certainly could have made it over the
bar at high tide) and that using troops from Fort Monroe would
weaken what he thought was a far more important garrison in
another state that seemed likely to secede from the Union at any
moment. But his age must also be taken into account (failing
health would force him to retire in November at seventy-five), and
he had possibly fallen into President Buchanan's bad habits of
hesitating, procrastinating, vacillating, and temporizing, trying
to be all things to all men.

To begin with, both Scott and Buchanan had delayed the
Sumter relief mission in order to appease the Southern peace
commissioners negotiating with them in Washington, thus giving the secessionists the chance to strengthen their weak harbor
defenses. Captain Doubleday, Fort Sumter's second in command,
felt that the general, "who at this time was quite pacifically
inclined, may have thought that if this vessel [the *Star*] could slip

in, and land its cargo unawares, he would have secured the harbor of Charleston without increasing the war fever in the South. Be this as it may, there is no doubt that his policy was too peaceful in the early days of the war. . . . The original plan to succor us was excellent: the substitute was an utter failure."

Whatever his reasoning, Scott convinced shilly-shallying Buchanan to let him rescind his orders for the vaunted *Brooklyn* and sent the toothless paddle-wheel steamer in her place. As the *Star of the West* wheeled out into the gray Atlantic toward Charleston Harbor, she passed the steamer *Columbia,* whose captain was an ardent secessionist. The northbound vessel sent up nine rockets as a salute, but McGowan ignored them. While he continued stealthily on his course that night, a Southern spy who signed himself simply "Jones" was wiring South Carolina Governor Pickens, or Rhett's *Charleston Mercury,* that the *Star* was on her way to reinforce the Yankees in Fort Sumter. Romantic tales might make the still unknown Jones the first Civil War spy, but in truth New York and Washington were swarming with Southern sympathizers only too glad to act as secret agents when the opportunity arose. Among them was Buchanan's secretary of the interior, mild-mannered Mississippi secessionist Jacob Thompson, who later admitted that he had given the Confederacy advance warning of the *Star*'s coming, sending two telegrams to Judge A. B. Longstreet in Charleston to this effect before resigning from the post to which his good friend Buchanan had appointed him. Predictably Senator Wigfall from Texas had also acted as an informer, wiring Governor Pickens that the *Star* was on her way.

Spies weren't needed anyway. Southern sympathizers could simply read the news in Northern newspapers and telegraph it to Charleston. *The New York Times,* for instance, reported on January 7 that "The *Star of the West* is, without doubt, already on her way to Charleston. . . . during Saturday night it is believed that some three hundred marines were put on board by a steam tug . . . they were undoubtedly received on board the steamer, which during the night proceeded to sea." The *New York Tribune* reported identical rumors that same day, and a day later the *Washington Constitution* advised that the *Star of the West* should be nearing Charleston at any hour. In fact, one New York paper had reported the *Star*'s mission even before she left her Warren Street pier, while below deck, *New York Post* war correspondent Church jotted in his notebook: "Our principal hope is in the ignorance of the Charlestonians; and if they get no whisper of our plan, we hope to slip in to Fort Sumter without opposition or hindrance, on Wednesday morning next at daybreak."

The very last people to hear of the mission were the men most deeply involved in it: those on board the *Star of the West* and Major Anderson and his troopers in Fort Sumter. It seems that in yet another error in this comedy of errors, Joseph Holt, the former postmaster general who had replaced the disgraced Southerner John B. Floyd as secretary of war, sent Anderson a detailed plan of the mission, but forwarded the vital message through the regular mails instead of by special courier. Since all mail to Sumter had been stopped by order of Governor Pickens, the letter didn't arrive until the mission ended, leaving Anderson with no knowledge at all that he was instructed to fire at South Carolina batteries if they opened fire on the *Star*. He, Doubleday, and the others did read about the relief ship in a copy of the *Mercury* brought to the fort by workmen on January 8, but Anderson dismissed the story as just another rumor in that rumormongering sheet and made no special preparations. Most of his officers agreed with him about the report. Noted Captain Crawford in his diary: "We do not credit it entirely. . . . Major A. thinks Genl. Scott would not send troops except by a War vessel."

Only Captain Doubleday paid much attention to the news stories. "We had seen a statement . . . that a steamer named the *Star of the West* . . . was to be sent to us under the command of Captain John M'Gowan, with a re-enforcement of several hundred men and supplies of food and ammunition," he wrote later, "but we could not credit the rumor. To publish all the details of an expedition of this kind, which ought to be kept a profound secret, was virtually telling South Carolina to prepare her guns to sink the vessel. It was hard to believe the Government would send to us a mercantile steamer—a mere transport, utterly unfitted to contend with shore batteries—when it could dispatch a man-of-war furnished with all the means and appliances to repel force by force. As the insurgents at this period had but few field guns, and a very scanty supply of cannon powder, the *Brooklyn* alone, in my opinion, could have gone straight to the wharf in Charleston, and have put an end to the insurrection then and there; for we all know what its distinguished captain, Farragut, was able to accomplish when left to his own resources. . . . Although I had little faith in the announcement, I scanned with increased interest every vessel that approached the harbor."

While Anderson's men and most aboard the *Star of the West* knew nothing of what was to come, there was no doubt the secessionists knew everything. Charleston telegraph operator Edwin F. Ludwig, a Pennsylvanian who had moved South, recorded in his diary the gist of many messages that clicked in over his instrument. Wrote Ludwig on January 3: "Rumored today that Federal Government sending troops to reinforce Fort Sumter. Preparations made to resist." Three days later he noted: "Rumor in streets steamer *Star of the West* started from New York with reinforcements for Fort Sumter. Great excitement and war commenced if true." Preparations to resist had actually been in progress since December 31, when Governor Pickens, having received telegraphic notice that the *Brooklyn* would be sent to reinforce Anderson's garrison at Fort Sumter, had instructed Major General Schnierle of the state militia to erect a battery on Morris Island beyond range of Sumter's guns. Major Peter F. Stevens, commander of Charleston's Citadel academy, was ordered to bring forty cadets to help a ninety-man company of infantry with the work at the northern end of the island and man the battery when it was constructed. Doubleday, looking through his spyglass at the young cadets "hard at work at the new battery," had his doubts about them: "The day was cold and rainy, and the wind blew fiercely. We wondered how long those boys would keep up their enthusiasm amidst the hardships and trials of the real war which was now fast approaching."

The young cadets would surprise Doubleday. Indeed, the Civil War could have been called "The Boys' War." No reliable figures are available for the South but, according to one estimate, of the North's 2.5 million soldiers about half were under eighteen years old, roughly 200,000 of these under sixteen, and some 100,000 fifteen or under. Of the last group, 300 were thirteen years old or under and 25 were actually under ten years of age (most of these ten-year-olds were drummers and fifers, but several of them were fighters)! The Citadel cadets would conduct themselves as well as any unit at the battle of Sumter, and one boy among them would fire the first secessionist shot of the war.

South Carolina's Governor Pickens had also heard rumors that the U.S. revenue cutter *Harriet Lane* was on her way to Charleston carrying 250 men to reinforce Fort Sumter. This same ship would eventually become part of the Sumter story, but she hadn't been ordered into action at this time. The *Harriet Lane* was later to figure in a touching Civil War tale. After the Confederates captured Galveston, Texas, shelling and seizing the ship, Confederate Major A. M. Lea boarded her with a party and found his son, a Union man and a lieutenant of the *Lane,* dying on the deck. But now, early in January 1861, Pickens waited in Charleston for both the *Harriet Lane* and the *Star,* and possibly the *Brooklyn.* He was a worried man.

Pickens ordered all fortifications in the harbor strengthened. He personally supervised the defense work at Fort Moultrie, where volunteers like peppery old Edmund Ruffin (just returned from stomping for secession in Florida) were "committing a little treason" by repairing and strengthening the fort on Sullivan Island. On the sandy wastes of Morris Island, the governor not only ordered the Citadel cadets to help build and man the crucial battery commanding the main ship channel into Charleston Harbor, he also ordered the Vigilant Rifles, a company of firemen turned soldiers, to camp in the open near a battery at Cummings Point on the southern end of the island. Guard ships were stationed in the main ship channel; one of them, the *General Clinch,* patrolled between 7:00 P.M. and daylight with a detail of twenty Irish Volunteers aboard who were instructed to sink any small boats entering the harbor from vessels outside the bar. Finally, all the lights in the harbor were turned off, and the buoys marking the way across the bar were removed. The Charleston lighthouse had already been pulled down, its powerful, costly fresnel-lensed lantern smashed, and now it was hauled away to Rattlesnake Shoal. Only Fort Sumter's beacon remained to light the night.

But nothing assuaged Governor Pickens or the people of Charleston. They were relieved that the *Harriet Lane* rumor finally proved untrue, but otherwise the future seemed bleak. Businesses closed. The banks suspended specie payment. Fort

106

Sumter itself was thought impregnable by the Carolinians. "Twenty-five well-drilled men could hold it against all Charleston," the *Courier* warned on December 31, unaware of Major Anderson's problems at Sumter. "Its batteries could level Fort Moultrie to the ground in a few hours and shell our city effectively."

Worse yet, General James Simons of the state militia, ordered by Pickens to survey the harbor defenses, made the gloomiest report possible: The cadets at what was to be called the Star of the West Battery on Morris Island north had never fired a 24-pounder or even seen one fired. At Fort Johnson on James Island were raw militiamen "who had never handled a heavy gun." At Fort Moultrie on Sullivan's Island the guns Anderson's men had so poorly spiked before leaving had been repaired, but there probably wasn't a single man in the garrison who had "ever loaded a siege gun," and the position was indefensible—it could easily be leveled with fire from Sumter by "the enemy," as U.S. forces were already being called.

General Simons, too, had no idea of how poorly Fort Sumter was armed, and was sure that the Yankees controlled the entire harbor. "Why, then, all this preparation and expense, if the work cannot but terminate in disastrous failure?" he asked. The enemy could "demolish our . . . posts when he pleases, from one of the most impregnable fortresses in the world, and so our posts live at his will, and remain in our possession at his sufference." In closing, he urged Governor Pickens to withdraw his troops and let Fort Sumter be reinforced with no resistance. Pickens predictably retorted, "I shall do no such thing!" Inexperienced South Carolinian troops could rise to the occasion and fight as well as regulars, he reasoned, and he suspected that the Yankee forces weren't as strong as the General reckoned. Besides, he would not so easily surrender all that Carolina had thus far won. Recruiting went on in the city and state for a ten-regiment army. Men who refused to serve were spurned by their sweethearts. Ladies made bandages from their petticoats, and defense work continued in a city where many felt fear and panic but few surrendered to their feelings.

Aboard the *Star of the West* most of the men didn't know what they were up to until the morning of Monday, January 7, when they reached Cape Hatteras, North Carolina, a point notorious for its rough seas ("If the Tortugas let you pass, / Beware of Hatteras"). There, in this continuing comedy of errors, a Federal officer chanced upon an article in a previous Saturday New York newspaper that related the *Star*'s mission in detail. At this point, Captain McGowan confirmed the rumor of war, the first time the troops were officially informed of their mission. McGowan quipped that it wasn't very pleasant to be shot at when one couldn't shoot back, and the men took his remark in the spirit of fun. They were ordered to remain below decks, but no one seemed overly concerned about the secret mission, the soldiers congregating in small groups, telling stories and singing. Their favorite tune turned out to be "Away Down South in Dixie," which songwriter and minstrel Daniel D. Emmett had composed on his violin in 1859 "while looking out on the cold dreary streets of New York City and wishing he were down home in Dixie." This would become the favorite marching song of the Confederates during the Civil War, but it was first sung as a war tune by these Yankees heading South. "In Dixie land I'll take my stand, to live and die in Dixie . . .": War correspondent Church reported that these words were heard again and again, over twenty times on the first day alone, as the ship sped through the waves.

While the warriors on the *Star* sang confidently, Secretary of War Holt in Washington was besieged with doubts. On January 5 he had read for the first time Major Anderson's official report written December 31, which had taken almost a week to reach him and which advised that the Carolinians were constructing one or two batteries on Morris Island commanding the main channel leading to Fort Sumter. The usually astute artillerist Anderson didn't seem to realize the importance of this—"Thank God we are now where the Government may send us additional troops at its leisure," he wrote—but Holt and his advisers knew that even an armed ship like the *Brooklyn* might have trouble running such a gauntlet, and they had sent an unarmed side-wheel steamer. Holt quickly tried to cancel the *Star*'s mission, but she had already left and was far out at sea. The war secretary conferred with Buchanan and General Scott, and they decided that the *Star* would now need protection to reach Sumter; but not until January 7, almost two days later, could Holt get word to Fort

Monroe ordering the *Brooklyn* under Captain Farragut to sail south immediately, find the *Star,* and assist her in any way possible.

Aboard the *Star* Captain McGowan reduced his speed when the ship rounded Cape Fear on the morning of the eighth, and that afternoon he stopped her entirely. Somewhere off Georgetown, South Carolina, only seventy miles or so from his destination now, he planned to reach Charleston Harbor by early the next morning and steal in to Sumter at dawn. The troops were encouraged to come up on deck and fish for the remainder of the afternoon, many trying their luck until nightfall when the *Star* steamed off again. In the dusk, yarns were spun by the old salts for the green, often seasick landlubbers.

Perhaps it was at this time that Captain McGowan tried calming his troops by reading them what could be called a bedtime story. We know as a matter of record that he chose "Some Adventures of Captain Simon Suggs, Late of the Tallapoosa Volunteers," humorous yarns of a backwoods gambler enjoying flush times on the old southwest frontier spun by Alabama newspaperman Johnson Jones Hooper. McGowan's strategy didn't work though, for as war correspondent Church observed, few slept that stormy night, and all singing ended. The *Star* churned through the night, all lights out save for a small cabin lantern. The troopers finally had to consider the reality of running the gauntlet unarmed, for Captain McGowan had assigned some of them stations below deck to plug up with mattresses any holes made by cannonballs; he had also rigged up a device to steer the ship from below if the wheelhouse were destroyed. Should the *Star* be disabled, he advised, they would ground her as close to Sumter as possible and ninety men and supplies would be rowed to the fort in six small boats. Few were eager to be among the ninety "volunteers."

It was three in the morning on January 9 when the *Star of the West* approached within a few miles of Fort Sumter. The *Star* stood off the Charleston bar, but Mr. Brewer, the pilot McGowan had brought along from New York, couldn't find the main channel in the dark harbor, where only a dim glow from Fort Sumter could be seen through the haze on the horizon. Captain McGowan, Brewer, two army officers, and war correspondent

Church waited for dawn on the upper deck. About three hours passed before light came, and they could see thick evergreens along the coast, then the spires of Charleston. All the troops were on deck now, the secrecy over. Fort Sumter itself became visible, the Stars and Stripes waving over the glistening red structure, and the men suppressed a cheer. The leadsman on a platform near the bow finally found a safe passage, and the *Star of the West* steamed boldly across the bar on the ebb tide, flushing out before her the guard ship *General Clinch,* ironically named after Major Anderson's father-in-law from Georgia, Bayard Clinch, a Seminole War hero.

The little *General Clinch* fled up the channel into the harbor ahead of the *Star,* all of her lights blinking, signaling the alarm with rockets and flares to alert the Citadel gunners. The *Star* moved slowly toward Sumter, Lieutenant Wood and his noncoms ushering all troops below deck again as daylight came and the sidewheeler assumed her pathetic disguise as a peaceful merchantman once more. For the rest of the battle they would wait there with loaded muskets, listening to the swish of the engines and the boom of artillery, hearing cannonballs thump against the planking, but seeing nothing.

Soon the *Star* was within two miles of Sumter. To her port bow was Morris Island, where the forty Citadel cadets waited under the command of Major Stevens. The cadets were now sharing quarters in the ramshackle buildings of an abandoned smallpox hospital with two militia infantry units, the Zouave Cadets and the German riflemen—stationed there to guard against an amphibious assault—but that night the well-trained young artillerists had slept on the beach. Their crude battery was concealed behind parapets of sand, which afforded the only protection to the guns and gun crews. A broadside from a warship like the *Brooklyn* would have leveled it, and any landing force would have found it open and unprotected at the rear. The cadets were aware of this, and they believed that Fort Sumter's guns, only three thousand yards away at their backs, could all but destroy them, yet they remained at their posts.

When he saw the *General Clinch* fire a rocket warning, the boy sentry on duty, Cadet William S. Simpkins, roused his companions, who rushed to their guns. Major Stevens sighted the

110

number one gun and turned it over to Cadet George Edward Haynesworth from Sumter County. Stevens had orders from Governor Pickens to fire upon any strange ship trying to enter the main channel. He quickly cried out, "Commence firing!" and Cadet Captain John M. Whilden gave the order, "Number one fire!" Cadet Haynesworth, a boy barely sixteen, snapped one end of his firing lanyard into the ring of the friction primer protruding from the gun's vent, uncoiled the lanyard full length, and drew it taut. "Fire!" Major Stevens cried again, and at exactly 7:15 A.M. young Haynesworth fired what has been called "the first shot of the Civil War at the American flag." Later a correspondent for the *Charleston Courier* reported: "From an eyewitness I learned that the 'first shot' was fired by Cadet G. E. Haynesworth who applied the match, and that the piece was commanded by Cadet John M. Whilden, senior captain of the Corps of Cadets."

An American ensign could clearly be seen fluttering from the *Star's* flagstaff, but when Lieutenant Wood saw a puff of smoke from the Morris Island battery and watched a shot about the size of a bowling ball skip across the water in front of his ship, he quickly raised the huge garrison flag she carried at the fore. This, he wrote angrily later, "was no more respected than the first," for less than a moment after Haynesworth's apparent warning shot, came another. The *Star* then increased her speed and continued steaming toward Sumter. All along the harbor, bugles and long drumrolls were heard calling gunners to their battle stations. The *Star* was definitely the target now. Guns under the red South Carolina flag were aimed at the *Star of the West* and began firing as she ran the gauntlet, sometimes less than three thousand feet from them. The second shot fell as short as the first one fired by the Citadel cadet, but the third skipped over the water like a stone for some three hundred feet and then bounded completely over the *Star* and into the sea, nearly taking a sailor's head with it. Still another shot ricocheted, and Captain McGowan thought the *Star* might make it. "Bah!" he shouted. "Give us bigger guns than that, boys, or you'll never hurt us!" As if in reply, a heavier gun sounded from shore and a shot hit the *Star of the West* about two feet above water in the fore chains, just below the feet of the leadsman, who was dropping the lead to take soundings. The leadsman ran in panic onto the deck. "Get back!" Captain Mc-

Gowan shouted. "You're much safer where you were—lightning never strikes twice in the same place!" His words hardly comforted the terrified leadsman, but other hands came forward to assess the damage done by the ball. War correspondent Church noted that it left "an honorable scar" but had been too spent to penetrate the side.

The young cadets behind the dunes kept firing, and shots whistled over the *Star of the West.* "One shot passed just clear of the pilothouse," McGowan wrote later, "another passed between the smoke-stack and walking beams of the engine, another struck the ship just abaft the forerigging and stove in the planking, while another came within an ace of taking away the rudder." Although the range for the old-fashioned 24-pounders was short, and the youngsters were green artillerists, at least seventeen shots were fired; two or three of them hit the ship and several whizzed over the deck just above the heads of the men as the *Star of the West* paddled on at undiminished speed. All Charleston knew of the action now, the Charleston correspondent of the *Washington Star* noting in his story that "our citizens were aroused by the loud and repeated reverberation of cannon to seaward, and a general rush was made from all parts of the city to the wharves . . . the excitement and anxiety intense . . ."

As the *Star* passed out of range of the Morris Island guns and almost within range of the bigger guns of Fort Moultrie to the starboard on Sullivan's Island, Captain McGowan anxiously wondered, despite the Stars and Stripes flying there, whether Fort Sumter hadn't fallen into Confederate hands. Sumter could plainly be seen, yet Major Anderson hadn't opened fire on either Morris Island or Fort Moultrie. What the hell was happening? McGowan, of course, had no way of knowing that Anderson and his men were completely unaware of the strategy to reinforce Sumter and were about the only ones in all of Charleston who didn't know all the details of the *Star*'s mission and had no inkling that they were supposed to use their guns to "silence such fire" if the *Star* was attacked.

Sumter's defenders had first noticed the *Star* earlier that morning, when Captain Doubleday had spotted her. "Soon after daylight . . . I was on the parapet with my spyglass," Doubleday

112

remembered later, "for I fancied from a signal I had observed the previous evening on a pilot-boat, that something must be coming. As I looked seaward, I saw a large steamer pass the bar and enter the Morris Island channel. It had the ordinary United States flag up; and as it evidently did not belong to the navy, I came to the conclusion it must the *Star of the West.* I do not remember that any other officers were on the lookout at this time. Anderson himself was still in bed. When the vessel came opposite the new battery, which had just been built by the cadets, I saw a shot fired to bring her to. Soon after this an immense United States garrison-flag was run up at the fore. Without waiting to ascertain the result of the firing, I dashed down the back stairs to Anderson's room, to notify him of the occurrence."

Anderson ordered Doubleday to have the drummer beat the long roll summoning men to guns on the parapet. The usually fastidious Anderson dressed hastily, clearly angry, yet confused and unable to act. No one is certain what happened next. Gunnery Sergeant James Chester reported that a conference of officers was held. "When the *Star of the West* was seen standing in," he wrote, "the novelty of a steamer carrying the national flag had more attractions for the men than the breakfast table. They soon made her out to be a merchant steamer, as the walking-beam, plainly visible as she rounded into the channel, was unknown on a man-o-war. She had taken the Morris Island channel, and was approaching at a fair rate of speed. Perhaps every man in Sumter was on the ramparts, but there was no excitement. But when the blue puff of smoke from a hidden battery on Morris Island advertised that she was being fired on, there was great scurrying and scampering among the men. . . . There seemed to be much perplexity among our officers, and Major Anderson had a conference with some of them in a room used as a laundry which opened up on the terre-plein of the sea-flank. The conference was an impromptu one, as Captain Doubleday and Lieutenant Davis were not of it. But Captain Foster was there, and by his own actions demonstrated his disappointment at the result. He left the laundry, bounding up the two or three steps that led to the terre-plein, smashing his hat, and muttering something about the flag, of which only the words [the

South Carolinians] 'trample on it' reached the ears of the men at the guns, and let them know that there was to be no fighting, on their part at least."

Captain Doubleday contended that there was at the time no "council of war," as he called it. "I know Foster was under this impression," he testified later, "but upon my recalling the circumstances to his recollection a short time before his death, he admitted his mistake. My memory is very clear and distinct on this point, and I am sustained in regard to it by both [Captains] Seymour and Crawford. . . . Indeed there was no time for deliberation while the troops were at the guns, for the vessel was moving very rapidly, and the whole affair was over in a few minutes. The council was held *after the steamer was gone,* to determine what action ought to be taken in consequence of the attack."

In either case, it was Major Anderson's decision not to return fire, despite the fact that the United States flag had been fired upon. Knowing nothing of his delayed instructions, Anderson felt compelled to obey his previous order from Washington to act "strictly on the defensive," though "defensive" could have been loosely interpreted to mean protecting any American flag, not merely the one fluttering from Fort Sumter. Anderson's officers gave conflicting advice. Young Virginian Lieutenant Meade searched his soul and urged the Major not to fire because he believed the firing upon the *Star* was the unauthorized work of secessionist hotheads and once Sumter's guns let fly, "It will bring Civil War upon us." Lieutenant Jefferson C. Davis advised Anderson to forget about Morris Island and concentrate on Fort Moultrie; the Major sent him below to take charge of two 42-pounders aimed at Moultrie and await further orders.

Doubleday, quite predictably, stamped his feet in frustration. "I think the people in Fort Moultrie, who expected to be driven out to take refuge behind the sand-hills, were especially astonished at our inaction," he wrote later. "It is very true that the Morris Island battery was beyond the reach of our guns. Still, we did not know this positively at the time; and our firing in that direction, even if ineffectual, would have encouraged the steamer to keep on its course. We had one or two guns bearing on Fort Moultrie; and as that was within easy range, we could have kept the fire down long enough to enable the steamer to come in. It was plainly our duty to do all that we could. For any thing we knew to the contrary, she might have been in a sinking condition. Had she gone down before our eyes, without an effort on our part to aid her, Anderson would have incurred a fearful responsibility by his inaction."

Most of Sumter's enlisted men yearned for action, believing by now that they were more than a match for the boy secessionists. Corporal Francis Oakes, manning a barbette 24-pounder facing Morris Island, held the lanyard, fingers itching to jerk it back. The wife of Private John H. Davis, though Virginia-born, was so enraged that she grabbed a friction tube and leaped behind a gun, which she swore she would fire herself if no one else did. Captain Doubleday finally calmed her.

By this time the big Fort Moultrie guns were ready to fire upon the *Star of the West.* Lieutenant Colonel Roswell Ripley, a West Pointer and Northerner who had joined the secessionists, gave the order. "Now, boys, we'll give 'em a shot or two," he cried, "and then we'll catch the devil from Sumter!" The ready Columbiad, nicknamed "Edith," immediately roared, but her shot went wild, the ship still out of range.

"Do let us give them one, sir!" an officer pleaded with Anderson inside Sumter.

"Patience—be patient," was the reply. Sumter gave no devil in return, nor any assistance at all to the *Star.* When the steamer tried signaling the fort with its flag, Major Anderson did attempt to answer, but the Sumter flag couldn't be raised because the halyards were fouled. Robert Anderson had decided not to fire; as much as part of him wanted to, he sacrificed his pride in the hope that all-out war could be avoided, and if only for the moment, he lost face in the eyes of many of his men.

Though she received no help or communication from Sumter, the *Star* continued side-wheeling on toward the fort; but the Carolinian balls were coming lower and closer every moment as the young artillerists sharpened their aim. The Carolinian cannonading could be heard for miles around, and Charlestonians rushed out half-dressed into the streets and down to the wharves, or sent their servants on fast horses to see whether the sound of the big guns meant war, as most of them guessed. Then just as the *Star* passed within range of Fort Moultrie, two armed schooners were spotted being towed into action by steamboats and getting ready to fire upon her. By now, over twenty shots had already been fired—some seventeen by the cadets and three or so from Fort Moultrie. Although only two of these shots had hit the *Star,* causing no serious damage, Captain McGowan thought it would be foolhardy to continue. He was only a half mile from Sumter when he shouted the order for the *Star* to reverse her course in an abrupt curve and head back to sea, a prudent action that perhaps saved his ship damage, if not sinking, and his men injury. Officers and crew had lost face, but most retained a sense of humor. After the *Star* scraped the bottom several times recrossing the bar, at about 8:50 A.M., an officer looked back at the spires of Charleston, glanced about the damaged ship, and quipped: "The people of Charleston pride themselves upon their hospitality, but it exceeds my expectation. They gave us several balls before we landed."

Captain McGowan was in a fouler mood. Out at sea the Liverpool sailing vessel *Emily St. Pierre* was encountered, and McGowan asked her where she was bound and under what flag she flew. Her captain replied that she sailed under the American flag and was bound for South Carolina.

"Then you can't go into Charleston," McGowan replied. "They will not let the American flag into that port. I was just driven out of there. They fired upon me when I was sailing under the American flag."

"I suppose I must go in under the palmetto flag of South Carolina then," said the *Emily St. Pierre's* captain.

"Then I ought to take you!" McGowan shouted angrily. "War has been declared. They have fired upon me, and you will be a lawful prize."

But thinking better of claiming the ship, realizing his orders gave him no such authority, Captain McGowan headed back to New York, which he reached in three uneventful days. No cheering crowds were on hand to greet the *Star of the West* at her Warren Street dock, though curious people did gather to examine the wounds of the defeated ship whose mission had accomplished nothing except to make M. O. Roberts $10,500 richer.

As for the mighty *Brooklyn* with her twenty-two 9-inch guns, it took her two days to get ready for battle after War Secretary Holt ordered her into action at Charleston. She didn't sail until the *Star* was already on her way back to New York; after searching the rough seas in vain, she headed back to Fort Monroe. The *Star of the West* was to serve her country one more time and earn M. O. Roberts a few more dollars. The United States soon rechartered her to sail to Indianola and evacuate Federal troops being withdrawn from Texas. This mission, too, failed, when she was captured by the Confederates on April 17 and escorted to New Orleans. The *Star* served the Confederacy more effectively than she had the Union, carrying stores up the Yazoo River to Vicksburg, where she was kept far beyond the reach of Yankee troops. Her career ended when she was sunk in the Tallahatchie River near Fort Pemberton to blocade the Federal fleet, and she lay there as an obstruction for many years.

In a letter to M. O. Roberts written as soon as he docked, Captain McGowan officially summed up his mission:

Sir: After leaving the [Manhattan] wharf on the 5th inst., at 5 o'clock P.M., we proceeded down the Bay, where we hove to, and took on four officers and two hundred soldiers, with their arms, ammunition, etc. and then proceeded to sea, crossing the bar at Sandy Hook at 9 P.M. Nothing unusual took place during the passage, which was a pleasant one for the season of the year. We arrived at Charleston Bar at 1:30 A.M. on the 9th inst. but could find no guiding marks for the bar, as the lights were all out. We proceeded with caution, running very slow and sounding, until about 4 A.M., being then in four and a half fathoms water, when we discovered a light through the haze which at the time covered the horizon. Concluding that the lights were in Fort Sumter, after getting the bearings of it we steered to the S.W. for the main ship channel, where we hove to, to await daylight, our lights having all been put out since 12 o'clock, to avoid being seen. As the day began to break, we discovered a steamer just inshore of us, which, as soon as she saw us, burned one blue light and two red lights as signals, and shortly after steamed over the bar and into the ship channel.... As soon as there was light enough to see, we crossed the Bar and proceeded on up the channel (the outer-bar buoy having been taken away), the steamer ahead of us sending off rockets, and burning lights until after broad daylight,

continuing on her course up nearly two miles ahead of us. When
we arrived about two miles from Fort Moultrie, Fort Sumter
being about the same distance, a masked battery on Morris's
Island, where there was a red Palmetto flag flying, opened up on
us—distance about five-eighths of a mile. *We had the American
flag flying at our flag staff at the time, and soon after the first shot
hoisted a large American ensign at the fore.* We continued on under
the fire of the battery for over ten minutes. . . . Our position now
became rather critical . . . and we concluded that, to avoid certain
capture or destruction, we would endeavor to get to sea. Conse-
quently we bore round and steered down the channel, the battery
firing upon us until the shot fell short. As it was now strong ebb
tide, and the water having fallen some three feet, we proceeded
with caution, and crossed the Bar safely at 8:50 A.M., and continued on our course for this port, where we arrived this morning, after a boisterous passage. A steamer from Charleston followed us for about three hours, watching our movements. In
justice to the officers and crews of each department of the ship, I
must add that their behavior while under fire of the battery
reflected great credit on them. Mr. Brewer, the New York pilot,
was of very great assistance to me in helping to pilot the ship over
Charleston Bar, and up and down the channel. Very respectfully,
your obedient servant,

John McGowan, Captain

In his report, or explanation of his failure, McGowan seemed
moved only by the fact that the flag—*two* American flags—had
been fired upon; he went so far as to underline the words. More
than half the country shared his sentiments, and it seems clear
from newspaper accounts, editorials, and letters that the act
turned the tide of Northern opinion entirely against the South:
there were very few now who wanted peace at any price. This
insult to the flag had steered the ship of state so close to war that
only a miracle might avert it. One reporter wrote of the *Star*'s
return to New York "to the great disappointment and humilia-
tion of all true men, who were hardly less disgusted at this
skulking mission than chagrined at its failure." Back at Sumter,
Doubleday acidly remarked when the South Carolinians restored
mail delivery: "After the *Star of the West* affair, they probably

118

thought we were a very harmless people and deserved some reward for our forebearance." Wrote stowaway war correspondent Church, back now at his *Evening Post* desk: "The war has begun in earnest . . . I do not believe anymore that this tremendous question can be settled peacefully. I rather anticipate civil war, fratricidal horror—hell let loose on earth—for a season."

Yet still there was faint hope. The American flag had been fired upon where it waved aboard the *Star of the West,* but it still flew unscathed over Sumter.

7

Cold War in a Ring of Fire

Calm as that second summer which precedes
 The first fall of the snow,
In the broad sunlight of heroic deeds,
 The city bides the foe.
> —Henry Timrod,
> "Charleston," 1861

THE Star of the West Battery on Morris Island is often credited with firing the first shot of the Civil War; most historians, however, insist that the first shot sounded months later when Fort Sumter itself was bombarded, and candidates for the actual firing range from the venerable fire-eater Edmund Ruffin to a two-year-old baby. In fact, Citadel Cadet Haynesworth's poorly aimed shot from the Star of the West Battery was the first fired at the American flag by a secessionist, but shots had been fired in anger the night before the *Star* reached Charleston Harbor. At that time a Federal guard at Fort Barrancas in Pensacola, Florida, opened fire on twenty rebel state troopers who advanced upon him, probably scouting to determine if Barrancas was garrisoned. Fort Barrancas's second in command, Lieutenant J. H. Gilman, later described the action there.

Near Fort Barrancas . . . is the post of Barrancas Barracks [Gillman wrote], and there, in January 1861, was stationed Company G. 1st United States Artillery, the sole force of the United States Army in the harbor to guard and hold, as best it might, the property of the United States. . . . With the new year, 1861, came to us at that quiet little post the startling news of the seizure of United States property at various points by State troops, and by January 7th rumors, to us still more startling, reached our ears, to the effect that the Navy Yard and forts in Pensacola Harbor were to be seized by troops already preparing, in Florida and Alabama, to march against us. . . . On January 8th the first step indicating to outsiders an intention on our part to resist was taken, by the removal of the powder from the [old] Spanish fort [San Carlos de Barrancas] to Fort Barrancas, where on the same night a guard was placed with loaded muskets. It was none too soon, for about midnight a party of twenty men came to the fort, evidently with the intention of taking possession, expecting to find it unoccupied as usual. Being challenged and not answering nor halting when ordered, the party was fired upon by the guard and ran in the direction of Warrington village, their footsteps resounding on the plank walk as the long roll ceased and our company started for the fort at doublequick. This, I believe, was the first gun in the Civil War fired on our side.

It is often said that Fort Pickens on Santa Rosa Island in Pensacola Harbor, to which the tiny Fort Barrancas garrison of forty-six men later withdrew for strategic reasons similar to those Anderson had in removing to Sumter, was held without a shot being fired by either side, but that story ignores this nameless sentry at Fort Barrancas, whose shots must be regarded as part of the Fort Pickens action. In any case, the shots at Barrancas were the first shots fired in defense of the Union, while the shots fired at the *Star of the West* were certainly the first fired at the U.S. colors, coming fully three months before Sumter was fired upon and about a week before one Horace Miller, a trooper in Captain J. F. Kerr's battery in Vicksburg, Mississippi, let loose a 4-pounder in front of a steamer out of Pittsburgh suspected of carrying arms and ammunition to Federal forces in New Orleans. (No supplies were found when militiamen searched the paddle wheeler, and she was allowed to sail on.)

Who fired the first shot concerned no one inside Sumter after the beaten and scarred *Star of the West* scampered out of the harbor. But there were misgivings about Union strategy. After the war, Sumter's Sergeant Chester claimed that even the unarmed *Star of the West* could have made it down the channel. "Sumter was master of the situation," Chester wrote. "[Fort] Moultrie had few guns mounted—only one, according to report— and that fact ought to have been known to the people on the *Star of the West*. It was known officially in Washington that fourteen days previously Major Anderson had spiked the guns and burned the carriages at Moultrie, and gun-carriages cannot be replaced in two weeks when they have to be fabricated. Hence Moultrie could not have been formidable, and as soon as it [the *Star*] passed the battery on Morris Island, it would have been comparatively safe."

124

General Scott and his staff were surely guilty of poor interpretation of intelligence if Chester is right, but nevertheless the *Star* probably would have needed the support of Sumter's guns to get through, although the evidence indicates that she had a chance of making Fort Sumter had McGowan dared, even without Anderson's artillery support. In retrospect the U.S. government, especially General Scott and President Buchanan, has to take most of the blame. The expedition should have been a bold, open one, defending what belonged to the nation, not a secret, skulking spy mission; the expedition should have sailed earlier, before there were any South Carolinian defenses to speak of, instead of being delayed out of deference to the Southern commissioners; orders should have been sent by special courier to Major Anderson, not through mails controlled by the secessionists; the *Star* should have had more specific orders, and the mighty *Brooklyn* should certainly have been sent in the *Star*'s place, or as an escort. Five "should haves" that didn't happen. Government bungling made Captain McGowan's lack of daring (out of concern for his men and M. O. Roberts's ship) and Major Anderson's confusion or vacillation seem negligible.

Carolinans crowed about their victory over the *Star,* and many considered it the beginning of a revolutionary war long in coming. Most believed that the *Star* had committed the first act of war by entering "their" harbor to begin with. "Yesterday the 9th of January will be memorable in our history," Rhett's *Charleston Mercury* pronounced. "Powder has been burnt . . . perhaps blood spilled. . . . The expulsion of the . . . *Star of the West* from the Charleston Harbor yesterday morning was the opening ball of the Revolution. We are proud that our harbor has been so honored. . . . Entrenched upon her soil she has spoken from the mouth of her cannon, and not from the mouths of scurrilous demagogues, fanatics and scribblers . . . she has not hesitated *to strike the first blow,* full in the face of her insulter. . . . We would not exchange or recall that blow for millions! It has wiped out a half century of scorn and outrage."

Clearly a case of the pot calling the kettle "scurrilous demagogues, fanatics," and so on, but the majority of Carolinians did agree with the *Mercury* in substance. As the local correspondent of the *New York Herald* wrote in a dispatch that same day: "War is unquestionably declared, and South Carolina resolute for it."

In the North, opinion ranged from the reactions of abolitionists such as William Lloyd Garrison, Wendell Phillips, and Horace Greeley, who believed that the United States could now rid itself of the evil of slavery by letting "the erring sisters go in peace," to that of New Yorker George T. Strong, who wrote in his diary: "The nation pockets this insult to the national flag, a calm, dishonorable, vile submission." Southern sympathizers like Democratic Congressman John Logan of Illinois compared the Carolinians to patriots of the American Revolution. But in Albany, New York, the *Atlas and Argus* argued, "The authority and dignity of the Government must be vindicated at every hazard. The issue thus having been made, it must be met and sustained, if necessary, by the whole power of the navy and army." Many called for the force of arms to put down this rebellion, but numerous Northerners, angry as they were, still hoped for another great sectional compromise like those of 1820, 1833, and 1850 to appease Southern tantrums and avoid war.

Buchanan obliged, to an extent. The President offered no great compromise, but he took no action remotely resembling war. Northern cartoonists soon began depicting the national eagle as a scrawny, sorry bird with its feathers plucked, its head drooping, and a thick chain choking it. For the most part "a gloomy, gnawing, fierce unrest pervaded the land," as a contemporary historian put it. What could be done without killing one's brothers?

The Fort Sumter garrison agreed almost to a man with Captain Foster when he declared in his official report: "The firing upon the *Star of the West* by the batteries on Morris Island opened the war." Major Anderson may have come down a peg in their estimation for failing to fire back, but he regained lost respect on advising his men that he proposed to close Charleston Harbor and loose Sumter's guns on any ship attempting to enter. The members of the council he convened to discuss this proposal varied widely in their reactions. Captain Doubleday, true to form, agreed without reservations, and Lieutenants Hall and Snyder went along with him. Young Lieutenant Meade voiced his opposition: Sumter could act only on the defensive, he insisted; such were their orders and anything else would be an act of war. Lieutenant Davis first wanted to know whether Governor

Pickens had ordered the attack on the *Star* or if it was unauthorized.

Surgeon Crawford seems to have been the hero of the piece, but then it is he who recorded the conference in his diary. Crawford claims that he urged Anderson to dispatch a message to Pickens letting him know just how determined they were. Soon after, Lieutenant Hall rowed a boat to Charleston under a white flag— whatever anyone *said,* North and South were clearly enemies at war now—and made his way to City Hall, where Governor Pickens hastily adjourned a cabinet meeting to receive him. Pickens, like the excited crowds of Charlestonians Lieutenant Hall passed on his way to City Hall, feared that Anderson would bombard Charleston itself and anxiously opened the letter Hall handed him.

"Sir," Anderson had written, "Two of your batteries fired this morning upon an unarmed vessel bearing the flag of my Government. As I have not been notified that war has been declared by South Carolina against the Government of the United States, I cannot but think that this hostile act was committed without your sanction or authority. Under that hope, and that alone, did I refrain from opening fire upon your batteries. I have therefore respectfully to ask whether the above-mentioned act, one I believe without a parallel in the history of our country or of any other civilized government, was committed in obedience to your intentions, and to notify you, if it be not disclaimed, that I must regard it as an act of war, and that I shall not, after a reasonable time for the return of my messenger, permit any vessel to pass within range of the guns in my fort. In order to save, as far as lies within my power, the shedding of blood, I beg that you will have due notice of this, my decision, given to all concerned, hoping, however, your answer may justify a further continuance of forbearance on my part. I remain, respectfully, Robert Anderson."

After reading the letter Governor Pickens quickly conferred with his cabinet again and wrote his reply to Anderson, which Lieutenant Hall carried back to Sumter. The major was surprised to read that Governor Pickens was making threats of his own. Pickens, far from disavowing the attack on the *Star of the West,* claimed the action had been perfectly justified because the *Star* had been warned not to enter the harbor and South Carolina had officially informed the President of the United States that any attempt to reinforce Sumter would be regarded as an "act of hostility." For Anderson to close the port would impose "upon the state the conditions of a conquered province," a condition that South Carolina would resist and that would be solely Anderson's responsibility. There is not a touch of humility in the governor's reply, written largely in the third person:

> Governor Pickens, after stating the position of South Carolina toward the United States, says that any attempt to send United States troops into Charleston Harbor, to re-enforce the forts, would be regarded as an act of hostility, and, in conclusion, adds that any attempt to re-enforce the troops at Fort Sumter, or to retake and resume possession of the forts within the waters of South Carolina, which Major Anderson abandoned, after spiking the cannon and doing other damage, can not but be regarded by the authorities of the state as indicative of any other purpose than the coercion of the state by the armed force of the government; special agents, therefore, have been put off the Bar to warn approaching vessels, armed and unarmed, having troops to re-enforce Fort Sumter aboard, not to enter the harbor. Special orders have been given the commanders at the forts not to fire on such vessels until a shot across their bows should warn them of the prohibition of the state. Under these circumstances, the *Star of the West,* it is understood, this morning attempted to enter the harbor with troops, after having been notified she could not enter, and consequently she was fired into. This act is perfectly justified by me. In regard to your threat about vessels in the harbor, it is only necessary for me to say, you must be the judge of your responsibility. Your position in the harbor has been tolerated by the authorities of the state; and while the act of which you complain is in perfect consistency with the rights and duties of the state, it is not perceived how far the conduct you propose to adopt can find a parallel in the history of any country, or be reconciled with any other purpose than that of your government imposing on the state the condition of a conquered province.
>
> F. W. Pickens

Major Anderson's hopes for peace were revived on reading that a warning shot had been fired at the *Star* before hostile fire was directed against her. Previously unaware of this, he now decided *not* to close the harbor until he received further instructions from Washington, much to Doubleday's consternation. The major sat down to write Pickens a second letter.

> Sir, I have the honor to acknowledge the receipt of your communication and say that, under the circumstances, I have deemed it proper to refer the whole matter to my government, and intend deferring the course I indicated in my note this morning until the arrival from Washington of such instructions as I may receive. I have the honor also to express the hope that no obstructions will be placed in the way, and that you will do the favor of giving every facility for the departure and return of the bearer, Lieutenant T. Talbot, who is directed to make the journey.
>
> Robert Anderson

What amounted to a de facto truce resulted when Governor Pickens informed messengers Crawford and Talbot that he was "very glad" the major had changed his mind about closing the harbor and gave Talbot safe passage to Washington. Relieved that the harbor wasn't bottled up and commerce still thrived in Charleston, the governor also granted permission for all the women and children in Sumter to leave at any time, allowed the hungry garrison to purchase food (except flour) in the city, and even let a chivalrous South Carolina officer send over a few cases of claret. It was still very much a gentleman's battle in what all too many still believed would be a gentleman's war.

Pickens, however, gentleman though he may have been, was thinking like a politician. Unlike Anderson, he very much wanted war, very much wanted to attack Fort Sumter. But wiser men, worried that war would begin before the South could be unified in a Confederacy, warned him to be patient. The "little garrison" at Fort Sumter "presses on nothing but a point of pride," the future president of the Confederacy, Jefferson Davis, wrote to him. "You can well afford to stand still . . . and if things continue as they are for a month, we shall then be in a condition to speak with a voice that all must hear and heed."

The voices Governor Pickens heard advising caution influenced him less than the fact that he lacked the means to take the

129

fort. There was some truth in the *Mercury*'s threat that South Carolina had more men under arms than the thousand U.S. soldiers scattered from fort to fort from Boston to New Orleans. But U.S. forces consisted of trained soldiers, and the United States boasted a powerful navy, especially when compared to the practically nonexistent South Carolinian "fleet" of four guard boats. Pickens knew there was much work to be done and seized the precious time the truce provided him.

For starters, the governor ordered four Southern artillery experts to "report the most favorable plan for operating upon Fort Sumter, so as to reduce that fortress, by batteries or other means." His experts took less than a day to report that more "batteries of heavy ordnance" and mortar batteries should be built on all the islands surrounding Fort Sumter. Such guns, they reasoned, would prevent any reinforcements from reaching Sumter and could blast the garrison until it was weak and demoralized enough to be taken by assault. Another option was to assist "the slow process of starvation" to deliver the fort to the state.

While Anderson thought of keeping the peace, the Carolinians were thinking of how to grow strong enough to break it. Carolina militiamen and as many as a thousand slaves began laboring day and night to strengthen the Star of the West Battery and the battery at Cummings Point on Morris Island, build batteries at Fort Johnson on James Island, and place cannon at various other places to extend their ring of fire around Sumter. Guns were taken from Castle Pinckney, a stone's throw from Charleston, and shipped to Fort Moultrie where they were ordered "to be used in the newly constructed battery at the east end of Sullivan's Island." Huge incandescent Drummond lights with their intense white light that utilized calcium oxide, or lime, were installed to light the harbor and prevent reinforcements from reaching the Sumter garrison at night—Fort Sumter was literally *in the limelight* now. As a further step, the steamers *Marion* and *Aid* were assigned as guard ships to help the *General Clinch* and *Nina* protect the harbor. Finally, Pickens ordered four old hulks, contributed by the citizens of Savannah, to be loaded with the granite stones being used to build the customhouse and sunk in the channels to block any future relief ships. Though the ships themselves would soon be swept away by strong tides, the rocks would remain to prevent any vessel drawing more than 13 feet of water from entering. Despite Doubleday's suspicion that this was "a mere *coup de théâtre,* to intimidate us," the channels were blocked so well that larger merchant vessels had to be diverted to Savannah, which lost Charleston much trade and led local humorists to quip that the citizens of Savannah would be glad to give Charleston all the old hulks she wanted to sink—no charge. As Doubleday quipped: "The Charleston people said they now fully understand and appreciated the kindness of the people of Savannah in furnishing them with old hulks to destroy the harbor of Charleston."

Major Anderson and his men in Sumter watched through spyglasses as the Carolinians began strengthening the semicircular ring around the fort (the ring would come almost full circle a month or so later with the completion of the celebrated ironclad Floating Battery). Second in command Doubleday urged Anderson to warn the secessionists to halt all work or have their still vulnerable forts blasted to bits. But the major ignored all such advice: he would still try to keep the peace.

Despite his conciliatory efforts, Anderson's stock kept rising in the North, mainly because of his love and respect for the flag. As *Harper's* editor Guernsey later noted: "In the first sentence of his demand upon the insurgent governor, the words 'the flag of my government' touched the sensitive public heart. [Anderson] had been the first to assert the existence of that government among the insurgent and to support its flag, and he rose higher than before in public favor." People sensed even then that the responsibility of war or peace rested entirely on Major Anderson's shoulders, that he would always wait for requested instructions that never came from a government that, as Doubleday put it, desired only "to have a peaceable death bed, leaving its burdens for Mr. Lincoln's shoulders." According to a contemporary historian, Buchanan's nickname was Old Buck but would better have been Old Buckpasser, the Sumter affair being "possibly the most flagrant instance of passing the buck in American history."

While awaiting orders from Washington, Anderson did begin to strengthen Fort Sumter, and by the end of January, fifty-one guns would be in position, including two 10-inchers placed in the parade grounds as mortars. Meanwhile, Governor Pickens kept thinking of ways "to negotiate us out of Fort Sumter," in Doubleday's words. On January 11, two days after the *Star* had fled, Pickens dispatched two representatives to Sumter in the little steamer *Antelope* under a white flag, their arrival coinciding with the stone-crammed hulks from Savannah being towed out in the channels to be sunk. Anderson escorted the two officials of the South Carolina republic into the fort's guardroom, where one of them, the diminutive Judge Andrew Gordon Magrath, the republic's secretary of state, handed him the governor's letter.

"Sir," Pickens had written, "I have thought proper, under all the circumstances of the peculiar state of public affairs in the country at present, to appoint the Honorable A. G. Magrath and General D. F. Jamison [Secretary of War], both members of the Executive Council and of the highest position in the State, to present to you considerations of the gravest public character, and of the deepest interest to all who deprecate the improper waste of life, to induce the delivery of Fort Sumter to the constituted authorities of the State of South Carolina, with a pledge on its part to account for such public property as is under your charge."

In other words, "Please surrender your garrison now." Major Anderson knew he would do nothing of the sort, but as a matter of form called a war council of his officers, who to a man, even the southerner Meade among them, also rejected the proposal. Anderson explained to the messengers that he must await Lieutenant Talbot's return from Washington with instructions, and the scholarly, eloquent Judge Magrath—a Harvard man and "the champion orator of the State," as Doubleday described him—made an impassioned speech to Sumter's officers in the cold, damp guardroom. Captain Doubleday remembered its gist being that "South Carolina was determined to have Fort Sumter at all hazards . . . that the other Southern states were becoming excited on the subject; that President Buchanan was in his dotage; that the government in Washington was breaking up; that all was confusion, dispair, and disorder there; and that it was full time for us to look out for our own safety, for if we refused to give up the fort nothing could prevent the Southern troops from exterminating us." Listen to reason, Magrath warned the officers, or "thou-

Fort Sumter on the Eve of War

When Federal troops occupied Fort Sumter in late December 1860, they found the place "filled with building materials, guns, carriages, shot, shell, derricks, timbers, blocks and tackle, and coils of rope in great confusion." The soldiers spent many weeks clearing away debris, distributing shot, and bracing up embrasures against a threatened Confederate attack. By April 1861 the fort looked much as it does below.

The principal parts of the 1861 fort are identified in the following list. Each is keyed by number to the illustration. The cutaway section of the illustration shows the arched first- and second-tier casemates behind the brick exterior. The second-tier casemates were unfinished and no cannon were mounted there.

apartments for officers and their families. Ordnance storerooms and a hospital were also located here.
9/Enlisted Men's Barracks, each designed to accommodate two companies.
10/Stair Tower, providing access to the barbette tier.
11/Hot Shot Furnace
12/Second Tier Embrasures
13/Fort Lantern
14/Bins containing oyster shells probably used in the fort's construction.
15/Sand and Brick-bat Traverses, erected by Federal engineers as protection

against Confederate cannon fire.
16/Sanding Traverse, built to protect Federal gunners against enfilading fire from Fort Moultrie.
17/Mackenomis Gallery, a wooden outcropping atop the parapet in which soldiers could stand to fire into or drop grenades onto an attacking force.
18/Sally Port
19/Granite Wharf

1/Left Face
2/Left Flank, facing Charleston and Fort Johnson.
3/Right Face, fronting Fort Moultrie across the main ship channel.
4/Right Flank, facing the Atlantic Ocean.
5/Gorge Wall, facing Confederate batteries on Morris Island.
6/Left Gorge Angle
7/Right Gorge Angle, where Capt. Abner Doubleday commanded a Federal gun crew in one of the lower casemates.
8/Officers' Quarters, consisting of several three-story

(National Park Service)

(above left) The Old Public Functionary, or Old Pennsylvania Fossil, President James Buchanan. (National Park Service)

(above right) President Buchanan's pro-Southern Secretary of War John B. Floyd. (National Park Service)

(right) General Winfield Scott, "Old Fuss and Feathers." *(Harper's Pictorial History of the Civil War)*

(left) Portrait of Abraham Lincoln after his inauguration. (Library of Congress)

(below left) Gustavus Vasa Fox, who had a "foolproof" plan to reinforce Fort Sumter (Library of Congress)

(below right) Lincoln's Secretary of State Seward hindered the Fox expedition to reinforce Fort Sumter (Library of Congress)

(above) All of Sumter's offic
except Lieutenant Hall, who w
on a mission to Washington w
the photo was taken. Front r
left to right: Captain Doublec
Major Anderson, Captain Cr
ford, Captain Foster. Back r
Captain Seymour, Lieutena
Snyder, Davis, Meade, Tal
(National Park Service)

(left) Major Anderson poses f
photographer with his wife, E
and their son Robert, Jr. (Nati
Archives)

(clockwise from top center) Governor Francis W. Pickens of South Carolina. *(Harper's Pictorial History of the Civil War)* Judge James Louis Petigru, South Carolina's staunch Unionist. (New York Public Library) Robert Barnwell Rhett, Jr., *Charleston Mercury* editor and, like his father, a confirmed fire-eater. (Library of Congress) Robert Barnwell Rhett, Sr., "the father of secession." *(Battles and Leaders of the Civil War)* Old Fire-eater Edmund Ruffin, in uniform during the battle for Fort Sumter. (New York Public Library)

(clockwise from top left) Virginia Congressman Roger Pryor. (Library of Congress) Senator Lewis T. Wigfall of Texas. (Library of Congress) Jefferson Davis, President of the Confederate States of America. (National Park Service) Robert Toombs, Confederate Secretary of State. (Library of Congress) General Beauregard or "Old Bory." *(Battles and Leaders of the Civil War)*

(clockwise from top) Fort Sumter before the hostilities in 1860. (Benton J. Lossing. *Pictorial Field Book of the Civil War)* Flag and motto of seceded South Carolina as it adorned a booklet of the day. South Carolina Secession Convention banner. It was hoped that all the states represented would secede. Secession Hall in Charleston where the South Carolina Ordinance of Secession was passed. *(Battles and Leaders of the Civil War)*

Secessionists rallying in front of Charleston's Mills House hotel after the Ordinance of Secession was signed. (Library of Congress)

(right) Major Anderson knew that Fort Moultrie, in disrepair with sand dunes rising to the top of its walls, would be difficult to defend. *(Harper's Weekly)*

Union secret evacuation of Fort Moultrie on December 26, 1860. *(Harper's Weekly)*

Union troops landing at Fort Sumter after leaving Moultrie. *(Harper's Weekly)*

Gun carriages burning after Major Anderson evacuated Fort Moultrie. *(Harper's Weekly)*

Families of the Sumter defenders wave their farewells as they depart for New York. *(Harper's Weekly)*

(above) Carolinians at the U.S. Arsenal after the state seized it following Anderson's escape. *(The Soldier in Our Civil War)*

(left) The U.S. Custom House in Charleston, seized by the Carolinians after Anderson's escape. (Benton J. Lossing, *Civil War in America*)

(below) Castle Pinckney just after Carolinians seized it. *(Harper's Weekly)*

The inauguration of Jefferson Davis as President of the Confederate States of America in Montgomery, Alabama, February 18, 1861. *(New York Illustrated News)*

The *Star of the West* as she neared Charleston on January 9, 1861. *(Harper's Weekly)*

(left) Lincoln's inauguration on March 4, 1861. *(Frank Leslie's Illustrated Newspaper)*

(below) The completed Floating Battery with its attached hospital to the right. *(Harper's Weekly)*

(above) Fort Sumter's officers quarters. *(Harper's Weekly)*

(right) Major Anderson in his quarters at Fort Sumter. *(Harper's Weekly)*

(below) Captain Doubleday getting ready to fire the first Union shell of the battle. *(Harper's Weekly)*

Big 10-inch Columbiad trained on Charleston from the Sumter parade could not be used due to dangerous enemy fire. *(Harper's Pictorial History of the Civil War)*

(right) Charlestonians watch from rooftops as Confederate guns bombard Fort Sumter. (National Park Service)

(below) Fort Sumter during the battle. (Library of Congress)

(left) Peter Hart raising the flag after Confederate shells felled it, an act of heroism celebrated throughout the North. *(Harper's History of the Great Rebellion)*

(below) Fort Sumter's main battery, bearing on Fort Moultrie. *(Harper's Weekly)*

Sumter sallyport and officers quarters after the battle. (National Archives)

The Charleston Mercury Extra.

Saturday Evening, April 14, 1861.

THE BATTLE OF FORT SUMTER!

END OF THE FIGHT!

MAJOR ANDERSON SURRENDERS!

Rhett's *Mercury* proclaims victory.

Sumter the day after surrender. (National Archives)

Confederate flag flies over Fort Sumter the day after Sumter fell to the rebels. (United States Military History Institute)

sands will howl around these walls and pull out the bricks with their fingers." But he ended with an affecting "May God Almighty enable you to come to a just decision," before yielding the floor to Major Anderson.

"I cannot do what belongs to the government to do," Anderson replied, as near as Surgeon Crawford remembered in his memoirs. "The demand must be made upon them, and I appeal to you as a Christian, as a man, and as a fellow-countryman, to do all that you can to prevent an appeal to arms. . . . Why not exhaust diplomacy as in other matters?" He offered to send another of his officers to Washington to report on the condition of Fort Sumter if Governor Pickens would send a commissioner to lay South Carolina's claims before the authorities there.

Back in Charleston, Pickens received Anderson's written offer with glee—he must have at least rubbed his hands together a few times—and immediately accepted it. The truce had been extended, there was more time, probably weeks, to continue work on the batteries around Sumter. He hastily appointed Attorney General Colonel Isaac W. Hayne as his commissioner to Washington, while Anderson sent young Lieutenant Norman J. Hall.

Doubleday "was strongly opposed to this fatal measure," which, he wrote, "ultimately cost us the loss of Fort Sumter." The agreement, he felt, "tied the hands of the United States for an indefinite period of time, and prevented the arrival of any war vessels until South Carolina was fully prepared to receive them. The delay gave the State time to complete and man its batteries, and to obtain an unlimited number of guns and quantities of shot and shell from the cannon foundry at Richmond, Virginia, known as the Tredegar Iron Works. Thus, while our supplies would be running out, theirs would be coming in. Every day's delay would weaken us and strengthen them."

The angry captain seemed to resent that Anderson's decision hadn't been submitted to a war council, that Anderson was "at the time at the height of his popularity, and everything he did was sure to be sustained at Washington." In a letter to his wife, at home in New York now, Captain Doubleday strongly expressed his dissatisfaction, and an angry Mary Doubleday passed the letter on to Abner's brother, Ulysses, a prominent no-nonsense Republican. He sent it to President-elect Lincoln along with a letter in which he wrote "that Maj. A's. heart is not with his duty" because, despite Captain Doubleday's protests, he had let the secessionists arm themselves when he could have prevented it. Lincoln would remember these words, but neither he nor anyone close to him tried to take any action or made any comment about the accusation. In fact, President-elect Lincoln was keeping a low profile as part of his plan to save the Union. There had long been many in the North who agreed with Buchanan's former Secretary of State Lewis Cass, who had resigned in December, that "The people in the South are mad [and] the people in the North are asleep . . . [and] the President is pale with fear." Now there were those who began to suspect that the new administration would offer nothing better on coming into power. Like Cass, they lamented: "God only knows what is to be the fate of my country!"

Major Anderson went on strengthening Fort Sumter as best he could under the circumstances. Over the remaining weeks more guns were mounted in the first tier of casemates and along the parapet, these including heavier 42-pounders and big Columbiads, so that by the time of the battle for Sumter a total of sixty guns were ready. Anderson also had five Columbiads mounted in the parade as mortars, positioned three howitzers about the sally port or gateway in the gorge, built "bombproof" shelters, and constructed overhanging galleries out from the parapet at strategic points for dropping shells on any assaulting force. He was forced to leave the second tier of casemates unarmed, however, and had to link up the 8-foot-square openings in the outer wall. He just did not have enough soldiers to man them.

As for the Carolinians, they were developing the "secret weapon" that would complete the ring of batteries around Sumter. Their experts felt that a battery should be placed between the fort and Charleston, and when Captain John Randolph Hamilton, Alexander Hamilton's grandson, who had recently resigned from the U.S. Navy, and Major J. H. Trapier presented plans for an ironclad Floating Battery to the South Carolina Executive Council, $12,000 was authorized for its construction. Work began on the Floating Battery in the middle of January, and it was completed by March 3. It is often forgotten that this ironclad vessel was the first such used in the Civil War, a full year before the historic clash of the *Monitor* and *Merrimac* (or *Virginia*) at Hamp-

134

ton Roads, though ironclad vessels had been used by the French and other nations, particularly against waterfront forts, for many years. Credit for the Floating Battery is usually given to Captain Hamilton, but Major Trapier wrote South Carolina's Secretary of War D. F. Jamison that he had originated the idea.

Be that as it may, Hamilton supervised the construction of the ironclad vessel in Charleston, within sight of Sumter's troops. No official details survive of its construction, but it was probably 100 feet long and 25 feet wide, built of pine logs, buttressed in front with palmetto logs, and armored with two layers of inch-thick railroad iron, enough to resist the heaviest shells. Resembling a barge with a three-sided, peak-roofed barn at the bow and sandbags extending the entire width of the stern, it had an 8-foot draft. There were four "windows" for cannon to shoot through and even a hospital in an attached shed. Sixty men were required to operate it.

People in the North were especially curious about this "secret weapon," and the *New York Herald* invited the public to its offices to see a palmetto log like the one used in its construction. It is said that P. T. Barnum was offered another palmetto log to exhibit at his American Museum on Broadway, but that the Prince of Humbug refused to pay the $150 requested for it. The Yankees at Sumter called the officially designated Floating Battery "the raft," but the Carolinians had a harsher name for the contraption, dubbing it "the slaughter pen," because the troops feared it would tip over and drown everyone on board once the first Yankee shell hit it. Captain Foster, Sumter's engineering expert, thought little of the battery and advised Washington that "it can be destroyed by our fire before it has time to do much damage."

Major Anderson was instructed that he would be justified in firing at the Floating Battery if he thought it was advancing to attack him but to leave it alone if it remained at a reasonable distance. The Carolinian command had planned to tow the monster out to Sumter and anchor it off the weak gorge of the fort where, in Doubleday's words, it would "beat down our main gates and make wide breaches in the walls for an assaulting party to enter." However, public opinion against the slaughter pen was so strong that this plan had to be abandoned. After its completion on March 3, the Floating Battery was tied up at a wharf at Cove

Inlet at the west end of Sullivan's Island. From there it would join in the bombardment of Sumter and do considerable damage.

Long before the Floating Battery was finished, Anderson and his men had secured the main gates of Sumter against any landing party assault by mining the wharf and building a wall of stone and mortar behind the gates, leaving what was called "a man-hole" for the entrance of one person at a time. This opening was covered by a twenty-five-pound howitzer loaded with canister shot, a collection of small projectiles in a case.

Doubleday estimated that some six hundred slaves were at work improving secessionist harbor defenses, which far outclassed Sumter's by now. Yet the resourceful little band in the fort—so few that only eight men could be stationed at each of its five walls—kept coming up with plans to trick the secessionists. Fougasses—heaps of stones, each concealing a magazine of gunpowder—were installed on the walls, where they could be detonated from inside the fort, like mines. The ingenious Captain Seymour had invented what Doubleday called an "infernal machine." It was in fact a "flying fougass," stones and powder in a barrel "so arranged that when the barrel was rolled off the parapet the powder would explode (by means of a long lanyard) about five feet from the base of the wall" and send stones flying every which way. Doubleday later tried out one of these secret weapons when he spotted a rebel ship sailing by. Several Carolinians soon told Lieutenant Hall that there was now some anxiety in Charleston about attacking Fort Sumter because "a schooner had just come in great danger from one of our 'infernal machines,' which had exploded and whitened the water for three hundred yards around."

Wittyman's Masterpiece, another "Yankee infernal machine," also scared the rebels and gave a few laughs to the men inside Sumter. "Wittyman," Artillery Sergeant Chester later wrote, "was a German carpenter, not very familiar with English, and wholly ignorant of military engineering. His captain had conceived the idea that a *cheval-de-frise* [an obstacle, sometimes in the shape of a sawhorse, covered with spikes and barbed wire] across the riprapping at the salient angles of the fort would confine the enemy on whatever face he landed until he had been treated liberally with shell-grenades. So Wittyman was ordered to build a *cheval-de-frise* at the angle of the gorge nearest Morris Island. It was easy to see that Wittyman was not familiar with *cheval-de-frise,* so the captain explained and roughly illustrated the construction. At last Wittyman seemed to grasp the idea and went to work upon it forthwith. Perhaps the work was not examined during construction, nor seen by any one but Wittyman until it was placed. But from that day forward it was the fountain of amusement for the men. No matter how sick or sad a man might be, let him look at the masterpiece and his ailments were forgotten. Not a steamer passed—and they were passing almost every hour—but every glass on board was leveled at the masterpiece. But it baffled every one of them. Not one could guess what it was, or what it was intended to be; and after the bombardment was over we learned, quite accidentally, that it had been set down by the enemy as a means of exploding the mines."

For his part, the inventive Captain Doubleday suggested that mâchicoulis galleries be built on all the flanks and faces of Fort Sumter. "The mâchicoulis," as Chester explained it, "looked like an immense dry-goods box, set upon the parapet so as to project over the wall some three or four feet. The beams upon which it rested extended inward to the terre-plein [the ground surface] and were securely anchored down. But the dry-goods box was deceptive. Inside it was lined with heavy iron plates to make it bullet-proof. That portion of the bottom which projected beyond the wall was loop-holed for musketry, and a marksman in the mâchicoulis could shoot a man, however close he might be to the scarp wall. But musketry from the mâchicoulis could hardly be expected to beat off a determined assault upon the flanks and faces of the work. To meet this difficulty, hand grenades were improvised. Shells of all sizes, from 12 pounders to 10-inch, were loaded, and the fuse holes stopped with wooden plugs. The plugs were then bored through with a gimlet, and friction primers inserted. Behind the parapet at short intervals, and wherever it was thought they might be useful, numbers of these shell-grenades were stored under safe cover in readiness for any emergency. The method of throwing them was simple. Lanyards of sufficient length to reach to within about four feet of the riprapping were prepared, and fastened securely at the handle and near the piles of shell-grenades. To throw a grenade, the soldier lifted it on the parapet, hooked the lanyard into the eye of the friction primer, and threw the shell over the parapet. When the lanyard reached its length, the shell exploded. Thus a very few men would be more than a match for all that could assemble on the riprapping."

Despite their fears about Yankee "secret weapons," the Carolinians still managed to play the chivalrous gentlemen. When Governor Pickens learned that Sumter was without meat and fresh fruit and vegetables, for example, he sent a supply boat out to the fort. To the disappointment of most of the garrison, on a monotonous diet of salt-pork and bread, Anderson refused the gift, deciding with "due thanks to his excellency, respectfully to decline his offer." Doubleday, true to form, thought "Anderson showed a good deal of proper spirit on this occasion."

The governor's action proved very unpopular with the radical Rhett faction in Charleston, who wanted to starve Anderson and his men out as soon as possible. Rhett himself hastened to inform Pickens that he demanded that Sumter be taken without any further procrastination or delay, but the governor shrewdly put him down. "Certainly, Mr. Rhett, I have no objection," he replied. "I will furnish you with some men and you can storm the fort yourself!"

Rhett drew back, a bit shaken, and replied: "But, sir, I am not a military man!"

Said the governor: "Nor I either, and therefore I take the advice of those that are!"

Toward the middle of January the Sumter garrison lost Lieutenant Meade, the Virginian whose father was minister to Brazil, when a dispatch arrived at the fort informing him that his mother was on her deathbed. Doubleday suspected foul play. "I never knew whether this telegram was founded on fact," he wrote, "or was a strategic move to force poor Meade into the ranks of the Confederacy, by detaching him temporarily from us and taking him where tremendous political and social influences could be brought to bear upon him. He had previously been overwhelmed with letters on the subject. He was already much troubled in mind; and some months after the bombardment of Fort Sumter the pressure of family ties induced him (very reluctantly as I heard) to join the Disunionists. It was stated that he never was a happy man afterward, and that before a year had passed death put an end to his sorrow and regret. He was among the few to fight on both sides."

Soon after Meade left for home, Lieutenant Talbot returned to Sumter from Washington with a dispatch from War Secretary Holt essentially assuring Major Anderson that he was doing a fine job and that everything would be left to his judgment. The buck-passing continued, Anderson always waiting for orders that never came. Talbot told of how President Buchanan put a trembling hand on his shoulder and asked him, a mere junior officer: "Lieutenant, what shall we do?" Buchanan appeared pitiful and almost senile to the astonished Talbot.

"The President seemed like an old man in his dotage," he told Lieutenant Snyder.

The end of bleak January was marked by the departure of all the women and children from Fort Sumter. Anderson found it necessary to move them despite the effect on morale, for the food supply was low and he was concerned about their safety should Sumter be fired upon. Arrangements were made to ship all 45 dependents to Fort Hamilton in Brooklyn; the women and children moved to Charleston with Governor Pickens's permission on January 30 and transferred there to the steamer *Marion,* which sailed on February 3. Anderson arranged a one-gun salute as the *Marion* passed Sumter out into the Atlantic, and the men "gave repeated cheers" for their loved ones "and displayed much feeling; for they thought it very probable they might not meet them again for a long period, if ever."

Among those who left was an orphan named Dick Rowley, later known as Sumter Dick. "He had been abandoned by his mother, and thus thrown out on the world," Doubleday related. "For a time he was sent after his arrival in New York, to the house of Dr. Stewart, who was a family connection of mine. After supper he reminded the ladies that he had not heard tattoo yet, and wished to know at what hour they beat the reveille. He evidently thought every well-regulated family kept a drummer and fifer on hand, to sound the calls. He was very unhappy until he had procured a small stick and a miniature flag." After the battle, Sumter Dick was not heard from again in history.

Morale among the plucky little band in Sumter remained good

139

despite the loss of their loved ones and the scarcity of food and other supplies. One recent Irish immigrant rowed out to Sumter from Charleston waving his shirt as a flag of truce and delivered a small supply of tobacco to the soldiers. "I did not cross the broad Atlantic to become the citizen of one state!" he reportedly said in a heavy brogue. Though none of the men of Sumter smoked Spanish cigars, drank champagne, and ate *pâté de foie gras* like some of the genteel Carolinian officers, they managed to keep their spirits high. Several of the officers later commented on this, and Sergeant Chester testified that "There never was a happier or more contented set of men in any garrison since the Sumter soldiers, nor one more willing to do the extremely heavy physical labor of moving cannon and ball from one part of a fort to another." Their efforts and their bravery did not go unappreciated in the North at the time, either, congressmen, preachers, and crowds in the street lauding "the glorious boys of Sumter."

8

The Confederate States of America—or the Washington Republic, or Alleghania

Hath not the morning dawned with added light?
And shall not evening call another star
Out of the infinite regions of the night,
To mark this day in Heaven?
—Henry Timrod,
"Ethnogenesis, Written During the Meeting
of the First Southern Congress,
at Montgomery, February 1861."

$\int$ UMTER'S morale definitely wasn't uplifted by the news of more Southern states seceding from the Union. First came Mississippi, on January 9; the same day the *Star of the West* tried to break through to Fort Sumter, a state convention at Jackson, Mississippi, voted 84 to 14 to join South Carolina. An eyewitness reported that "A great wave of excitement swept the audience, and grave and dignified men, swayed by a common impulse, joined in the deafening applause. In an instant the hall was the scene of a wild tumult which soon spilled out into the streets." It was here that the famous patriotic song of the South "The Bonnie Blue Flag" was inspired by an immense blue silk banner with a single star that someone carried through the crowd. According to one old story, Arkansas comedian Harry Macarthy witnessed the scene and began writing the song's lyrics, which he finished when the rest of the Southern states seceded:

> First gallant South Carolina nobly made the stand;
> Then came Mississippi, who took her by the hand;
> Next, quickly Florida, Alabama and Georgia,
> All raised on high the Bonnie Blue Flag that bears a
>   Single Star . . .
> Hurrah, hurrah! for Southern Rights Hurrah!

A day after the *Star of the West* had been turned back, on January 10, Florida joined her sister states of South Carolina and Mississippi, adopting an ordinance of secession by an even more lopsided vote of 62 to 7. Five days before the convention at Talla-hassee two Federal forts in Florida had been seized by the state and more were expected to fall.

143

SUMTER

Alabama joined the seceded states a day later on January 11, by a vote of 61 to 39 at a convention in Montgomery. The vote proved closer here, primarily because there were strong pockets of antisecessionist sentiment in northern Alabama, and there was considerable debate on the floor. Nevertheless, Alabamians danced in the streets that night, setting off firecrackers and blazing rockets. "All Alabama is in a blaze," wrote one observer. The state also became the first to call for an affiliation, or confederation, of seceded states and states thought ready to secede. "In order to frame a revisional as a permanent Government," the convention declared, "the people of the States of Delaware, Maryland, Virginia, North Carolina, South Carolina, Florida, Georgia, Mississippi, Louisiana, Texas, Arkansas, Tennessee, Kentucky and Missouri ... are hereby invited to meet the people of the state of Alabama, by their delegates in convention, on the 4th day of February next in Montgomery."

Georgia—inflamed by fire-eaters like Toombs, who had assured Georgians that secession would be their "best guarantee for liberty, security, tranquility and *glory*"—became the fifth state to secede on January 19, by a vote of 208 to 89, which revealed some Union support and a hard core of moderates like Alexander Stephens, who voted against secession but later became vice-president of the Southern Confederacy. Georgia adopted the legendary Don't Tread on Me rattlesnake emblem of the Revolution for its secessionist banner.

Only a week later, on January 26, Louisiana left the Union at a convention in Baton Rouge by an overwhelming vote of 114 to 7. When told of this back in South Carolina, Judge Petigru found some humor in her secession. "Good Lord," he said. "I thought we *bought* Louisiana." In any case, golden pens were given to each signer of the Louisiana secession ordinance, and crowds marched in the streets all through the night. Not long after, Texas became the seventh state to secede, on February 1, by a vote of 166 to 7.

Senators and representatives from the seceded Southern states resigned from Congress in droves. In a particularly dramatic scene on January 21, five senators from Alabama, Florida, and Mississippi left the Senate chamber, several of their parting speeches calling tearfully for conciliation, though acknowledging their loyalty to their native states. Mississippi's Jefferson Davis, soon to be president of the Confederacy, rose to say in a quavering voice that there would be peace if the North willed it, but should war come "we will invoke the God of our fathers, who delivered them from the power of the lion, to protect us from the ravages of the bear." While fellow senators wept, he went on: "I concur in the action of the people of Mississippi, believing it to be necessary and proper, and should have been bound by their action if my belief had been otherwise . . . I am sure I feel no hostility to you, Senators from the North. I am sure there is not one of you, whatever sharp discussion there may have been between us, to whom I cannot say now, in the presence of my God, I wish you well . . . Mr. President, and Senators . . . it only remains for me to bid you a final adieu." His wife later wrote: "Inexpressibly sad he left the chamber, with but faint hope." That night in his room he prayed for peace.

More and more that always ominous and even sinister word *glory* was being heard in Southern speeches. With South Carolina and the six Gulf states gone from the Union, all the nation, including the small band trapped in Sumter, knew that a confederacy of the seceded states—a new nation—wasn't far off, especially since Federal property, including forts, arsenals, mints, customhouses, and ships were being seized by the rebels with abandon. In fact the Confederacy came into being even sooner than most expected, on February 9, less than eight weeks after South Carolina had seceded.

Reading the letters, speeches, and articles written by those who urged secession on the Southern states, one is amazed at how many thought that no war would result or that if war did come it would be a practically bloodless exercise. "Why, I'll drink all the blood that is spilled in a war between North and South," fire-eaters commonly quipped when urging secession. One false prophet would pull out a handkerchief and claim he'd wipe up all the blood spilled with nothing more than that small piece of cloth. Such was the dominant feeling among the delegates from the seven seceded states who met at Montgomery, Alabama, on February 4 to form the Confederate States of America. They were a varied bunch: the loud, hard-drinking Georgian Robert Toombs; Robert Barnwell Rhett, Sr.; former U.S. Senator James Chesnut from South Carolina; and the sharp-tongued but moderate little

145

congressman from Georgia, Alexander Hamilton Stephens, who at 90 pounds was no bigger than a child (once an enemy had laughed that he could eat him "without any trouble" and Stephens replied, "In which case you would have more brains in your belly than in your head.") Yet few of these men, whether prominent or unknown, even vaguely suspected what the future would bring as they made speeches and listened to Herman Arnold lead his Montgomery Theatre Band through catchy tunes like "Dixie." Electing Howell Cobb of Georgia president of the convention, the delegates proceeded to work out a provisional constitution very similar to the U.S. Constitution—for they considered themselves the defenders of the Constitution and the Yankees its violators. Their charter, however, by implication gave each member state the right to secede from the Confederation, guaranteed all citizens the right to own slaves, and provided for fugitive slaves to be returned to their owners when escaping from one state to another. In order to keep peace with foreign nations, most of which had outlawed slavery, resumption of the foreign slave trade was prohibited, though slaves could of course be bred and traded from state to state.

Robert Toombs might well have been selected president of the Confederacy by the convention, but Toombs, like Cobb, had made many political enemies, and when he got a little too drunk and loud one night, he lost any chance he had. "Toombs got quite tight at dinner," Alexander Stephens later wrote, "and went to a party in town tighter than I ever saw him—too tight for his character and reputation by far. I think that evening's exhibition settled the Presidency where it fell."

The delegates instead chose the inoffensive Jefferson Davis, who had alienated few people in his long career and was a cool, astute political manager who appealed to both moderates and fire-eaters. The forty-two-year-old Davis, a West Pointer who like Lincoln had served in the Black Hawk War and who had been a hero of the Mexican War at Buena Vista, would rather have been appointed a general, but he was clearly the best man available. Not long after his selection, a Northern journalist commended his singlemindedness and tenacity: "He is not, like Toombs, a boaster and bully of the fire-eating school; but he has a cool and almost serene audacity, which accomplishes his ends at least as effectively as noisier methods, and in a manner much better suited to his taste and his temperament. His nature is not rich, his soul not magnanimous, or his mind either strong or subtle. He influences men neither by convincing nor by winning them. His talent is that of clear perception; his power, that of nervous energy; and these are directed by an inflexible will. While other men pause over their scruples, and endeavor to reconcile their purpose and their conscience, he strikes directly at success. Devoid alike of enthusiasm and sentiment, he yet knows the exaltation of entire commitment to a great purpose. His body is spare; his brain large; his face attenuated and purely intellectual in expression; his manner placid and precise but decided. He could not have aroused the storm of insurrection, but he is just the man to guide its destructive energies."

Word that he had been selected—with Alexander Hamilton Stephens as his vice-president—reached Davis while he and his wife tended their flower garden at Brierfield, their plantation near Vicksburg, Mississippi. His face pale as he read the news, he again told Varina Davis that he didn't want the presidency, would much rather command the Confederate Army, but he would do his duty. On February 18 he took his oath of office while the sun shone brightly over Montgomery and in his inaugural address tried to reassure both North and South. Approaching his duties "with a humble distrust of my abilities," he said he was sure that there should be little rivalry between an "agricultural community" like the Confederate States of America and a "manufacturing community" like the "American Union," their "mutual interest would invite good will and kind offices." However, if the "Northern states" be dictated by "a desire to inflict injury upon us" then "a terrible responsibility will rest upon it, and the suffering of millions will bear testimony to the folly and wickedness of our aggressors." His address was generally temperate, but this last sentiment appealed to radicals like Yancey and Ruffin, as did his appointment of Toombs as secretary of state. A good number of Northerners liked Davis's speech, but it wouldn't be very long before almost all of them would be singing about how they'd hang him from a sour apple tree. It should be added that this quiet man, whom Yancey had introduced to the crowd at Montgomery with the line "The man and the hour have met," did have a vague vision of the future. "The audience was large and brilliant," he wrote home to his wife. "Upon my weary

147

heart was showered smiles, plaudits and flowers, but beyond them, I saw trouble and thorns innumerable."

He could not have anticipated rabid reactions to his newfound glory like that of Reverend J. W. T. McMullen of Centerville, Indiana, which surely belongs in everyone's *Book of Uncommon Prayer*: "I pray God that I may be one of the men who will pull the rope to hang Jeff Davis; and that the spirit of Washington, Jefferson, Jackson and Adams may look over the battlements of Heaven down upon the bleaching carcass, as the flesh drops from the bones, and listen to the winds, whistling Hail Columbia and Yankee Doodle through the decaying ribs which once enclosed his corrupt and traitorous heart. Amen."

At about the same time that Davis was being sworn in as president of the Confederacy, on February 6, U.S. Secretary of War Holt was framing an answer to South Carolina's Attorney General, Colonel Isaac W. Hayne, who had been sent to Washington as still another commissioner of Governor Pickens's to demand that Fort Sumter be sold to the state (which somehow had the right of "eminent domain" over it). Wrote Holt, on President Buchanan's instructions: "The title of the United States to Fort Sumter is complete and incontestable. . . . [The U.S.] has . . . absolute jurisdiction over the fort and the soil on which it stands. . . . This authority was not derived from any questionable source, but from the peaceful cession of South Carolina herself, acting through her legislature, under a provision of the Constitution of the United States. . . . South Carolina can no more assert the right of eminent domain over Fort Sumter than Maryland can assert it over the District of Columbia. . . . The President . . . can no more sell and transfer Fort Sumter to South Carolina than he can sell and convey the Capitol of the United States to Maryland. . . . If, with all the multiplied proofs of the President's anxiety for peace and of the earnestness with which he has pursued it, the authorities of that State shall assault Fort Sumter and peril the lives of the handful of brave and loyal men shut up within its walls, and thus plunge our common country into the horrors of civil war, then upon them, and those they represent, must rest the responsibility."

It was one of the handful of resolute actions Buchanan had

taken during the entire crisis, and to those who read it closely enough it spelled *war* in the near future. Yet Buchanan still left the responsibility for going to war on Major Anderson's shoulders, for his last instructions, in the dispatch from Holt that Lieutenant Talbot had brought back with him from Washington on January 19, made Anderson responsible for deciding when and if reinforcements were needed *and whether they should be sent.* Holt also stated in the message that any attempt to reinforce Sumter would "be attended by a collision of arms and the effusion of blood—a national calamity," that, in short, reinforcements meant war. Therefore, speaking for Buchanan, he was leaving the lives of millions and the fate of the country in the hands of a mere major in the U.S. Artillery.

The situation at this point could be summed up by a rhyme popular in Northern streets at the time:

James is in his Cabinet
    Doubting and debating;
Anderson's in Sumter,
    Very tired of waiting.

Pickens is in Charleston,
    Blustering of blows;
Thank goodness March the Fourth is near,
    To nip Secession's nose.

The only difference was that the proud, haughty, often rude Francis Pickens no longer would decide if and when Fort Sumter would be attacked, much as he wanted to. This decision rested now with the Confederacy and Jefferson Davis, who on February 12 wired Pickens that any question about U.S. forts or any U.S. property in the Confederacy would be answered by the Confederate States of America. Not only was Pickens no longer the leader of a Republic of sorts, he suffered the further indignity of losing the $3,000 he arrogantly had claimed the United States owed him on his salary as U.S. minister to Russia, where he had served for two years before being elected governor in 1860. Secretary of the

Treasury John Adams Dix simply sent him a draft on the U.S. subtreasury in Charleston for the $3,000. Since the governor had in his ongoing harassment of the government already ordered that all Charleston subtreasury payments be stopped, the check could never be cashed.

But Pickens still had his plantation with over two-hundred slaves, plenty of food to eat, liquor to drink, tobacco to chew, horse races to watch, and balls to waltz at, while the Yankees in Fort Sumter tightened their belts, drank nothing stronger than water, and were down to chawing on bits of cotton. Their only entertainment was their mail, which the Carolinians were opening before it reached them. Still their morale remained high. Doubleday seemed to relish the fact that he had received an "insulting letter" from Charleston threatening to tar and feather him as a snake of an abolitionist if he was ever caught in the city. The captain was most critical of Major Anderson's letting photographers, artists, and even known Carolinian military men visit Sumter and roam at will through the fort—considering that at least some of them probably were spies—but he and the others were delighted by the publicity they were getting, especially the stage dramas, like the pantomime *Fort Sumter by Moonlight,* that were popular in the North: "We saw advertisements now in the Northern papers showing that dramas founded on our occupation of Fort Sumter, and confinement, were being acted both in Boston and New York. It was quite amusing to see our names in the play-bills, and to find that persons were acting our parts and spouting mock heroics on the stage." Doubleday did not know about, or did not mention, the burlesque show playing at the Laura Keane Theatre in New York in which an actor playing Major Anderson waved a flag while surrounded by scantily clad dancers representing Liberty, Justice, Pocahontas, and the Spirit of '76.

Among the Sumter officers, both Doubleday and Crawford had reservations about Major Anderson. Captain Foster got along with him worst of all, feeling that Anderson had no authority over his engineering assignment and refusing for a time to let his engineering officers serve as officers of the day. Doubleday later reported that Anderson had said "if his native State, Kentucky, seceded, he should throw up his commission and go to Europe.

The fact is, as I have stated, he was a strong pro-slavery man, and felt bitterly toward the North for not carrying out the Fugitive Slave Law. He contended that slavery was right in principle, and expressly sanctioned by the Bible. One day, while we were conversing on the subject, I called his attention to the fact that slavery in ancient times was not founded on color; and if white slavery was right, I saw no reason why someone might not make a slave of *him,* and read texts of Scripture to him to keep him quiet. He was unable to answer this argument."

The truth is that Anderson had also come to detest the secessionists, as had his Georgian wife, and though he badly wanted peace, for unselfish reasons as well as a way out of his dilemma, he felt guilty that he hadn't defended his flag when it was fired upon during the *Star of the West* incident. He clearly remained a man who didn't know which way to turn, and no one came to rescue him from his indecision. What instructions he had from Washington seemed to range between orders for him to keep the peace at practically any price to orders for him to decide whether and when there should be war. Not that there were many instructions—or any intelligence. Most of what Major Anderson knew he read in the papers, a few of which, up North, were questioning his loyalty, and many of which, down South, were calling for his head on a platter next to Doubleday's.

Wishful thinking still prevailed in the South and the North, even after the formation of the Confederacy. War would either be avoided, or it wouldn't amount to more than a few drops of blood. Such sentiments could even be found in the Sumter garrison. Writing home to his father in Ireland late in February, Private Thompson proved a poor soothsayer. "That they intend to bombard us is evident," Thompson wrote, "and that they will attempt to breach the work at its weakest point is equally sure, but we are sure their attempt will prove a failure. . . . To tell the truth in spite of all their bluster I am almost sure they never will fire a shot at us."

Northerners often directed their wishful thinking to the vain hope that most people in the South were loyal Unionists. But despite the pipe dreams of Lincoln's future Secretary of State Seward and many others, the citizens of South Carolina and the rest of the Confederate states were almost all for secession. There were different shades of secessionists (including incendiaries who seriously considered seceding from the seceders because they weren't quick enough on the trigger), but possibly the only vocal pro-Union man in Charleston was Judge Petigru, who clearly thought his fellow Carolinians crazy and continued to say so. (When the Episcopal church eliminated the words *the United States* from one of its prayers, Judge Petigru walked out of the church.) Almost to a man, rich and poor Charlestonians joined the crusade against the damn Yankees, the companies of soldiers sporting dashing costumes decidedly bright and colorful but so unlike one another that they could hardly be called uniforms. Among South Carolina's huge volunteer army, one company consisted entirely of college students, another, led by a minister, had in its ranks a dozen or so theology students, and a third company had so many planters in its ranks that it was said to be one of the richest outfits that ever went to war.

Whether they were poor dirt farmers or millionaire planters, the rebel soldiers were sure that their cause was just, that it was the cause of George Washington and the founding fathers. In fact, at dawn on February 22 the Southern troops at Castle Pinckney fired thirteen shots in honor of the father of our country—after all, one of the names suggested for the new Confederacy had been the Washington Republic, which was better liked than Alleghania, but lost out to the Confederate States of America. Everybody loved George Washington. Not to be outdone, the Yankees at Fort Sumter fired their own thirteen-gun birthday salute to him a little after noon. Both sides, of course, would always claim the Founding Father as their own, just as they both claimed providence as their staunch ally.

Though there were differing opinions about who had George Washington and God on their side, there was no argument about who had the most guns and battalions. The lowliest greenhorns at Sumter knew that the fort was vastly outgunned and outnumbered, and they observed through their spyglasses that more and more big guns were being pointed at them every day; the Confederates were relentless in fortifying their positions. Desperate to do something, anything, Captain Foster mounted heavy barbette guns aimed at Cummings Point, only a mile or so away. One big 10-inch Columbiad was even aimed at Charleston, three miles distant, in the event it should prove advisable to bombard the city. Sergeant Chester later told of a misfiring of this gun that frightened both sides.

"Some of the officers," he wrote, "were anxious to try how [the gun] would work, and perhaps to see how true its alignment was, and to advertise to the enemy the fact that we had at least one formidable mortar in Fort Sumter. At any rate they obtained permission from Major Anderson to try the gun with a 'very small charge.' So, one afternoon the gun was loaded with a blind shell, and what was considered a 'very small charge' of powder. The regulation charge for the gun, as a gun, was eighteen pounds. On this occasion only two pounds were used. It was not expected that the shell would be thrown over a thousand yards, and as the bay was clear no danger was anticipated. Everything being in readiness, the gun was fired, and the eyes of the garrison followed the shell as it described its graceful curve in the direction of the city. By the time it reached the summit of its trajectory, the fact that the charge used was not a 'very small' one for the gun fired *as a mortar* became painfully apparent to every observer, and fears were entertained by some that the shell would reach the city, or at least the shipping near the wharves. But fortunately it fell short, and did no damage beyond scaring the secessionist guard-boat then leaving the wharf for her nightly post of observation. The guard-boat put back, and Sumter was visited by a flag of truce, perhaps to find out the meaning of our performance. No doubt the explanations given were satisfactory. No more experiments for range were tried with that gun, but we knew that Charleston was within range."

The shell had, in fact, missed Broad Street by only 516 feet (and would easily have hit the Battery had the shell been made eccentric). This accident nearly began the Civil War instead of just frightening everyone concerned. In fact, accidents had already caused what could be called the first deaths of the Civil War. The spirited young Confederate militiamen at Fort Moultrie were bored with all the waiting for the real thing and indulged in a lot of horsing around. In one tragic instance Private Thaddeus Strawinski was killed when a revolver went off accidentally. In another, Private James Allen died after he slipped and a friend's bayonet ran through his eye.

9

Point of No Return

We know not; in the temple of the Fates
God has inscribed her doom;
And, all untroubled in her faith, she waits
The triumph or the tomb.
—Henry Timrod,
"Charleston," 1861

OUR BETTER ANGELS BEATEN! Some tabloid North or South might well have run this headline even before President Lincoln called upon "the better angels of our nature" in his inauguration speech. It already seemed to many that the point of no return had been passed and war was inevitable when Brigadier General P. G. T. Beauregard, under the authority of the Confederate States of America, assumed command of all secessionist forces in Charleston on March 3. Anderson praised his former pupil in a letter to Washington and desperately prayed: "God grant that our country may be saved from the horrors of a fratricidal war!"

Pierre Gustave Toutant-Beauregard, hero to the South and colorful villain to the North, hailed from a Louisiana Creole family long devoted to lost aristocratic causes. One of his French royalist ancestors, for example, had a history of the life of Louis XVI in his library and under the frontispiece of the volume wrote in a fine hand: "Pierre Toutant a été heureux jusqu'à '93"— Pierre Toutant was happy until '93 (the year of Louis XVI's death). Beauregard joined the U.S. Army at the age of sixteen against the wishes of both his father and his mother, the daughter of Italian royalty. The short, swarthy, handsome young man mastered artillery under Anderson so well and quickly that his Nestor made him an assistant instructor while he was still a West Point cadet. A twice-wounded hero in the Mexican War who was mentioned in Scott's dispatches, he did not hide his light under a bushel like Anderson, even writing a book about his experiences with the windy title, *Personal Reminiscences of an Engineer During the Campaign in Mexico Under General Winfield Scott in 1847-48.*

Beauregard was quick to see any advantage for himself. On entering the Point, from which he graduated second in a class of forty-five in 1838, he took the hyphen out of his surname, Toutant-Beauregard, in order to be placed higher alphabetically on the academy class lists. After his graduation he served as a second lieutenant with the army engineers constructing coastal defenses at Fort Adams, Rhode Island, and Pensacola, Florida, before moving on to make a survey of Louisiana's Barataria Bay Islands, former home of Jean Laffite and his pirates. He then did tours in Fort McHenry, Baltimore, and various forts at the mouth of the Mississippi prior to the Mexican War. Before the battle of Vera Cruz, Beauregard climbed a tall tree to scout enemy positions and then refused an order for his men to dig trenches in the vicinity, figuring that enemy guns could wipe out half his command if they remained there. He moved his troops to a safer position and won the day. His brilliant objections to the plan for the battle of Mexico City led to his own tactics being successfully employed there. Only one soldier received more brevets under Scott in Mexico, and this was another young Southern engineer, Robert E. Lee, who received three to his two because Scott thought him a more original thinker. Touchy Beauregard did complain that he *deserved* three, however.

Disgusted that he remained only a captain after the Mexican War, Beauregard came close to resigning from the army, but he realized on marrying a second time that his new brother-in-law, Louisiana Senator John Slidell, could be of great help to him. Ever the politician, Beauregard had the Louisiana boss secure his appointment as military superintendent of the New Orleans customhouse. The ambitious Creole even fought a losing election battle for mayor while on active duty, and then he convinced Slidell to secure his appointment as Superintendent at West Point. Amazingly, Beauregard, a Southerner outspokenly committed to leaving the army as soon as his state seceded from the Union, landed the post late in 1860. To young cadets from Louisiana he offered the advice, "Watch me, and when I jump, you jump." The War Department, aside from Floyd, didn't look kindly on such advice and realizing its mistake, revoked his incredible appointment the day after he arrived at the Point.

A perturbed Beauregard couldn't understand why the army had removed him from a position where a Southerner could do the army great damage. "So long as I keep my opinions of the present unfortunate condition of our country to myself," he wrote, "I must respectfully protest any act which might cast . . . reflection upon my reputation." Beauregard returned home fully intending to resign from the army and fight for the South, yet was quite peeved when the niggardly U.S. government refused to pay his $165 travel expenses! He did indeed resign when a telegram reached him that Louisiana had seceded on January 5 and on reaching New Orleans embarked upon a campaign to win a high rank in the state army. The Little Peacock found that Braxton Bragg, another hero of the Mexican War, who later became nominal commander in chief of the Confederate Army, headed this militia, and convinced that he himself deserved the position, Beauregard turned his nose up at Bragg's offer of a colonelcy and volunteered himself as a lowly private in the Orleans guard. This, as he well knew, would be an enlistment of only a short duration, for good old brother-in-law Slidell was hard at work behind the scenes.

By early March the Grand Creole had made the most rapid advancement in American military history, rising from militia private to brigadier general in the Confederate Army when Jefferson Davis ordered him to Charleston to command all Southern forces there. When he got to Charleston, he impressed most people, though not Mrs. Chesnut, who wrote in her diary: ". . . a hero worshipper was struck dumb because I said that so far he has only been a Captain of artillery or engineer or something."

Beauregard would, however, prove an excellent choice, a buoyant, peppy little man, who despite his touchiness and vanity was a social lion and goodwill ambassador for the Confederacy in Charleston. One story has him throwing a victory party where champagne was piped into his courtyard fountain and flowed all night. He would become one of the best-known figures of the Civil War, his fame exceeding Major Anderson's at the time, and be remembered as "the Man of Sumter" in American history because he headed the attacking forces. As for his military abilities, Anderson wrote: "The presence here, as commander, of General Beauregard, recently of the U.S. engineers, insures, I think, in a great measure, the exercise of skill and sound judgment in all operations of the South Carolinians."

Even Anderson's second in command, Captain Doubleday, who

159

had little good to say of any rebel, noted that Beauregard had been "highly trusted and honored" while serving in the U.S. Army, that he "displayed a good deal of feeling at finding himself opposed to the flag under which he had served so long," and that the Confederate general "expressed much sympathy for his old friend Anderson, who, he stated, was merely fulfilling his duty as a soldier in fighting for his own government."

Beauregard was such a vain, dapper little man that he became the butt of a number of jokes among rebel and Yankee troops. When his black hair began turning gray later in 1861, for instance, some people blamed the stress of command, while others insisted that the Union sea blockade had made hair dye impossible to get. The Northern press dubbed him Boar-a-guard and represented him in cartoons as a pig. But there was no doubt of Old Bory's excellence among either Anderson's men or his own troops, who were sure "Peter" would soon and soundly whup the Yankees.

The rebels indeed saw everything going their way and couldn't imagine why fortune wouldn't always favor them. Since December 27, secessionists throughout the South had seized some forty poorly defended, undermanned U.S. ships, forts, and other installations, not counting all the U.S. military posts in Texas that the half-senile General David E. Twiggs surrendered to state authorities on February 21. What had begun with South Carolina had spread first to Fort Pulaski on the Savannah River, which Georgia seized on January 2, and the United States Arsenal at Mount Vernon, taken the next day by Alabama troops. Seeing that Buchanan took no retaliatory actions, the South became bolder and bolder, as the following list shows.

> January 5—Fort Morgan and Fort Gaines, vital points for the protection of Mobile, were seized by Alabama.
> January 6—Florida seized the Federal arsenal at Apalachicola.
> January 7—Fort Marion, at St. Augustine, was taken by Florida.
> January 9—Secessionists from Smithville and Wilmington took Fort Caswell, North Carolina.
> January 10—State authorities seized the U.S. Arsenal and barracks at Baton Rouge, Louisiana.

January 11—Forts Jackson and St. Philip, in Louisiana, were occupied by state authorities.

U.S. marine hospital near New Orleans was taken by Louisiana.

January 12—State authorities took over Barrancas barracks; Fort Barrancas; Fort McRee; and the navy yard at Pensacola, Florida, leaving only Fort Pickens, out in the harbor, still in Federal hands.

January 14—Fort Pike, Louisiana was seized by the state.

January 15—U.S. coast survey steamer *Dana* was seized at St. Augustine, Florida.

January 20—Fort Massachusetts on Ship Island, potentially important as a staging and supply point controlling the mouth of the Mississippi, was taken by Mississippi after several attempts by state militia.

January 24—Georgia authorities took the U.S. Arsenal at Augusta.

January 26—State authorities occupied Fort Jackson and Oglethorpe barracks in Georgia.

January 28—Louisiana seized Fort Macomb.

January 28—U.S. property in the hands of army officers was seized at New Orleans, Louisiana.

February 1—Louisiana seized the U.S. Mint and Customhouse at New Orleans and the schooner *Washington.*

February 8—Arkansas seized the U.S. Arsenal at Little Rock, the Federal garrison of Captain James Totten evacuating under force.

February 12—State troops took possession of U.S. Arsenal at Napoleon, Arkansas.

February 16—Texas took the U.S. Arsenal and barracks at San Antonio.

February 21—Brevet Major General David E. Twiggs, one of the four highest-ranking U.S. generals, surrendered all U.S. military posts in Texas to the state, relinquishing some $1.5 million in U.S. property, exclusive of the forts.

March 2—U.S. revenue cutter *Dodge* seized by the state at Galveston, Texas.

To this list could be added three more marine hospitals, plus lighthouses or light vessels at Rattlesnake Shoal, Bull's Bay, Oyster Beds, Tybee, Wolf Island, Cat Island, Dog Island, Southwest Reef, Pelican Spit, Half Moon Shoal, Swash, Aransas Pass, Red Fish Bar, and many other points, bringing the total close to one hundred. An estimated two hundred thousand muskets and huge supplies of ammunition were taken with the six arsenals seized, while the forts captured were valued at about $7 million and the customhouses were worth another $6 million. All and all, the U.S. properties seized by the South must have totaled well over $25 million, if any dollar value could be computed for those strategically essential locations. In addition over one-third of the 1,108 officers of the U.S. Regular Army had resigned, or were preparing resignations, to join the Confederate forces. Often they kept their swords, carving the *U.S.* out of the handles.

George Templeton Strong's diary entry on these seizures of U.S. property reflected the general feeling in the North. "No revolution," the New Yorker wrote, "no great political movement ever combined so much and so various crime, dirty and bold, sneaking and insolent, as this, unless there be a parallel case in the history of France, or that of the Roman Empire in its days of rotting. Southerners have lost all moral sense. Their nerves of moral sensation seem smitten with paralysis. The 'chivalry' exults in treachery, bad faith, oppression of the weak, and everything that distinguishes the churl from the knight." Strong did not know, or he would certainly have mentioned it, that General Scott had recommended in a letter of October 29 that the President reinforce and strengthen six of these seized Federal forts, and that timorous Buchanan had turned down his proposal.

Most Southern seizures met with little or no resistance, despite outraged public opinion in the North about incidents like the U.S. marine hospital takeover in New Orleans, where all of the two hundred patients who could leave their beds were immediately turned out. The only exceptions were the firing on invaders at Fort Barrancas before it fell (see Chapter 7), and the refusal of young Lieutenant Adam Slemmer to evacuate Fort Pickens when the governors of both Florida and Alabama demanded its surrender on January 12. Slemmer and his forty-six troops and thirty seamen held out at Fort Pickens on Santa Rosa Island at the mouth of Pensacola Bay, having withdrawn (in a tactic similar to

Anderson's) from the indefensible Fort Barrancas, and waited for reinforcements. "A governor is nobody here," Slemmer declared. He endured until the middle of April, when a relief expedition, sent on January 24, finally reached him, and the Stars and Stripes flew over Fort Pickens until the end of the war without a shot being fired. Even here, however, Buchanan had vacillated some, holding to the so-called Fort Pickens truce with the secessionists, in which he agreed not to reinforce Slemmer so long as the rebels did not attack. Only when Lincoln came into power and considered the truce ended with his inauguration did Slemmer get the help he needed; this was accomplished despite the meddling of Secretary of State Seward, who had not yet learned that Lincoln was the better man and the boss.

That Buchanan did at least agree to send reinforcements to Fort Pickens under certain conditions is evidence of his contradictory nature. About the only other positive things he did were to garrison Fort Taylor at Key West with Federal troops and to challenge seventy-one-year-old General Twiggs to a duel for surrendering all the U.S. military posts in Texas, seeing to it that Twiggs was almost immediately dismissed from the service as a traitor.

It is rarely noted that from President Lincoln's inauguration, the day after General Beauregard took command in Charleston, until the battle for Fort Sumter, there were no more secessionist seizures of Federal property, compared with the one hundred or so under Buchanan's administration. The rebels obviously expected a tougher stance and were feeling Lincoln out. His inauguration on March 4 before thirty thousand onlookers was held with troops posted all over the city, however, and people were so certain violence would strike that great numbers deserted the city. Squads of sharpshooting snipers were stationed on rooftops covering the inauguration route and speaking platforms; all sewers were searched for bombs. America had never before had a President hated by so many. Already the hate mail was coming, including a drawing from Charleston showing Old Abe tarred, feathered, and chained, with a rope dangling from his neck. If Southern wishes could kill, Lincoln would have been dead months before election day. Evidence of an assassination plot uncovered by private detective Allan Pinkerton forced the

President-elect to travel incognito to Washington disguised as an invalid and accompanied by a woman detective, though he did not wear the ridiculous Scotch-plaid cap and long military coat depicted in scores of cartoons, this being the hoax of *The New York Times* reporter Joseph Howard, who managed to trick his editors.

There were rumors that the inauguration platform would be blown up while Lincoln spoke, and a squad of soldiers had to be stationed under it. Lincoln was a minority President who won election with 180 electoral votes, but whose combined opposition outpolled him by almost a million popular votes, and he was of course the South's *bête noire*, Rhett's *Charleston Mercury* calling him "the beau ideal of a relentless, dogged, free soil Border Ruffian, a vulgar mobcat and a Southern hater." But those who hated the new President would have to contend with loyal supporters like General Scott, who said of anyone with plans to harm Lincoln or the Union: "[He] should be lashed to the muzzle of a 12-pounder and fired out the window of the Capitol. I would manure the hills of Arlington with fragments of his body."

Outgoing President Buchanan had already predicted that he was the *last* President of the United States. Most Northerners couldn't agree with that, but many agreed that "such a pei fect imbecile never held office before," as an Iowa senator wrote, and that Buchanan's government was a laughing stock. One widely distributed cartoon depicted "a White Old House with a gray old rat, / fidgeting ever and blind as a bat." Walt Whitman described Buchanan and the President's cabinet members as "deformed mediocre, sniveling, unreliable false-hearted men." A few zealots even demanded that Lincoln's first act of office be to "hang the old traitor James Buchanan as high as old John Brown." Lincoln himself had said, in anger, on hearing a false rumor that Buchanan had instructed Anderson to surrender Fort Sumter if attacked: "If that is true they *ought* to hang him."

Lincoln was supposed at the very least to be a welcome relief from Buchanan. It was to have been good-bye to all that, hello to a man with backbone. So his remark in a Columbus, Ohio, pre-inaugural speech that "there is nothing going wrong" in the Union had been received with puzzlement if not shock by some Unionists. "Have not our forts and vessels been seized, our arsenals invaded, our mints robbed, by men and States in arms?" asked a New York congressman on the floor of the House. "Has not our flag been fired into, our mails rifled and intercepted, our commerce on the Mississippi obstructed? Is not the public mind today, North and South, convulsed as never before?" Loyal supporters tried to explain that the new President had only meant to calm a troubled nation. After all, hadn't Lincoln declared in another pre-inaugural speech that he would rather be assassinated than give up the principles of his country. His inaugural address would show exactly where he stood. People anxiously awaited what he would say as he and a much-relieved Buchanan rode in the presidential carriage to the Capitol through streets bristling with bayonettes. The *Star* reported that "never in the history of Washington was so immense a crowd of spectators seen on Pennsylvania Avenue," nor so many "oddish people, some decidedly crazy, and some about half-and-half."

After witnessing Hannibal Hamlin sworn in as vice-president in the Senate chamber, Lincoln was escorted to the outdoor platform to take his Constitutional oath of office. As he began to deliver his inaugural address, there were cheers saluting the new President but no violence. The rifles gleaming on the rooftops and from windows of the Capitol wings were silent as Lincoln, wearing his spectacles, began to speak. He would only be interrupted —and startled—once, when a limb cracked in a tree not far from him and a spectator crashed to the ground.

Lincoln spoke in a calm, patient voice, but his rugged powerful presence suggested a raw strength to many onlookers. In his speech of some three thousand words he vowed to avoid war but to maintain the Union, which was by its very nature indissoluble: ". . . no state, upon its own mere motion, can lawfully get out of the Union," he said firmly. "The power confided in me will be used to hold, occupy and possess the property and places belonging to the government," he stated, not naming any place in his speech but clearly meaning Fort Sumter. In closing he told all the South: "In your hands, my dissatisfied fellow-countrymen, and not in mine, is the momentous issue of civil war. . . . You can have no conflict without being yourselves the aggressors. *You* have no oath registered in heaven to destroy the government, while *I* shall have the most solemn one to 'preserve, protect and defend it.'"

And then, in the last and most poetic passage of his speech, the President nobly pleaded for peace: "I am loth to close. We are not enemies, but friends. We must not be enemies. Though passion may have strained, it must not break our bonds of affection. The mystic chords of memory, stretching from every battlefield and patriot grave to every living heart and hearthstone, all over this broad land, will yet swell the chorus of the Union, when again touched, as surely they will be by the better angels of our nature."

But the better angels of most American natures and the guardian angel of the nation had taken a long holiday. Though Lincoln's speech impressed many in the North, sending the signal that he was firm and unfawning—"a Man," as the *New York Tribune* put it—relatively few there seemed touched by his plea for peace. And it was too late for Lincoln to make friends in the South. Senator and spy Louis Wigfall, bored with the eloquent speech, telegraphed back to Charleston: "Inaugural means war."

Great men, and the wisdom of their words and deeds, are rarely known until they are gone. Few newspapers North and none South recognized the heartfelt conciliatory tone of Lincoln's impassioned peace offering. "It is our wisest policy to accept it as a declaration of war," announced the *Charleston Mercury*. "Sectional war awaits only the signal gun," predicted the *Richmond Enquirer*. Most Southerners were agreed that Lincoln would reinforce and try to hold Fort Sumter. In Charleston, Emma Holmes wrote in her diary that President Lincoln's speech was "just what was expected of him, stupid, ambiguous, vulgar and insolent" and "is everywhere considered as a virtual declaration of war." Former President John Tyler, a cultivated Virginia gentleman who had presided over a last-minute February "peace conference" in Washington to avoid Civil War, complained about Lincoln's grammar.

After his swearing in by old, palsied Chief Justice Taney and the firing of an artillery salute, Lincoln rode back to the Executive Mansion with Buchanan, who left him with these last words: "If you are as happy, my dear sir, on entering this house as I am in leaving it and returning home, you are the happiest man in this country." Then almost seventy, eighteen years older than Lincoln, he would live seven more years, dying in his sleep at his

Wheatland estate in 1868, perhaps his only distinction as President being that he remained a bachelor all his life.

As for Lincoln's happiness, it lasted only until the morning after the inaugural ball, when a letter arrived from Major Anderson (it had actually come to Buchanan on inauguration day, but he had typically refused to deal with it) advising that he would need *twenty thousand* good and disciplined troops to hold Fort Sumter, that his position was just about hopeless, and that even if not attacked he would soon have to surrender or see his men starve to death—he reckoned his food supplies would last from a month to forty days. Lincoln no doubt remembered the letters Captain Doubleday's brother Ulysses had written him questioning Anderson's loyalty, but there was no real evidence here of even faintheartedness on the major's part. Though he had previously advised Washington that in his new position at Sumter "the government can reinforce me at its leisure" and that he could hold down the fort as long as desired, the rebel forces in the harbor were now far stronger. Anderson had not been reinforced when he should have been. Captain Foster agreed with him that huge numbers of reinforcements were needed if any relief expedition were to succeed; Captain Seymour doubted that *any* size expedition would work; and even eager Doubleday called for ten thousand men.

General Scott, perhaps influenced by Seward, agreed with his officers at Fort Sumter, Old Fuss and Feathers advising that the time for reinforcing Sumter had "passed away nearly a month ago." But Lincoln decided to confer with Postmaster General Montgomery Blair's brother-in-law, thirty-nine-year-old former Navy Captain Gustavus Vasa Fox, who was widely known to favor a naval expedition to supply Sumter, his plans even published in the press. Fox, a distinguished strategist besides being by marriage part of the most politically influential family in America, advised the President to send an expedition of two warships, a troop transport, and three tugboats, their engines protected by bales of cotton. Under cover of night in Charleston Harbor the troops and supplies would be transferred to the tugs and run down the main Swash Channel to Sumter, so that they would have to pass only the Cummings Point and Fort Moultrie batteries. Just in case the tugs, racing along at 14 knots, were fired upon and hit, however, there would be sufficient empty launches being towed behind to carry all personnel to Sumter, and if Confederate gunboats ventured across the bar to fire on the launches, the U.S. warships and the guns of Sumter could surely deal with them. His plan would not require a large force of men, would take only a few days, *and would work,* Fox insisted—he'd be glad to risk his own life leading it.

Lincoln took Fox's plan to his cabinet on March 14 and only the Captain's brother-in-law, Postmaster General Montgomery Blair, agreed that Fort Sumter should be reinforced. Gideon Welles, secretary of the navy, entertained doubts; Simon Cameron, secretary of war, saw no benefits in reinforcements; Edward Bates, the attorney general, wanted to evacuate Sumter; Salmon Chase, secretary of the treasury, straddled the fence; and Caleb B. Smith, secretary of the interior, was for evacuation. Secretary of State Seward, the disappointed but proud presidential candidate who still thought he should be President, had decided that an appeased South would return to the Union, and told Lincoln that it wasn't time for the use of force.

But though six out of seven opposed him, as did General Scott, Lincoln did not give up on reinforcing Sumter. The entire U.S. Army consisted of less than sixteen thousand men and he knew that the only twenty thousand men available were the twenty thousand or so office seekers pounding at his door, as the *New York Herald* quipped. And there had to be a better idea than the balloon landings, submarine expeditions, and similar harebrained schemes suggested in the hundreds of letters the President received about the troubled fort. He decided to send Captain Fox to Charleston to study the situation firsthand and report back to him.

In Charleston, a city now awash with more rumors than its shore was with waves, the *Courier* had already announced in a headline on March 11: "The Evacuation of Fort Sumter Determined on. Anderson to Go to Fort Monroe." But then there were also rumors that Anderson had resigned from the army, that his troops had mutinied, and that that hated Black Republican dog Doubleday had gone stark raving mad and been clamped in irons.

Doubleday wasn't mad, but he was angry. It seems that on

March 7 the Confederate battery at Cummings Point had been practicing with blank charges when without warning a ball was blasted out the muzzle of one of the cannons and soared over the water to land on the mined Sumter wharf. Luckily none of the mines exploded. It developed that one of the Palmetto Boys on duty had grown bored with the blanks and slipped in a ball, just for the fun of it! Ashley Halsey, Jr., an editor of the *Saturday Evening Post,* relates in his book *Who Fired the First Shot?* that it was a twenty-three-year-old private who remarked on the night of the sixth of March that he was "tired of this nonsense—there will be some fun in the morning," when he fired the shot. "The shot was no accident," Halsey insists. "I can say that with certainty, for the man who loaded the gun during the night was my grandfather, E. L. Halsey of Charleston. Grandfather was not the patient type. The explosive gesture seemed entirely representative of his feelings. If action was what he wanted, he soon got it. Transferring from harbor defenses to horse artillery, he became first lieutenant and then captain of a battery which fought in 143 battles and skirmishes from start to finish. Of the unit's original 147 men, only twenty-three answered the final muster. At the surrender they cried as they kissed their cannon good-bye. Grandfather broke his saber and kept his revolver. . . . He lived out his days totally unreconstructed."

In any case, the commander of the Cummings Point battery company, Major Peter F. Stevens, rowed over to Sumter with an explanation and apology. Doubleday was not appeased. "Our men were dissatisfied that the affair ended in nothing," he wrote later. "They were becoming thoroughly angry and disgusted at their long confinement, and at the supervision South Carolina exercised over them. One and all desired to fight it out as soon as possible."

Captain Gustavus Vasa Fox was to prove instrumental in satisfying that desire to fight. Fox, despite his reputation, somehow got Governor Pickens's reluctant approval to visit Fort Sumter shortly after Lincoln dispatched him to Charleston, though Pickens did send a Southern naval officer along with him to spy on the spy, who was quite aware he was being spied upon! Fox managed to spend a few moments alone with Major Anderson and learned that if Anderson put his men on short rations he had enough supplies to hold out until April 15, a little longer than he had previously estimated. Fox did mention to the major a good spot for landing reinforcements at the fort, but he was unable to convey much of his plan to Anderson, or perhaps he did not want to, distrusting Anderson's loyalty.

Despite the fact that Anderson told him relief from the sea would be impossible, Captain Fox's brief visit made him more confident than ever that his plan would work. Returning to Washington, he reported this to Lincoln on March 25. The President spent a sleepless night deciding, but determined that evacuation of Sumter could do nothing but discredit and weaken the Federal government, forestalling war only a short time, whereas reinforcing Sumter, while probably resulting in war, would place the burden of striking the first blow on the South. He knew as well that it would be sure political death to abandon Fort Sumter, which, though not of great strategic importance to the North in the overall scheme of things, had become of immense emotional significance, a symbol of the Union almost as much as the flag.

The next morning all of Lincoln's cabinet except Seward approved his decision and the President implemented it by ordering the necessary ships and three hundred troops to be assembled at New York and placed under Fox's command. The expedition was to sail no later than April 6.

All the time that Lincoln wrestled with plans for reinforcing Sumter by sea, Secretary of State Seward had been politicking for the *evacuation* of the fort. It was a lie Seward had fed his friend James Harvey of the *New York Tribune,* a South Carolinian, that led to the *Courier*'s headline claiming Fort Sumter would be evacuated, since Harvey had promptly telegraphed this information to Charleston. For a man who could coin grandiose moral maxims like "There is a higher law than the Constitution," Seward certainly could lie with the best of them. The secretary also led Jefferson Davis's three Confederate commissioners to believe that Sumter would be evacuated, giving them this impression not once but several times. Eight years older than Lincoln at sixty, Seward, a former senator from New York, was slim and white-haired; "eyes secret but penetrating, lively with twinkling, a subtle quick man, rejoicing in power," he had been the Merlin behind the White House throne in the William Henry

Harrison and Zachary Taylor administrations, and only bad luck and his uncompromising free-the-slaves-at-any-cost position on abolition (a line he had since softened) had kept him from getting the 1860 Republican nomination over Lincoln. A chain cigar smoker who brought a smoke-filled room with him wherever he went, he was a consummate thick-skinned politician, who could say to an opponent in the Senate who had heaped abuse on him, "Benjamin, give me a cigar and when your speech is printed send me a copy." One journalist described Seward's smile as a "sly Jesuit" one. Though often wild-haired and disheveled, he was said to be "politically the uncleanest politician in the United States, but personally the cleanest." This great constitutional lawyer, among the best of his day, genuinely liked Lincoln, but as was the habit of so many people, vastly underestimated the Rail-splitter, having a notion of him as something of a pleasant, gentle, rawboned rube, a lanky, small-town lawyer who tripped all over himself and was given to buffoonery and flippancy. He did not know, as Samuel Eliot Morison among others has pointed out, that Lincoln was always most flippant when thinking deeply, that his remarkable mind easily worked on two levels at the same time. Seward was sure he would dominate this President, as he had two previous ones.

The imperious Seward finally had the effrontery to write Lincoln one of the most insulting memorandums ever written by a cabinet member to a President. Submitted on April Fool's Day, it was wild enough to be a joke, but dead serious. "Some thoughts for the President's Consideration" stated that Lincoln's government had no policy "either domestic or foreign," that Fort Sumter should be abandoned and Fort Pickens defended, so that (for some unexplained reason) "the question before the Public [would change] from one upon Slavery . . . for a question upon Union or Disunion." He then suggested that war be declared on Spain or France, or possibly England and Russia as well, to unite both North and South against a common foe, and concluded by saying in a roundabout way that he, the secretary of state, would be glad to take full command!

Lincoln might understandably have demanded his resignation for insubordination, or stupidity, but he appreciated the man's huge talents, realized Seward would be of great help in the future, and calmly but firmly said *no*. It wasn't until about this time that Seward realized he would never dominate Lincoln and became one of the first men around the President to sense his greatness.

Seward, however, had already managed to place many obstacles in the way of the Fox expedition, mainly by creating confusion about which ships were being sent to Sumter and which were to be used for a second expedition Lincoln had ordered sent to Fort Pickens (the President was unaware that the first Pickens expedition, sent on January 8, hadn't failed but was merely resupplying at Key West). Because of Seward's interference the Fox fleet wasn't able to sail until April 10, and if Fox had sailed just a few days sooner the final outcome might have been much different at Sumter.

Knowing nothing of any of these political complications, Gustavus Vasa Fox sailed from New York on April 8 in the chartered steamer *Baltic* with two hundred troops and enough supplies for Sumter to hold out at least another year. He expected to rendezvous outside Charleston Harbor with the four-gun paddle wheeler *Harriet Lane*, the three tugs *Yankee, Uncle Ben,* and *Freeborn,* and the men-of-war *Pawnee, Pocahontas,* and *Powhatan.* He had no idea that Seward's manipulations had taken the *Powhatan* from him and given her to the Pickens expedition, where she wasn't needed. The President had instructed Seward to telegraph the New York naval yard ordering the *Powhatan* to be delivered to the Sumter expedition, instead of the Pickens expedition, to which, Lincoln now realized, it had been assigned under a Seward order that he had routinely approved without knowing its contents. Seward, however, signed his own name to the telegram instead of Lincoln's, and the officer in charge of the yard let the *Powhatan* go with the Pickens force, reasoning that the previous order signed by the President was supreme. It is entirely possible that Seward had this in mind when he signed his own name though there is no proof one way or another. Whatever the case, the mistake would cause trouble never dreamed of by Captain Fox as he began the 658-mile trip to Sumter. But then he didn't know any of a half-dozen things that could and would go wrong.

Before Fox steamed out of New York, Lincoln ordered Secretary of War Cameron to advise Major Anderson that a relief expedition was coming, would proceed if resisted, and that he should hold the fort until it arrived, although he was authorized to surrender if necessary. Anderson, who didn't receive the letter *(sent as ordinary mail)* until April 7, answered in a letter that *never* reached Washington, falling into Beauregard's hands. With a heavy heart he replied that he and his men would "strive to do our duty." Knowing that the war he had so desperately tried to avert, at the cost of losing respect among his men, could not be avoided now, he repeated that "my heart is not in the war which I see is thus to be commenced."

Anderson had felt this deep inside for some time now, even when, on April 3, the Confederate guns on Morris Island fired a warning shot across the bow of the *Rhoda Shannon,* a little schooner carrying a cargo of ice, whose rather incompetent skipper had steered her into Charleston Harbor through the fog, somehow thinking that he was in Savannah. In Doubleday's words, Captain Joseph Marts, the *Rhoda Shannon*'s master, "very much astonished at this proceeding, ran up the Stars and Stripes to show that he was all right. This was regarded as a direct defiance, and a heavy cannonade was at once opened on the vessel. Very much puzzled to account for this hostility, he lowered the flag, and the firing ceased."

Little damage was done to Marts's ship, thanks to inept gunners—one ball went through the ship's mainsail—but the incident frightened a lot of people. "A ship was fired into yesterday and went back to sea," Mrs. Chesnut wrote in her diary. "Is that the first shot? How can one settle down to anything? One's heart is in one's mouth all the time. Any minute . . . cannon may open on us, the fleet come in, & c&c." As for the Sumter troopers, they rushed to their posts after the Confederate shots, eager to do battle, five out of eight officers favoring firing on the Southern guns in return. Anderson said no, and he was right. It did turn out to be a shot fired in error because one of the guard boats hadn't been at its station to halt the *Shannon,* and would have been a foolish incident to go to war over. But most of Major Anderson's men disapproved, had been preparing for a fight so long that they were itching to have it.

Doubleday later spoke for the majority: "In amplifying his [previous] instructions not to provoke a collision into instructions

173

not to fight at all, I have no doubt [Major Anderson] thought he was rendering a real service to the country. He knew the first shot fired by us would light the flames of a civil war that would convulse the world, and tried to put off the evil day as long as possible. Yet a better analysis of the situation might have taught him that the contest had already commenced and could no longer be avoided. The leaders of the South at this period . . . needed blood and the prestige of a victory to rouse the enthusiasm of their followers, and cement the rising Confederacy."

Anderson was completely misunderstood, at this point, by his men, who were either shortsighted or victims of their own patriotism and claustrophobia, and by President Lincoln, who did not fully understand his problems, who worried that the infamous Floyd had appointed him in the first place, and who made a private remark at the time that "Anderson has played us false."

While Fox made his way toward Fort Sumter, all of Charleston wondered what would happen next. "And so we fool on, into the black cloud ahead of us," Mrs. Chesnut wrote in her diary, noting that her only consolation was her suppers of *"pâté de foie gras, salad, biscuit glacé, and champagne frappe."* Another evening she reported: "The plot thickens. The air is red-hot with rumors. The mystery is to find out where these utterly groundless tales originate." Her compatriot Judge Petigru, who had seen his summer house demolished by the secessionists to make room for more guns, was positive now that the world was an insane asylum, while belligerent old Edmund Ruffin's picture was on sale all over town as an inspiration to Confederate patriots. As for the dangerously romantic and bellicose Senator Wigfall, he had just returned from secretly recruiting soldiers for the Confederacy in Baltimore. Mrs. Chesnut told of his being summoned from her dinner table to address a crowd assembled outside the Mills House. In his combative speech Wigfall spoke of the new Confederate flag that "has not yet been baptized in blood" and must be. Again we find Sir Walter quoted by a fool. Vowing to be back in Washington "in the saddle," presumably in Lincoln's place, within a year, Wigfall recited from Sir Walter Scott's *The Lady of the Lake* where Fitz James, the Lowland king of Scotland who subdues the rebellious clan Alpine, says with great assurance:

Twice have I sought Clan-Alpine's glen
In peace; but when I come agen,
I come with banner, brand and bow,
As leader seeks his mortal foe.

As soon as Fox steamed out of New York with his relief expedition aboard the *Baltic,* President Lincoln had dispatched a messenger to Charleston with a letter to Governor Pickens that was delivered only a day after Anderson received his message. Unaddressed, unsigned, delivered by a mere clerk unauthorized to accept an answer—as if to say there could be no answer to it—Lincoln's message is generally acknowledged to be a minor political masterpiece. It read: "I am directed by the President of the United States to notify you to expect an attempt will be made to supply Fort Sumter with provisions only, and that if such attempt be not resisted, no effort to throw in men, arms or ammunition will be made, without further notice, or in case of an attack against the Fort."

In other words, Lincoln had maneuvered the Confederates into a corner. If they withheld their fire at this "peaceful" limited expedition, Sumter would be resupplied and U.S. sovereignty would be upheld, the flag still flying unviolated over the fort. However, if the Confederates decided to fire on the expedition, *they* would be firing the first shots of a civil war, not the United States, as Lincoln had promised in his inaugural address.

But more to the point is the often overlooked fact that the Confederates had already decided to shoot first, long before Governor Pickens turned Lincoln's famous April 6 message over to Jefferson Davis and his cabinet in Montgomery. The Confederates were tired of Seward's lies, which they took to be Lincoln's lies as well, and the Confederate commissioners had informed Davis that the Lincoln government "declines to recognize our official character or the power we represent."

Then there was General Beauregard's warning to Confederate Secretary of War Leroy Pope Walter that "if Sumter was properly garrisoned, it would be a perfect Gibralter to anything but constant shelling, night and day, from the four points of the compass," but that as it stood "the weakness of the garrison consti-

175

tutes our greatest advantage, and we must for the present, turn our attention to preventing it from being reinforced."

Fort Sumter was also a symbol, a chip on the Union shoulder, as Carl Sandburg has called it, that the South had to knock off. Above all, Davis knew that unless the flag flying over Sumter came down, the Confederacy's claim to independence looked ridiculous in the eyes of the world. "Unless you sprinkle blood in the face of the Southern people they will be back in the old Union in less than ten days," a friend warned him.

Even more likely, South Carolina would strike out on its own, and there was no chance that other Southern states would join the Confederacy unless action were taken. People in the South were clamoring for action. Urged a *Mercury* editorial: "Let us be ready for war.... Border states will never join us until we have indicated our power to free ourselves—until we have proven that a garrison of 70 men cannot hold the portal of our commerce. The fate of the Southern Confederacy hangs by the ensign balliards of Fort Sumter."

Reflecting on such intelligence, President Davis determined as early as April 3 that Fort Sumter was the place to use force, not the easier to defend Fort Pickens. When he learned of the relief expedition steaming toward Sumter, he laid before his cabinet his proposal that General Beauregard be instructed to demand the fort's surrender and to open fire if Major Anderson refused. When all but one of his cabinet concurred, a telegram was sent instructing Beauregard to demand Fort Sumter's immediate evacuation and if it was refused to "proceed . . . to reduce it." Ironically, fire-eating Robert Toombs, the Confederate secretary of state, was the only cabinet member who disagreed.

"The firing on that fort will inaugurate a civil war greater than any the world has ever seen," Toombs said, pacing back and forth; "it is suicide, murder. . . . You will wantonly strike a hornet's nest which extends from mountain to ocean; legions now quiet, will swarm out and sting us to death. It is unnecessary; it puts us in the wrong; *it is fatal.*"

As for President Lincoln, his state of mind about the inevitability of war might be indicated by a note he sent Pennsylvania's Governor Andrew G. Curtin on April 8: "I think the necessity of being ready increases.—Look to it."

176

10

The First Shot

Nor would we shun the battle-ground,
    Though weak as we are strong;
Call up the clashing elements around,
    And test the right and wrong!
                —Henry Timrod,
                "Ethnogenesis"

W ITHIN hours "the hoarse voice of the dogs of war" would be heard again, as the pseudonymous correspondent "Virginius" of the *Richmond Dispatch* put it. There were war correspondents from many papers in Charleston now, including the *New York Herald*'s F. G. de Fontaine and *The New York Times*'s George Salter, all as impressed as the Carolinians by the martial fever. Carolinian militiaman Augustus Dickert was thrilled, as any child of fifteen would be, with the "high glee—palmetto cockades, brass buttons, uniforms and gaudy epaulettes . . . seen in every direction." Ah, war was a marvelous thing! He later wrote of a town "ablaze with excitement, flags waving from the house tops, the heavy tread of embryo soldiers . . . heard in the streets," of high-toned gentlemen with their fine hands blistered and bloodied from moving guns and digging emplacements. "The gage is thrown down," proclaimed Rhett's *Mercury*, "and we accept the challenge. We will meet the invader, and the God of Battle must decide the issue between the hirelings of Abolition hate and Northern tyranny, and the people of South Carolina defending their freedom and their homes."

Former Union supporter Michael P. O'Connor called the Union "a dead carcass stinking in the nostrils of the Southern people!" Former Virginia Congressman Roger Pryor, urging his state to join the Confederacy, "making great play with that long hair of his, tossing it aside," gave a fiery speech from the balcony of his hotel on the night of April 10, urging an attack on Sumter and thanking the Carolinians for having "at last annihilated this accursed Union, reeking with corruption and insolent with excess of tyranny." To tremendous applause, fists clenched and looking out toward Sumter, he cried: "Strike a Blow!"

Similarly, the *Charleston Courier* cursed Lincoln, demanding

179

that the military "let the strife begin." Marching soldiers and enthusiastic civilians jammed Charleston streets, bonfires burned, drums rolled, parades snaked through the city. Old Ruffin, marching along musket in one hand and carpetbag in the other, had on April 9 been welcomed as an honorary member of the Palmetto Boys manning the Stevens Ironclad Battery and, positively salivating for battle, was given three cheers by men young enough to be his grandsons as a pioneer hero and prophet of secession. His commander, George Cuthbert, was glad to have him, for Ruffin had been wined and dined throughout the city by officers eager to enroll him in their companies. Ruffin had insisted that he be enlisted as an infantryman as well as an artilleryman so that he could join in any storming of Sumter after firing the big guns at the fort. He was but one of many who believed, in the words of an anonymous newspaper writer, that "the last aspiring spark of affection between Americans North and South must be quenched in blood," even if "we must transmit a heritage of rankling and undying hatred to our children."

War came with Major Anderson's rejection of the demand Jefferson Davis made for Fort Sumter's surrender. Mrs. Chesnut's husband, Colonel James Chesnut, a former U.S. senator and now one of Beauregard's top aides, delivered the ultimatum, along with Captain Stephen D. Lee and Colonel A. R. Chisholm. Mrs. Chesnut noted in her diary that former South Carolina Governor John Hugh Means fitted her husband out with a red sash and ceremonial sword for the occasion. "And now patience —we must wait," she added, as he left to meet the Yankees.

At about three-thirty on the afternoon of April 11 the sentries at Sumter noticed Chesnut's small boat flying a white flag approaching the fort. Ironically, the officer of the day greeting the emissaries bearing President Jefferson Davis's demand was young Union Lieutenant Jefferson Davis; he ushered them to the guardroom where Anderson accepted Beauregard's dispatch. "I am ordered by the Government of the Confederate States to demand the evacuation of Fort Sumter," Beauregard had written his former teacher. "All proper facilities will be afforded for the removal of yourself and command . . . to any post in the United States which you may select. The flag which you have upheld so long and with so much fortitude, under the most trying circumstances, may be saluted by you on taking it down."

Anderson conferred with his officers and to a man they rejected the proposal, "refused to give up our trust," as Captain Crawford put it. In his reply the major thanked General Beauregard for his "manly and courteous terms," but refused to comply. Yet as he escorted Chesnut to his boat he asked if Beauregard would fire on the fort without further notice and was assured that he would not. It was then that Anderson replied, "Gentlemen, if you do not batter us to pieces, we shall be starved out in a few days." This widely repeated remark has been criticized as unsoldierly, and it certainly wasn't taught as an example of proper military behavior at the Point, but it does show that Anderson's desire for peace remained unabated.

The major was still, however, much a soldier in all other ways, still filing his daily reports, for example, even though the mail to Washington had by now been cut off by the rebels. In any event, a rather surprised Colonel Chesnut asked and received Anderson's permission to repeat the starvation remark to General Beauregard. In less than an hour Beauregard, who much preferred to avoid bloodshed and seize an undamaged fort, telegraphed the information to President Davis in Montgomery and Davis had Secretary of War Walker send him instructions:

Do not desire needlessly to bombard Fort Sumter. If Major Anderson will state the time at which, as indicated by him, he will evacuate and agree in the meantime that he will not use his guns against us, unless ours should be employed against Fort Sumter, you are authorized thus to avoid the effusion of blood. If this, or its equivalent, be refused, reduce the fort as your judgment decides to be most practicable.

After dining with his wife at what she described as "the merriest maddest dinner we have had yet," where the men were "audaciously wise and witty" and he "was not inclined to be communicative," Colonel Chesnut spent the evening waiting for Walker's telegram, and when it came Beauregard ordered him to deliver an answer to Anderson. At 12:45 A.M. he, Chisholm, and

Lee docked again at Fort Sumter, Roger Pryor, now another of Beauregard's colonels, waiting behind in the little boat while they went inside. How long will it be before you are "starved out"? the note from Beauregard asked, in effect. "If you will state the time at which you will evacuate Fort Sumter," it said, "we will abstain from firing upon you."

Anderson withdrew with all his officers and discussed the question for nearly three hours, with Chesnut interrupting them because he felt they were stalling. Dr. Crawford estimated that the garrison could hold out for five more days, the last three of them without food, but Doubleday apparently did not agree, writing later that "As we had pork enough on hand to last for two weeks longer, there was no necessity for fixing so early a date." Nevertheless, none of the Sumter officers, not even the Virginian Lieutenant Meade, who later joined the Confederates, wanted immediate surrender. Finally they agreed to an evacuation date of April 15, though Doubleday felt that this "left too little margin" for any naval expedition that might have been sent to reinforce Sumter. Major Anderson accordingly wrote Beauregard that he would "evacuate Fort Sumter by noon on the 15th instant . . . should I not receive prior to that time controlling instructions from my Government or additional supplies."

To Colonel Chesnut this reply was "manifestly futile" and unacceptable; it had too many conditions attached to it. Authorized to reply for Beauregard, he and young Captain Lee, who at twenty-seven was soon to become the youngest lieutenant general in the Confederate Army, wrote a blunt rejection, which they signed and handed to Major Anderson:

> Fort Sumter, S.C., April 12, 1861, 3:20 A.M.—Sir: By authority of Brigadier General Beauregard, commanding the Provisional Forces of the Confederate States, we have the honor to notify you that he will open the fire of his batteries on Fort Sumter in one hour from this time.

Well written, courteous and chivalrous, with of course, that important Southern word *honor* in it, the message deeply moved Major Anderson, for he was more aware than its authors of all that it meant. Escorting the emissaries to their boat, he pressed

182

their hands and told them, "If we never meet in this world again, God grant that we may meet in the next."

Rowed across the water to old Fort Johnson, Colonel Chesnut listened to the bells of St. Michaels in Charleston pealing as, on General Beauregard's authority, he ordered Captain George S. James, a hero of the Mexican War, to fire the signal shell that would open the bombardment of Fort Sumter and the Civil War at exactly 4:30 A.M. He gave the instructions under Beauregard's general order number 14: "In case an alarm is given [in darkness] the mortar batteries will open at any rate on the firing of a shell from Fort Johnson." Captain James, a great admirer of Roger Pryor, turned to the colonel and told him, "You are the only man to whom I would give up the honor of firing the first gun of the war."

Strangely enough, the incendiary Pryor, who could strike so many blows in his speeches, was as timid as Toombs when it came to action. He seemed horrified by the thought, shaking his head. "I could not fire the first gun of the war," he said in a hoarse voice.

From the moment Pryor refused the awesome responsibility of pulling the first lanyard, there has been controversy over who did fire the first shot of the Civil War. As noted, at least a half dozen shots were fired before the battle for Fort Sumter, but since the Sumter battle is regarded by almost all historians as the start of the war, the "first shot" had to be fired when it began. Many favor Captain James himself because of his statement to Pryor that Pryor was the *only* man to whom he would give up the honor of firing the first gun of the war. General Beauregard, for example, maintained after the war in Colonel Alfred Roman's book on his military operations that "From Fort Johnson's mortar battery at 4:30 A.M. issued the first shot of the war. It was fired not by Mr. Ruffin of Virginia, as has been erroneously supposed, but by Captain George S. James of South Carolina." Yet Beauregard was not present when the first shot went off. Neither was Captain Lee, who all his life insisted that James pulled the lanyard and stated in an 1896 *Southern Historical Society Papers* article that Captain James replied to another officer who wished to take Pryor's place: "No, I will fire it myself."

Among the many unlikely candidates that the press at the time nominated for the South's first cannoneer was little two-year-old Frances Eugenia Olga Neva Pickens, born in Russia to Governor Pickens's wife while Pickens served as American ambassador there and nicknamed Douschka, or "little darling," by her godmother the Czarina. One story has General Beauregard holding Douschka in his arms, bending down, and letting her pull the lanyard, ignoring the facts that Beauregard wasn't present when the first shot sounded and that Douschka was fast asleep in her parents' quarters at the Charleston Hotel, to which Pickens had moved from the state capital at Columbia to be nearer the coming storm in Charleston. The youngest person to fire a gun in the battle for Sumter would be thirteen-year-old Paul B. Lalane, who had been visiting an older brother at the Iron Battery and was permitted to fire several shells.

A more reasonable candidate for the first cannoneer of the war is young Lieutenant Wade Hampton Gibbes, a West Pointer who had served in the cavalry. As Gibbes put it later: "The first shell was fired by Captain James's battery, and, incidently, by me as his first lieutenant. . . . My orders were to fire a shell, to burst high up in the air, as a signal to commence the general bombardment."

However, it seems more likely that Gibbes's subordinate Second Lieutenant Henry S. Farley, who enjoyed some prestige for being the first Southern cadet to leave West Point without waiting to graduate, was the man who fired the first shot, which Ashley Halsey, Jr., aptly calls "a crepe-draped distinction." The *Charleston Mercury* first reported this a week after the battle: "We are informed that Lt. H. S. Farley of Captain James' company had the honor of firing the alarm or first gun of the battle on Friday last." It seems that there were two batteries, not one, in the sand dunes near Fort Johnson, the west, or hill, battery and the east, or beach, battery. Lieutenant Gibbes commanded the hill battery and Captain James commanded the beach battery. Two doctors at the scene testified that Gibbes in the hill battery fired the *second* shot of the war, a shot that destroyed a private home in front of and concealing the hill battery, enabling that battery to fire effectively at Sumter.

Of the first shot, Dr. W. H. Prioleau (Pray-low), the post surgeon, later wrote: "On the morning of April 12, 1861, as soon as orders were received to open fire on Fort Sumter, we repaired to our posts, and 25 or 30 minutes after 4:00 A.M., by my watch, which I held open in my hand at the time, the first gun was fired, this being the righthand mortar in the battery on the beach. I cannot recall who pulled the lanyard, but the gun was directly in charge of Lt. Henry S. Farley, who, as well as I can recollect, sighted the gun, Captain James giving the order to fire."

Dr. Prioleau's colleague Dr. Robert Libby later wrote a paper published in 1911 in the *South Carolina Historical and Genealogical Magazine* confirming Prioleau's observations. "As to the question of who pulled the lanyard," he wrote, ". . . certain it is that either James or Farley fired it, but as Captain James gave the order to fire, it must have been Farley, as James would never have given himself the order to fire." Dr. Libby appended a letter from Farley to his article. Wrote Farley, by then a colonel and the head of New York's Mount Pleasant Military Academy: "The circumstances attending the firing of the first gun at Sumter are quite fresh in my memory. Captain James stood on my right, watch in hand, and at the designated moment gave me the order to fire. I pulled the lanyard, having already carefully inserted a friction tube [a copper encased fulminate of mercury primer] and discharged a 13-inch mortar." The only discrepancy in Farley's account is that official records reveal that a 10-inch mortar was used, there being no 13-inch Southern mortars at the battle of Sumter. But if Farley confused the calibre of the weapons, what else might he have confused!

Lieutenant Farley seems to be the odds-on favorite, yet due to his error Captain James remains a strong contender. What is absolutely certain is that old Edmund Ruffin, full of fleas from sleeping in his uniform on the sand, did not fire the first shot of the Civil War as countless historians have claimed. This canard can be traced to Ruffin's diary, where he wrote: "The night before, when expecting to engage Capt. [George B.] Cuthbert had notified me that his company [the Palmetto Guard] requested of me to discharge the first cannon to be fired, which was their 64 lb Columbiad, loaded with shell. By order of Gen. Beauregard, made known the afternoon of the 11th, the attack was to be commenced by the first shot at the fort being fired by the Palmetto Guard, & from the Iron Battery. In accepting & acting upon this highly appreciated compliment, that company had made me its instrument. . . . Of course I was highly gratified by the compliment & delighted to perform the service—which I did. The shell struck the fort."

Captain Doubleday denied this in his recollections of Fort Sumter, noting that Dr. Crawford and others on the parapet at the time saw the first shot come from the mortar battery at Fort Johnson. And in his official report of April 17, 1861, Captain Cuthbert stated: "The mortar battery at Cummings Point opened fire on Fort Sumter in its turn, after the signal shell from Fort Johnson, having been preceded by the mortar batteries on Sullivan's Island and the mortar battery of the Marion Artillery. . . . At the dawn of day the Iron battery commenced its work of demolition. The first shell from Columbiad No. 1, fired by the venerable Edmund Ruffin, of Virginia, burst directly upon the parapet of the southwest angle of the fort."

It is obvious then that Ruffin fired from the Iron Battery on Morris Island, so called because the battlement in front of it was iron plated. He was thus among the *last* of about a dozen batteries to open fire, for after the Fort Johnson shots sounded from James Island, guns from Sullivan's Island were heard, these finally followed by the guns on Morris Island. When Ruffin *did* fire in clockwise rotation, however, he performed with much panache, stepping forward, yanking the lanyard of a 5-ton siege cannon and after inspecting the horizon shouting gleefully that he had scored the first hit on Fort Sumter. It seems unlikely that a sixty-seven-year-old man could see so well three-quarters of a mile away on a foggy morning, so this, too, must be regarded as possibly myth. Yet Doubleday—who had willed himself to sleep soundly through the night to gird himself for battle the next day, but had been awakened by the cannon—did write of an early shot that "seemed to bury itself in the masonry about a foot from my head, in very unpleasant proximity to my right ear." He added: "This is the one that probably came with Mr. Ruffin's compliments." One stalwart to another.

Whether Farley fired it, or James, or Gibbes, or, by some strange improbability, Mr. Ruffin; whether it went off at 4:25 A.M., 4:27, 4:30, or 4:40, as various contemporary accounts have it, on that Friday, April 12, 1861, the signal or alarm shot from the beach battery was the first shot of the battle for Fort Sumter.

Wrote a teenager watching from the shore: "A perfect sheet of flame flashed out, a deafening roar, a rumbling deafening sound, and the war was on." Noted a Charleston correspondent: "The conscious shell went up shrieking and wailing along its fiery curve and, lingering reluctantly before its downward plunge, burst as it fell directly over the doomed fortress." As another reporter put it: "No meteor of more dire portent ever lit the sky." The 10-inch mortar belched flame and smoke, the round shell arched across the water leaving a scarlet train from its fuse, exploding over Sumter and briefly illuminating the brick fort in the darkness. To a gunner on Morris Island tracking the shell, it looked "like a firefly," while several romantic Charlestonians were convinced that it formed a perfect palmetto when it exploded in flame. "The firing of the mortar woke the echoes from every nook and corner of the harbor," Captain Lee later wrote, "and in this the dead hour of night before dawn, that shot was a sound of alarm that brought every soldier in the harbor to his feet, and every man, woman, and child in the city of Charleston from their beds. A thrill went through the whole city. It was felt that the Rubicon was passed."

Mrs. Chesnut certainly awoke: "The heavy booming of a cannon. I sprang out of bed. And on my knees—prostrate—I prayed as I never prayed before." Out in Sumter, Sergeant Chester saw "a flash of distant lightning . . . followed by the dull roar of a mortar. . . . The eyes of the watchers easily detected and followed the burning fuse which marked the course of the shell as it mounted among the stars, and then descended with ever-increasing velocity, until it landed inside the fort and burst. . . . Then the batteries opened on all sides, and shot and shells went screaming over Sumter as if an army of devils were swooping around it."

Back in Charleston the *Courier's* man described how the circle of batteries "with which the grim fortress of Fort Sumter is beleaguered" opened fire after the first signal shot: "The outline of this great volcanic crater was illuminated with a line of twinkling lights; the clustering shells illuminated the sky above it; the balls clattered thick as hail upon Sumter's sides . . . and so, at the break of day, amidst the bursting of bombs, and the roaring of ordnance, and before thousands of spectators, whose homes, liberties and lives were at stake, was enacted this first great scene in the opening drama of this momentous history."

"No meteor of more dire portent ever lit the sky."

The Civil War had begun.

The men of Sumter knew a very bad time was coming.

11

War! War! War!

One hour of life, crowded to the
full with glorious action, and filled
with noble risks, is worth whole
years of those mean
observances of paltry decorum.

—Sir Walter Scott,
"Count Robert of Paris"

A FTER the red dawn before daybreak, Confederate guns pounded Fort Sumter for more than two hours without any fire being returned. The sun rose at 5:37 A.M., the morning dark and cloudy with a heavy mist covering Charleston Harbor. "It is getting to be warm work for Major Anderson," a *Charleston Mercury* reporter scrawled in his pad as Sumter received the concentrated fire of the Confederate guns and mortars nearly encircling it. "Off goes the fifth shot," the pseudonymous "Virginius" wrote. "Its deep terrible report, the jarring of the windows and shaking of the house only tells the power and its destructiveness. . . . Off go Nos. 6, 7, 8, 9, 10 in rapid succession. . . . Quick flashes of lurid light . . ." Noted the *Mercury*'s man: "Shell followed shell in quick succession; the harbor seemed to be surrounded with miniature volcanos belching forth fire and smoke. Still Major Anderson gave no sign of resentment."

Most correspondents watched "the magnificent pyrotechnics" from the Battery in Charleston, along with a crowd estimated at over five thousand men, women, and children who had rushed from their houses awakened by the booming first shots. "Old Charleston looks from roof, spire and dome across her tranquil bay," Henry Timrod had written of the anticipation of war in his poem "Charleston." Now Charleston's bay was far from tranquil and the roofs, spires, and domes were packed with people. Mrs. Chesnut hurried to the rooftop of her hotel, the posh Mills House. "The women were wild there on the housetop," our diarist wrote. "Prayers from the women and imprecations from the men, and then a shell would light up the scene." She was "so weak and weary" that she sat down on something that looked like a black stool. "Get up, you foolish woman—your dress is on fire!" an old man shouted as her friends rushed to beat the fire out. She had sat down upon a chimney.

It seemed that all Charleston had turned out to see the battle; every available place, including church steeples, was packed with people, many regarding it all as some giant fireworks or diorama, others tense and nervous. Recalled F. G. de Fontaine of the *New York Herald* years later: "Lights flash on as if by magic from the windows of every house, and in the twinkling of an eye, as it were, an agitated mass of people are rushing impetuously toward the waterfront of the city. Grave citizens, whose dignity under ordinary circumstances is unimpeachable, are at the top of their speed dressing as they run, and sending up wild hurrahs as if they must have some such safety-valve for their enthusiasm or be suffocated. There are men *sans* coats, women *sans* crinolines, and children in nightgowns."

Cheers went up for South Carolina, the Confederacy, for Old Bory (or "Peter") and his gunners. "The houses were in a few minutes emptied of their excited occupants," a *Courier* reporter observed, "and the living stream poured through all the streets leading to the wharves and Battery . . . our beautiful promenade . . . crowded thickly with human forms. On no gala occasion have we ever seen nearly so large a number of ladies on our Battery as graced the breezy walk on this eventful morning. There they stood with palpitating hearts and pallid faces, watching the white smoke as it rose in wreathes upon the soft twilight air, and breathing out fervent prayers for their gallant kinsfolk at the guns. Steadily alternating, our batteries spit forth their wrath at the grim fortress rising so defiantly out of the sea. Still Major Anderson received the shot and shell in silence."

By this time "Virginius" was reporting from Charleston that "all is enveloped in smoke and I can see neither Sumter nor the Islands. . . . a heavy shower of rain comes up, but it stops not the heavy throats of the ordnance, nor drives away the thousands of spectators lining the wharves and housetops. . . . there goes the Stevens [battery], the earth trembles again. . . . that is a terrible gun. . . . all is now enveloped in smoke, and the spyglass aids me not." Fire-eaters like Ruffin were becoming anxious that the Yankees crouching in Sumter's casemates wouldn't fight back. They felt like bullies. "I was fearful that Major Anderson did not intend to fire at all," Ruffin explained. "It would have cheapened our conquest of the fort, if effected, if no hostile defense had been made—and still more increased the disgrace of failure."

But Anderson, growing more lines and gray hairs, had good reason to withhold his fire as long as possible, even as the heavy rain of metal fell on Sumter. His primary concern was the Confederate guns far outnumbering his. Almost directly ahead, about one and a half miles away, were two batteries facing him on James Island: the Fort Johnson battery with one 24-pounder, and a battery south of it with four 10-inch mortars. To his right flank and farthest out to sea, only 1,210 yards away, were four potentially deadly batteries on Morris Island at Cummings Point. One was Ruffin's much-heralded Ironclad or Iron Battery with three 8-inch Columbiads; another of these batteries contained four 10-inch mortars; and another contained three 10-inch mortars. The fourth battery consisted of two 42-pounders and a rifled Blakely gun. The Blakely was a new British weapon, the gift of one of Dr. Prioleau's relatives, Charles K. Prioleau, a Charleston businessman living in Liverpool. Extremely accurate with its patented side-sights, it could throw a shell or a 12-pound shot and marked a great advance in gunnery.

To Major Anderson's rear was the Mount Pleasant battery, some two miles away on the mainland and nearest Charleston, which boasted two 10-inch mortars, and Sullivan's Island, about a mile away, containing five batteries plus Fort Moultrie. In Fort Moultrie were three 8-inch Columbiads, two 9-inch seacoast howitzers, five 32-pounders, and four 24-pounders. Behind Moultrie stood a battery of two 10-inch mortars, and next to it, a battery of three 10-inchers. Just to the west of this was a battery of two 32-pounders and two 24-pounders, and flanking this a battery containing a lone heavy 9-inch Dahlgren gun. At the westernmost end of Sullivan's Island, deepest into Charleston Harbor, lay the Floating Battery (or "Slaughter Pen," or "incongruous looking rig" as one reporter called it), with two 32-pounders and two 42-pounders. The Floating Battery had been anchored near land there behind a stone seawall, probably out of deference to public opinion—so many people being sure that it would tip over and sink!

That made for a total rebel force of forty-eight guns—thirty cannon and eighteen mortars—aimed at Sumter from four different directions. To counter, a much-worried Major Anderson had but twenty-one working guns—all 32-pound and 42-pound cannon—sheltered in the casemates on the fort's lower level. For he had decided, rightly, it developed, that the twenty-six cannon, including eight heavy Columbiads, on the top level, or barbette tier, of the fort could not be used. Though they were his biggest and most effective weapons, they stood out in the open, providing no protection for the crews manning them, and were within easy range of Confederate guns. Not an officer to sacrifice his men like cattle, and fearing that so many would be killed on the barbette tier that there wouldn't be enough men left to repel a landing attempt, Major Anderson would try to make do with the smaller weapons on the lower level, which were more effective against ships than forts, masonry, earthworks, and ironclad batteries.

To complicate matters further, Anderson had no fuses for explosive shell and could fire only solid shot. Moreover, his guns lacked breech sights and couldn't be aimed accurately in the dark, and he had a supply of only about seven hundred powder bags, the cartridges used to discharge the cannon. Another obvious problem was manpower. Anderson commanded just seventy-seven soldiers, including himself and the eight other officers, in addition to eight musicians and forty-three civilian laborers who weren't expected to fight. These 128, or 129 counting the black waiter employed in the fort, were opposed by a force of over seven thousand men ranging from young boys and trained soldiers to old men like Ruffin. Outnumbered almost one hundred to one and outgunned more than two to one by an enemy with far superior weapons, Anderson had to be cautious and conserve his men and supplies. After a breakfast of fatty pork ("very rusty indeed"), water, and a little farina for the officers, he had his men assemble and ordered them to stay under cover of the casemates whenever possible while the shells were falling, advising them to be careful of their lives. "Make no imprudent exposure of your person to the enemy's fire," he told them, "do your duty cooly, determinedly and cautiously. Indiscretion is not valor." By this time there was enough light in the lower casemate of guns, surrounded by 60-foot-high walls, to make firing practical, and the major decided to open "a judicious counterfire," defending the flag but conserving his ammunition and manpower.

Anderson put his gun crews on four-hour shifts, appointing Captain Doubleday commander of the first shift, with Lieutenant Davis and Surgeon Crawford, also an expert artilleryman, working alongside him. Doubleday's battery of 32-pounders would fire on Cummings Point, where the formidable Ironclad Battery and the Blakely were already blasting Sumter. Lieutenant Davis would take on the Confederate batteries on James Island, and Dr. Crawford had the Floating Battery and Fort Moultrie on Sullivan's Island to contend with. Forsaking his privilege of firing the first gun, Anderson most appropriately gave Captain Doubleday the honors.

At just before 7:00 A.M. Captain Doubleday aimed a 32-pounder at the Iron Battery, stepped back, shouted "Fire!" and his gunner (the man's name unrecorded in history) yanked the lanyard that sent the first Union ball speeding across the water. Doubleday was a happy soul; it was the greatest moment of his career. Another of those people like Ruffin, he was completely sure of the moral rectitude of his actions. "In aiming the first gun fired against the rebellion," he later testified, "I had no feeling of self-reproach, for I fully believed that the contest was inevitable, and was not of our seeking. The United States was called upon not only to defend its sovereignty, but its right to exist as a nation. The only alternative was to submit to a powerful oligarchy who were determined to make freedom forever subordinate to slavery. To me it was simply a contest, politically speaking, as to whether virtue or vice should rule."

Fortunately for the secessionists, Doubleday's aim wasn't as good as his rhetoric. His shot missed, bouncing off the slanting roof of the Ironclad Battery, according to Captain George Cuthbert of the Palmetto Boys. Eyewitnesses reported that the Ironclad Battery, which Judge Petigru called "The Boomerang," seemed impervious to Union cannonballs, which were bouncing like "peas or marbles off a turtle's back." Ball after ball "rebounded from the close layers of railroad iron, and splashed their way harmlessly through the marsh beyond," a reporter from Charleston noted. "Most shots were aimed too high, and whizzed above the battery without striking it. These went ricochetting over the surface of the water, tearing up vast masses of seaweed, and giving a terrible fright to hundreds of sea fowl, which rose in every direction from the marsh." Southern soldiers even emerged from their "ratholes," large chambers burrowed into the immense slopes of sandbags flanking the Iron Battery, to run after spent Yankee cannonballs. Ruffin, wandering from battery to battery on Cummings Point, and stopping happily to pull a lanyard whenever offered another honorary shot, saw ten men jogging along the shore and thought that they were deserting before he realized that they were chasing such "memorials or trophies." In fact, of all Doubleday's shots, over four hours, only seven hit their target and these did little damage.

The same held true for Davis's guns and Crawford's blasts at Fort Moultrie and the ironclad Floating Battery behind its stone wall. Crawford and his men did manage to damage Moultrie's wooden structures within and without, causing flying splinters of wood to pelt the rebel gunners, but they could not silence a single one of the Confederate guns, which had been heavily padded with cotton bales and sandbags when Beauregard ordered the fort and all other batteries in the harbor strengthened and better protected. The gunners in Moultrie were so confident that they began playing a game when the Yankee balls hit. Each time a bale of cotton was knocked over, someone would cry: "Cotton is going down!" When a direct hit was made on an oven in the kitchen, scattering loaves of bread, a gunner shouted, "Bread is going up!"

Captain Doubleday, full of bravado, also tried joking to make a bad situation tolerable when Captain Seymour came with a fresh detachment to relieve him.

"Doubleday!" Seymour shouted over the sound of rebel shells, "What in the world is the matter here, and what is all this uproar about?"

Replied Abner Doubleday: "There is a trifling difference of opinion between us and our neighbors opposite, and we are trying to settle it."

He then gave Seymour the elevation and range to the Ironclad—five degrees, 1,200 yards—and Captain Seymour settled down to four hours of futile work. Almost automatically now the

Sumter gun crews were sponging barrel, loading cartridge, ramming it, loading ball and wad, ramming it—firing. Again and again, to the point of exhaustion, they bent over the cannons, while Sumter's noncombatant laborers carried ammunition and powder, or worked as burly "seamstresses" sewing shirts into makeshift cartridge bags with the six needles that could be found in the fort. But the 32-pound cannonballs weren't powerful enough to do much damage at such distances; the Union guns were like peashooters, many a soldier thought. About the only damage done to the Ironclad Battery resulted when a Union ball put one of its guns out of action by jamming the steel shutter protecting its embrasure, though this was soon repaired.

Major Anderson refused to use the big guns mounted as mortars in the parade ground to drop cannonballs on Charleston, three miles away, despite the fact that Doubleday had proved weeks ago that by loading them with eccentric shells this could be done. Anderson knew the parade ground was a dangerous place for his gunners to be, and he certainly didn't want to kill or maim any of the five thousand or more civilians watching the show from the Battery. Doubleday had no such qualms and would later write: "It seemed to me there was a manifest desire [on Anderson's part] to do as little damage as possible."

When all was going wrong for the Yankees, new hope suddenly appeared on the horizon. By early afternoon, as early as 10:30 A.M. according to Doubleday, the first vessels of Captain Fox's relief expedition were sighted beyond the bar at the mouth of Charleston Harbor. The troops were sure they were going to be reinforced, the fleet was coming in flying the Stars and Stripes—one, two, three ships! Major Anderson dipped his flag, signaling the vessels that Fort Sumter still fought on, and the gunners renewed their efforts even after a rebel shot hit the flagpole halyards and ominously stuck the flag at half-mast. Even a group of laborers joined in the fight for a time, learning how to handle the guns by watching the soldiers, trying their hand as cannoneers, and hitting their targets "square in the middle." An idea occurred to Private John Carmody of Company F that resulted in what Sergeant Chester called "the war of Carmody against the Confederate States." Carmody decided to disobey Anderson's orders and furtively made his way to the barbette tier and the powerful big guns of Sumter with their 65-pound and 108-pound projectiles, which could set fire to Moultrie instead of merely pounding the fort with shot. The guns were already loaded and roughly aimed, and the "wild Irish soldier" dashed along the rampart under the rebel barrage, firing one by one every big gun. One or two good shots hit the Cummings Point battery, but unable to reload the guns single-handedly, Carmody had to come down.

Inspired by Private Carmody, two grizzled old sergeants on the other side of the fort stole up to the barbette guns to try a similar tactic. "There, in the gorge angle," Sergeant Chester wrote, a 10-inch Columbiad was mounted, en barbette, and as the 42-pounders of the casemate battery were making no impression on the Cummings Point Iron Battery, the two veteran sergeants . . . were determined to try a shot at the Iron Battery from the big gun. As this was a direct violation of orders, caution was necessary. Making sure that the major was out of the way, and that no officers were near, the two sergeants stole upstairs to the 10-inch gun. It was loaded and aimed already, they very well knew, so all they would have to do was to fire it. This was the work of a few seconds only. The gun was fired, and those in on the secret down below watched the flight of the shot with great expectations. . . . Unfortunately the shot missed; not a bad shot—almost grazing the crest of the battery—but a miss. A little less elevation, a very little, and the battery would have been smashed; so thought the sergeants, for they had great faith in the power of their guns; and they determined to try a second shot. The gun was reloaded, a feat of some difficulty for two men, but to run it 'in battery' was beyond their powers. It required the united efforts of six men to throw the carriage 'in gear,' and the two sergeants could not budge it. Things were getting desperate around them. The secessionists had noticed the first shot and had now turned every gun that would bear on that 10-inch gun. They were just getting the range, and it was beginning to be uncomfortable for the sergeants, who in a fit of desperation determined to fire the gun 'as she was.' The elevating screw was given a half turn less elevation, and the primer was inserted in the vent. Then one of the sergeants ran down the spiral stairs to see if the coast were clear, leaving his comrade in a very uncomfortable position at the end of the lanyard, and lying flat on the floor. It was getting hotter up there every second, and a perfect hurricane of rebel shot was sweeping over the prostrate soldier. Human nature could stand it no longer. The lanyard was pulled and the gun was fired. The other sergeant was hastening up the stairway, and had almost reached the top when he met the gun coming down, or at least trying to. Having been fired 'from battery,' it had recoiled over the counter-hurters, and, turning a back-somersault, had landed across the head of the stairway. Realizing in a moment what had happened and what would be to pay if they were found out, the second sergeant crept to the head of the stairway and called his comrade, who, scared almost to death—not at the danger he was in, but at the accident—was still hugging the floor with the lanyard in his hand. Both got safely down swearing eternal secrecy to each other; and it is doubtful if Major Anderson ever knew how that 10-inch gun came to be dismounted. It is proper to add that the second shot was a capital one, striking just under the middle embrasure of the Iron Battery and half-covering it with sand. If it had been a trifle higher it would have entered the embrasure."

There were many close calls. A spent Yankee ball hit the sandbags above Captain Robert Jones while he stood at the Cummings Point Battery and fell, striking him on the back of the neck without doing serious injury; Arthur P. Lining of the Palmetto Guard just missed being hit while he waved the palmetto flag from the Iron Battery in defiance of Fort Sumter's guns to the cheers of his companions. Union guns came close to sinking the Confederate schooner *Petrel* off Hog Island Channel when they put a shot into its bow. At one point it was Fort Moultrie versus Fort Sumter, each side firing some forty shots—the first battle recorded in history in which two forts fired at each other.

But in general the Union guns were ineffectual, inflicting, for example, a total of 163 hits on the Floating Battery in the course of the battle without doing any real damage. In contrast to the Union gunners, without big guns, mortars, or fuses to fire their plentiful supply of shells, the Confederate forces inflicted great damage on Fort Sumter. After firing too high initially, they improved their aim and began dropping shells into Sumter almost at will, making the fort a hell of flying metal, brick, and wood.

Lieutenant John Mitchell was credited with dismounting two of Sumter's parapet guns with just one shot from one of the big rebel Columbiads. Explosions "shook the fort like an earthquake," Captain Crawford noted in his diary. "Our quarters are riddled with shot and shell." Fortunately, the men were well protected in the casemates, but Crawford early on recorded in his diary four slight casualties. The first, and thus the first of the Civil War, probably was Sergeant Thomas Kirnan of Doubleday's company, who continued fighting after suffering "severe contusions" when the powerful Blakely gun delivered a ball that blasted through the embrasure brick and knocked him to the ground. The Sumter troops began to think the relief expedition was their only hope and began cursing it for not having come in yet.

Sumter's barracks were particularly vulnerable. Supposedly fireproof because they were faced with brick, they were repeatedly set on fire by Confederate "hot shot," cannonballs heated red-hot in a specially constructed heavy-duty oven before being fired. At least three times during the day the barracks caught fire. Peter Hart, a former New York City policeman who served as Anderson's personal aide, volunteered to put the fires out. Hart had been Anderson's sergeant orderly during the Mexican War, and when Eliza Anderson arrived back in New York from Charleston she searched for him throughout the city, having no idea where he was but never relenting because she believed he would be a great comfort to her husband at Sumter. By sheer chance she found Hart working as a city policeman, and he agreed to return to Charleston with her, where the chivalry let him sign on as laborer in Fort Sumter and allowed Eliza Anderson a final brief visit with her husband. Now the stocky Hart led a volunteer force of laborers into the flames throughout the battle, carrying buckets of water from the cisterns and extinguishing blazes that threatened to skeletonize the fort. Providence or Tyche lent the heroes a hand with the final fire of the day, however, when an enemy shot shattered three cisterns near the roof and let loose a tsunami that combined with a sudden heavy rainstorm to drown the blaze. Why Anderson hadn't ordered all the wood removed from the barracks and officer's quarters during the long "cold war" between North and South is not known—probably he simply assumed they were fireproof, as he had been advised—but ultimately it was clearly Major Anderson's responsibility and the fires that resulted proved to be the Confederates' most devastating weapon.

Before the day's battle ended Captain Doubleday, back on duty again for another bully shift, would deal with the crowds of hated rebels watching the fray from the Battery and every other possible vantage point, as if this were some jolly Fourth of July celebration. In Charleston ladies and gentlemen mingled on the Battery and rooftops with officers wearing swords and red sashes, among many colorful uniforms. Some ladies reportedly wept for that "stout-hearted soldier" Major Anderson and all the gallant Yankees trapped in Sumter fighting on against impossible odds. One newlywed wept for her husband with the Palmetto Guards. Mrs. Chesnut complained that the constant sound of the guns "makes regular meals impossible" and didn't wonder anymore about Floating Battery inventor John Randolph Hamilton's baby, whose first words had been "Boom Boom," a sound he kept repeating, so often did he hear the big guns. "Some of the anxious hearts lie in their beds and moan in solitary misery," Mrs. Chesnut wrote in her diary. But a "satisfying faith" comforts most. "'God is on our side,' they cry. 'Why?' we ask. We are told: 'Of course He hates the Yankees.'"

Of course He did, young Emma E. Holmes, lamed by a recent illness, agreed while writing in her diary of the Battery "thronged with anxious hearts" watching the battle. "There are some few ladies who have been made perfectly miserable and frantic by their fear for the safety of their loved ones," Emma Holmes wrote, "but the great body of the citizens seem so improved with the justice of our Cause that they place entire confidence on the God of Battles."

She felt "calm and composed" though "every shot is distinctly heard and shakes our house," noting that "not a sign of fear or anguish is seen," everybody "relieved that what has been so long dreaded has come at last and so confident of victory that they seem not to think of the danger of their friends." She had great faith in "our Palmetto boys."

Honor in the Cause was of course of great concern to all those watching. At Mrs. Chesnut's, gallant Sir Walter made another of his frequent appearances. The ladies and gentlemen discussed

Scott's *St. Valentine's Day; or, the Fair Maid of Perth* (1828), in which the Highland chief, nursed as an infant "with milk of a white doe," fails of nerve on the battlefield, fulfilling an ancient prophecy.

As for the slaves in the city, they seemed "silent and invisible," forced to row the foolishly curious out into the harbor closer to the action, but reluctant to do so even at the high prices many were willing to pay. Some slaves were strangely trusting. A Confederate officer on guard boat duty "met a negro out in the bay rowing toward the city" with plantation supplies. "Are you not afraid of Colonel Anderson's cannon?" the officer asked. "No, Sar," the man replied. "Mars Anderson ain't daresn't hit me. He know Marster wouldn't 'low it."

A similar tale was told about a slave sailing a cargo of wood into the harbor. Warned of the danger of running the gauntlet of gunfire, he is quoted by a *Courier* reporter as saying: "Cain't hep that. Must go to de town tonight; if anybody hurt dis boat, Massa see him about it, shuah."

Most slaves weren't so brainwashed, though. Wrote Mary Chesnut: "Not by one word or look can we detect any change in the demeanor of these negro servants. Lawrence sits at our door, as sleepy and respectful and as profoundly indifferent. So are they all. They carry it too far. You could not tell that they hear even the awful row that is going on in the bay, though it is dinning in their ears night and day. And people talk before them as if they were chairs and tables. And they make no sign. Are they stolidly stupid or wiser than we are, silent and strong, biding their time?"

As previously noted, there was but one black out in Fort Sumter, a waiter who served the officers. Doubleday the abolitionist described this "spruce-looking mulatto from Charleston" in terms worthy of a paternalistic slave owner, writing things like: "He leaned back against the wall, almost white with fear, his eyes closed . . . his whole expression one of perfect despair." The man was an untrained, frightened noncombatant, no more scared than many of the white laborers, some of whom, it will be remembered, hid in closets or beneath beds at Castle Pinckney under far less trying circumstances. But never mind, Doubleday was a child of his time; and to be fair, he did add that the waiter was "an exception to most negroes" he had encountered in the Army.

Captain Doubleday would like to have done something about the rebels watching on the Battery in Charleston, but Major Anderson specifically forbid any such action. He could, however, deal with the large group of Charlestonians watching the war like a spectator sport along the shore on Sullivan's Island. This was all the more pleasurable because Lieutenant Colonel Roswell Ripley, commander of the Fort Moultrie artillerymen, might just happen to be walking about. Doubleday despised the Ohioan more than any native-born secessionist, considering the former Union officer a "renegade fighting against his old comrades" since he had gone over to the South. He also knew that Ripley "took pains to denounce me as an Abolitionist" and recommended that "I be hanged by the populace as soon as caught."

Whatever Doubleday's most urgent motives, he opened fire on the unsympathetic spectators on Sullivan's Island. Sergeant Chester blamed the incident on the Captain's weary and angry men, vouching that no officers were present and claiming that two shots struck about fifty yards short, "bounding over the heads of the astonished spectators" and crashing through the large wooden Moultrie House resort hotel, which was flying a yellow hospital flag at the time. The chivalrous Southerners and their newspapers regarded the action as "barbaric." Doubleday, however, proudly took full credit in his reminiscences, though he didn't quite admit that he fired on civilians, as both Chester and a later article in the *New York Herald* claimed, and he mentioned no hospital flag flying.

"Just before the attack was made upon us," he wrote, "the Palmetto flag, which had waved over the building, was taken down; but I noticed with a spy-glass that there were still quite a number of people, *apparently troops* [my italics], remaining in the house. I saw no reason why the mere lowering of the flag should prevent us from firing at them. I therefore aimed two forty-two pounder balls at the upper story. The crashing of the shot, which went through the whole length of the building among the clapboards and interior partitions, must have been something fearful to those who were within. They came rushing out in furious haste, and tumbled over each other until they reached the bottom of the front steps in one writhing tumultuous mass."

There were those, North and South, who would have regarded Doubleday's action as barbaric indeed, whether the captain fired at civilians on the beach, or troops in an unarmed hospital, or civilians or troops in a hotel, and irrespective of whether or not the Sumter hospital, too, was "treated to red-hot shot during the bombardment," as Chester claimed. But Doubleday thought it all a big joke. Later a Confederate officer would ask him why he fired at the hotel and he replied "that the true reason was that the landlord had given me a wretched room there one night, and this being the only opportunity that had occurred to get even with him, I was unable to resist it." His Confederate counterpart also thought this funny.

Major Anderson could hardly have failed to notice Doubleday's disobedience, or Carmody and his compatriots breaking orders either, for that matter, but at this point Sumter's survival completely occupied him. Where was the fleet, why hadn't it come in from beyond the bar? The constant Confederate bombardment and hot shot fires were making a ruin of the fort. The supply of seven hundred cloth gunpowder cartridges he had begun his counter-fire with was so badly depleted by midday that he was forced to take all but six guns out of action, leaving Sumter outgunned by over eight to one. The burly "seamstresses" sewed cartridge bags as fast as they could, even using "several pair of woolen socks belonging to Major Anderson," but couldn't keep up with the gunners' demand. Iron rained on Sumter all afternoon, and the return fire from Sumter grew slower every hour; by day's end only two Union guns were firing sporadically on Cummings Point, two on Fort Moultrie, and two on the Sullivan's Island batteries. That night an inspection by Surgeon Crawford and Lieutenant Snyder at twilight would find the fort's outside walls deeply cratered by Confederate cannonball on all five sides, and a hole almost two feet deep in one spot carved out by repeated fire from the fearsome Blakely gun. The main gate had been badly damaged, as had the parapet, and many guns were dismounted, though Sumter was still defensible.

As darkness fell Major Anderson told his men to cease firing in order to conserve ammunition. The deafening general fire from Beauregard's guns also ceased, but all through the night the eighteen rebel 10-inch mortars kept up a steady fire on the fort at fifteen minute intervals, each of them lobbing four shells an hour into Sumter. With so many shells landing, most of the men slept fitfully, if at all, in the casements, though a few, like Surgeon Crawford, "slept all night well but hungry," and others, Private Thompson among them, were so exhausted that they "slept all night as sound as ever I did in my life."

Major Anderson got no sleep through the stormy night, worrying about a possible rebel invasion under cover of darkness. How could the enemy be distinguished from a relief expedition? Sergeant Chester wondered: "Both would come in boats, both would answer in English. It would be horrible to fire upon friends; it would be fatal to not fire upon enemies."

But by midnight the relief boats had not come in, and Major Anderson began to wonder if they ever would. He had no idea that Captain Gustavus Vasa Fox was in a Murphy's Law situation— everything that could possibly have gone wrong with his expedition did go wrong. After inching South through a raging storm, Fox had arrived in the *Baltic* at 3:00 A.M. to find that of his seven-ship fleet only the five-gun cutter *Harriet Lane,* under the command of Captain John Faunce, had made the specified rendezvous ten miles out of Charleston Harbor. In another three hours the man-of-war *Pawnee,* captained by Commander C. Rowan, made her appearance. Fox decided to head these ships in toward Sumter, but on reaching the bar at about 7:00 A.M., he heard the guns booming and knew that war had begun. Now his orders were not only to resupply Sumter but to reinforce the fort with the two hundred troops aboard the *Baltic.* Realizing that his big ships could not make it through the intense Confederate fire, he turned back to sea and waited for the three tugs and the man-of-war *Powhatan* with the three hundred sailors aboard her who were supposed to man the tugs and fight their way into Sumter, according to his plan. Fox did not know that Secretary of State Seward had commandeered the *Powhatan* and sent her to Fort Pickens, which had been reinforced early that morning by another ship and would be reinforced again on April 17 by the *Powhatan,* now at sea. Neither did he know that none of the three tugs essential to his plan would show up in time. The *Uncle Ben* had been driven into Wilmington, North Carolina, by the storm and seized by secessionists; the *Yankee* had been blown past Charleston into Savannah; and the owner of the *Freeborn* had refused to let her leave New York after considering her dangerous mission.

All day as the battle raged and Federal troops cursed him, Captain Fox had waited off the bar for the *Powhatan* and the tugs. Now, while Sumter slept, he considered sending longboats in to the fort but realized that the seas were too heavy. The sea was so rough that the *Baltic* touched ground at Rattlesnake Shoals as she steamed in closer to the bar. An excellent target in the light of the anchored fire barges the rebels had ignited in the inner channels, she had to move farther out to sea again. Fox waited through the night, desperately signaling with lights for his missing ships in the darkness, trying to formulate some alternate plan. But none would come to him, as much as he continued to hope and the soldiers at Sumter continued to curse and pray. His plan had been sabotaged and ruined by Seward and bad luck, drastically changing the outcome of the battle.

12

The Inferno

Sing a song of Sumter
   A fort in Charleston Bay;
Seven and seventy brave men
   Fight there night and day.

—Popular rhyme of the day

WHILE Sumter slept or tried to sleep, the rest of the country was awakening to screaming tabloid headlines.

"War!!! War!!! War!!!" cried an early edition of the *Philadelphia Inquirer* read by people going to work, and one young man reading such bulletins posted outside the *Inquirer* office "had his nasal organ violently peeled" for calling the Stars and Stripes "only a rag." A second *Inquirer* dispatch began: "Charleston, April 12—The ball has been opened at last and the war is inaugurated ..." Philadelphia streets were so crowded that it was hard to get to work. Proclaimed the *Philadelphia Press*: "Henceforth each man, high and low, must take his position as a patriot or a traitor—as a foe or friend of his country—as a supporter of the Stars and Stripes or of the Rebel banner." Mobs of people responded to such rhetoric by surging through the City of Brotherly Love, gathering outside the houses of known pro-Southerners, and demanding that they raise the Stars and Stripes or be lynched from a lamppost.

Headlines throughout America screamed of war. Heralded the *St. Paul Pioneer & Democrat,* misspelling Sumter's name:

> The War Begun
> First Bloodshed!
> Sumpter Bombarded!

Headlined the *Washington Star*: "Conflict at Charleston—Immense Excitement."

"The War Commenced," cried *The New York Times*, which also spelled Sumter's name "Sumpter."

Though many throughout the country grieved for the future as

209

they read the often inaccurate bulletins, the national mood out-side the South was mostly one of shock and then angry patriot-ism. "Nothing for years . . . [has] brought the hearts of all the people so close together," *The New York Times* editorialized. In Printing House Square, in downtown New York City, crowds gathered outside James Gordon Bennett's *New York Herald* office and shouted, "Come out, you yellow-bellied secessionist!" to the editor, commonly called His Satanic Majesty and known for his support of concessions to the South. Bennett came out "energeti-cally and unconditionally" for putting down the rebels "by force of arms," and his son even offered his new yacht to the navy. All of New York City rallied behind Major Anderson, even Mayor Fernando Wood, who had supported the South and proposed that New York establish itself as an independent city. At the Stock Exchange there were cheers for Anderson every time a new dispatch was read, and the market held firm, as did the Chicago Exchange and the market in Baltimore. On Broadway at the Laura Keane theatre, those dancers did their bumps and grinds even more enthusiastically as the actor playing the major waved his American flag.

Two men in Baltimore wearing Southern cockades were mobbed and assaulted, while in Connecticut, April fourteenth was proclaimed "Battle Sunday," and one citizen donated one hundred tons of iron to be made into cannonballs and "sent South from the mouths of guns." It was the same everywhere, from the great cities to little hamlets like Keosauqua, Iowa, where "knots of men could be seen on every corner excitedly speculating on what should be done," the dominant feeling being: "Avenge the Union!" As a *Tribune* reporter put it: "Everybody was up to war point."

Meanwhile in Charleston, where the news was happening long before the North got it, a gamecock alighted on the tomb of Calhoun at dawn and crowed, flapping its wings—surely an omen of victory, some Charlestonians thought. Yet there were still "lively times on the Palmetto Coast," as a reporter wrote. After a breakfast of more fatback, which a Charleston wag said was served with "hot rolls" compliments of the Confederate gunners, the troops in Sumter came under the relentless general fire of the rebels again and could still do little in return, since

Major Anderson's lack of cartridges forced him to cut back the rate of fire to only one round every ten minutes. Sumter's men cursed the fleet off the bar, not realizing how powerless it was, and the Confederate gunners joined in their condemnation, considering the Yankees off the bar mere cowards and expressing contempt for their "timorous inaction." From the Battery the same huge crowd of over five thousand watched. The Confederate forces had swollen with even more volunteers, among them several of Eliza Anderson's brothers, who, as Doubleday put it, "in the final attack on Fort Sumter were on the opposite side, fighting against her husband," the first known example of divided family loyalties in a war of brother against brother.

At 8:00 A.M., just as the weather suddenly turned bright and sunny, into "a morning clear and brilliantly beautiful," in Emma Holmes's words, a hot shot from one of Colonel Ripley's guns at Fort Moultrie set the Sumter barracks on fire again, and "a wild shout of triumph heartily echoed across the water" from the Confederate batteries. Hart and his volunteers extinguished this blaze, too, but Colonel Ripley's hot shot kept striking like red-tailed hawks at wounded prey. Again and again the barracks caught fire, again and again the flames were subdued, only to spring up with new shots. The Sumter gunners fought back desperately, pouring shots at Moultrie and fighting "a grand duello" for over an hour. Cannonballs, or grape as the soldiers called them, whistled over the heads of the rebels and tore their barracks to pieces, though to no avail; Moultrie's fire was increasing. "We saw red flames piercing the top of the [Sumter] barracks," a Southern correspondent at Cummings Point wrote. "The sight inspired new confidence into our men, and the bombardment immediately became more rapid and fierce than at any previous time. . . . The bombs flew so thick and fast that we could see them exploding in groups over the flaming fortress. . . . The fire blazed furiously" sweeping away "the whole line of the barracks on the south side of Sumter."

By about 10:00 A.M. Sumter was an inferno again, over one-fifth of it on fire. The fires were out of control, had destroyed several barracks, the officers' quarters, most of the main gate, and were creeping toward the powder magazine, which had foolishly been established on the ground floor of another barracks.

211

Three hundred barrels of gunpowder were inside, and there was much loose powder spilled on the floor from Friday's action. Major Anderson ordered every available man to work rolling the barrels of powder from the wooden room, across the parade ground, under Confederate shelling, and into the masonry casemates. But after fifty to a hundred barrels had been moved, flying cinders from the fire made the work so dangerous that it had to be abandoned. The men closed the copper-sheathed door to the barracks-magazine, banking the door with dirt and digging a trench in front of it that they kept filled with water.

Sumter began firing upon *itself* when shells and grenades stored at strategic points on the parapets and the stair towers were detonated by flying sparks. A stair tower on the left gorge angle was completely destroyed, forcing Surgeon Crawford to climb up over rubble when Anderson ordered him to check on the still inactive fleet from the parapet. Sumter "didn't burn up in a cheerful way," according to Sergeant Chester: "Everything was wet [from the rain and cistern water] and burned badly, yielding an amount of pungent piney smoke that almost suffocated the garrison." Thick black smoke from which there was no escape was swirling in the high winds and choking the men throughout the fort. Gunners lay on the ground with wet handkerchiefs over their mouths, gasping for air; others, sweating, choking, and red-eyed were forced outside the gun embrasures, risking enemy fire for fresh air.

"We came very near being stifled with the dense livid smoke from the burning buildings," an officer later said. "By 11:00 A.M. the conflagration was terrible and disastrous," Doubleday agreed. "It seemed impossible to escape suffocation... Had not a slight change of wind taken place, the result would have been fatal to most of us."

But the wind gave only partial relief. Nearly asphyxiated, the troopers in the blazing fort manned their guns so valiantly that each time a shot sounded from Sumter after a prolonged silence, the Confederate gun crews sent up cheers and applause for their bravery. "Three cheers for Major Anderson!" someone shouted from the Floating Battery, and the cheers were given. A Confederate officer watching from Morris Island was moved almost to tears at the thought that the entire Sumter garrison might be suffocated. Ladies at the Battery wept for the Yankee defenders, who would surely be burned to a crisp.

Yet the rebel batteries redoubled their efforts to destroy the fort and bring the flag down. "The roaring and crackling of the flames, the dense masses of whirling smoke, the bursting of the enemy's shells, and our own, which were exploding in the burning rooms, the crashing of shot and the sound of masonry falling in every direction, made the fort a pandemonium," Doubleday wrote. One hot shot rolled across the parade ground and into a casemate, setting a trooper's bed afire. Sparks filled the air, and the powder stored in the casemates for safety became endangered now. On an anxious Anderson's orders, men dumped all but five barrels into the sea. "If the tide had been high we would have been well rid of it," Sergeant Chester recalled. "But the tide was low and the pile of powder-barrels rested on the riprapping in front of the embrassure." Confederate gunners noticed this and turned their cannon on the barrels bunched against the base of the fort, finally finding their aim and hitting them. The huge explosion that followed shook the wharves in Charleston, showering the fort with brick and blazing timbers and flinging an unmanned casemate gun off its mounting and clear out of the battery.

From a fort that looked like an erupting volcano, with all its shell and powder explosions, Sumter's gunners kept firing, aiming mostly at Moultrie. They were down to their last five barrels of gun powder, for a rebel ball had hit the magazine door and jammed it closed so that no more powder could be removed. Then at 12:48 P.M., in the midst of the raging inferno, a shot aimed by Moultrie's Lieutenant William C. Preston, Jr. broke the thick mastlike flagstaff, which had already been hit nine times by competing rebel gunners, and toppled Sumter's huge garrison flag to the instant cry of "The flag is down!" from Southern onlookers. ("Well done, Willie!" his "sweet gentle old grandmother," widow of the Revolutionary War hero General Wade Hampton, later wired Preston.)

Racing out through the searing heat and exploding shells in the parade ground, Lieutenant Hall recovered the flag, at the cost of singed hair and the loss of his eyebrows, which had completely burned off. Hall's gold epaulets became so hot that he had to rip them from his uniform. He beat out the flames on the flag and within ten minutes hastily improvised a flagpole from a long spar, assisted by Peter Hart and one of the laborers. Nailing the flag to the spar they dashed to the parapet where, under Captain Seymour's direction, Hart fastened the pole firmly to a pile of gun carriages while rebel guns concentrated their fire on him. "Without undue haste," as Doubleday put it, Hart raised the tattered Stars and Stripes again in an heroic scene that would be depicted many times by Northern artists, often most imaginatively.

The moment Sumter's flag had come down, General Beauregard concluded that blazing, smoldering Fort Sumter was ready to surrender and immediately ordered Captain Stephen Lee, William Porcher Miles, and Roger Pryor to row over to the fort from Moultrie and offer Major Anderson assistance in putting out the fires—a tactful way of saying he was so bad off he might as well surrender. But Senator Louis Wigfall, now a colonel on Beauregard's staff (all Southern politicians of any consequence seem to have been made colonels), was stationed on Morris Island much closer to Fort Sumter, and he had gotten the same idea. The battle lapsed into ludicrous comic opera again. Possibly against the objections of his superior, Brigadier General James Simons, though some hold that Simons agreed, Wigfall commandeered a small boat and had Confederate Private H. Gourdin Young and three slaves row him over to the fort.

Through stray shot and shell coming from everywhere but Morris Island, Wigfall's little boat made its way across the mile of water to Sumter, the colonel holding aloft a sword with a white handkerchief attached. The oarsmen rowed faster with each shot that narrowly missed them and made the fort in record time, Private Young forcing the reluctant slaves to wait at pistol point when Wigfall got out by the main gate, which was ablaze, and walked around to an open embrasure waving his little white flag.

Still undetected by anyone in the thick smoke, Wigfall pulled himself up by the hands to the sill of the embrasure and stuck his head in beside the mouth of a cannon just as gunners were preparing to fire it. He came face to face with Private Thompson, who at first refused to admit the wild-eyed Texan but finally allowed him to crawl into the smoking fort, when Wigfall pleaded that he might be killed by his own shot and shell. Wigfall soon encountered Lieutenants Snyder and Davis and put his unauthorized surrender proposals to Davis while Snyder went looking for Anderson. Here stood a burly, wild-eyed, black-bearded man brandishing a huge sword with a white flag attached to it demanding Sumter's surrender—one possibly apocryphal account has him resembling a pirate: naked to the waist, wearing a crimson-red sash, long hair tied in a braid. "Your flag is down, you are on fire, and you are not firing your guns," he told Davis. "General Beauregard desires to stop this."

"No, sir," Lieutenant Davis countered. "Our flag is not down. If you will step this way you will see it floating on the ramparts."

"Let us stop this firing," Wigfall said, offering him his white flag. "Will you hoist this?"

"No," Davis replied, "it is for you to stop it." But he let Wigfall wave the white flag-handkerchief out the embrasure and then, without any authorization and for no good reason (except that a Confederate had waved the white flag first), ordered young Corporal Bringhurst to do the same, which Bringhurst did until a shot from Moultrie drove him back from the embrasure cursing: "God damn it! They don't respect this flag either—they are firing upon it!"

"I have been fired upon with that flag two or three times," Wigfall replied, referring to his hazardous boat ride. "I should think you might stand it once."

By then Major Anderson had approached, and Wigfall came directly to the point. "I am Colonel Wigfall," he announced. "You have defended your flag nobly, sir. It is madness to persevere in useless resistance. You have done all that is possible for men to do. General Beauregard wishes to stop the fight and asks on what terms you will evacuate this fort."

Anderson, calm and collected despite the heat and his lack of sleep, must have already asked himself the same question. Authorized by Secretary of War Cameron to surrender whenever necessary and directed not to subject his men to any danger or hardship unusual in military life, he must have thought he had more than met those conditions. Fort Sumter was a smoldering hell with 275 barrels of powder threatening to blow up at any minute; his men were hungry and exhausted, some of them a bit mad from their thirty-three hour ordeal, at least six of them wounded; 3,307 shots, about two a minute, had been fired at Fort

Sumter, which was by now barely recognizable. Outnumbered a hundred to one, vastly outclassed in artillery, his men had fought bravely and well, firing almost one thousand balls at the enemy. There were just four usable kegs of powder and three cartridges left, almost no food, and no fuel. Even if the major had had more powder, his guns were doing little real damage against the Confederate batteries, and the Federal fleet showed no sign of coming to his aid.

Of course it could have been different. Fully manned, all her guns working, with the proper ammunition, Sumter would have held out much longer and the contest would have been close, with many deaths on both sides—up to this point, despite the terrible fires and barrages, the fort's basic defenses were unimpaired. On the other hand, if the Confederates had known how weak and helpless the Union fleet really was, they could have simply blockaded the fort and starved Anderson out—the supreme irony is that there actually was no need to fire a single shot at Fort Sumter. But the "ifs" of military history are as legion as all the legions dead in war. As it stood, Anderson knew that nothing could be gained, there was no point continuing the fight with the only prospect before him serious injuries and death to his men. He knew, in short, that Wigfall was right.

"I have already stated my terms for evacuation to General Beauregard," he told his visitor, referring to Beauregard's early offer. "Instead of noon of the fifteenth, I will go now."

"Then I understand you will evacuate the fort upon the same terms proposed to you by General Beauregard?"

"Yes, Sir," Anderson said, "and upon those terms alone."

Anderson ran up a hospital sheet that had evaded the cartridge makers in place of the torn flag as an elated Wigfall rowed away from the fort with a verbal surrender agreement permitting the major to leave Fort Sumter with all his men and their arms, and allowing the Yankees to salute their flag as they left. The colonel was carried ashore triumphantly on the shoulders of Morris Island troops who waded out to greet him. Later, "black with rage" at Anderson's account of the fall of Sumter, which didn't credit his peacemaking efforts, he would say: "Catch me risking my life to save him again . . ."

But while a wild, whooping Wigfall began celebrating his coup on the shoulders of the other boys, Beauregard's *legitimate* emissaries wondered what was happening out at Fort Sumter. During the first half of their longer row from Fort Moultrie, Sumter's flag had been down. When they saw the Stars and Stripes raised again, by Sergeant Hart, they turned back to Moultrie, but on reaching Sullivan's Island they sighted the white flag Anderson had raised for Wigfall. They rowed back to Fort Sumter, arriving there by 2:00 P.M.

Diplomatically offering Southern assistance to Anderson in putting out the fires, the emissaries were surprised when the puzzled major refused their aid and informed them that he had already surrendered "by authority of General Beauregard" and that the terms had been agreed upon. The mild-mannered Anderson was uncharacteristically outraged to learn from them that Wigfall had had no authority at all to propose surrender terms, and that they certainly could not guarantee the major permission to salute his flag before leaving the fort. Anderson ordered his men to immediately hoist the Stars and Stripes and begin firing again.

Beauregard's aides were quick to convince the major to reconsider and write down the substance of the Wigfallian agreement for Beauregard, when act three of the farce began with the arrival of *three more* emissaries from the Confederate general! These representatives, however, were authorized to offer Anderson terms essentially the same as those offered by Wigfall, not demanding an unconditional surrender but allowing him to salute his flag (the most important condition of all to him, symbolic as it was of his only reason for defending Sumter, of all his physical and mental suffering) "as an honorable Testimony to the gallantry and fortitude with which Major Anderson and his command had defended their post."

Anderson, worn and haggard as his men, face smudged with soot, accepted, and the first battle of the Civil War was over, Confederate bells ringing and salutes called the "magic seven" fired from the cutters *Lady Davis* and *Cadet's Battery* as soon as the surrender was announced.

The farce, however, continued. While the emissaries parlayed with Anderson in the casemate Surgeon Crawford used as his quarters, Roger Pryor had picked up what he thought to be a

217

whiskey bottle and without asking permission gulped down a large portion of it—he needed something bracing. The "whiskey" turned out to be poisonous iodide of potassium, and Pryor began gagging on it. "Do something for me, Doctor!" he pleaded to Crawford, and the Surgeon saved him from being the only fatality of the battle by dragging him out on the parade ground and applying a stomach pump.

"He was soon out of danger," Doubleday tells us, not without a humorous reservation: "Some of us questioned the doctor's right to interpose in a case of this kind. It was agreed that if any rebel leader chose to come over to Fort Sumter and poison himself, the medical department had no business to interfere with such a laudable intention. The doctor, however, claimed with some show of reason, that he himself was held responsible to the United States for the medicine in the hospital, and therefore he could not permit Pryor to carry any away."

13

In Eighteen Hundred and Sixty-one/The Cruel War Had Just Begun

In Eighteen Hundred and Sixty-one
The cruel war had just begun.
We'll all drink stone blind;
Johnny, come fill up the bowl.
—North Carolina folk ballad sung to the tune of
"When Johnny Comes Marching Home"

CHIVALROUS as they were, most Southerners celebrated their victory on Evacuation Day Sunday, April 14, 1861, without realizing that the South merely defeated 128 relatively unarmed soldiers and laborers—with a force of over seven thousand soldiers, unlimited arms, and all the free laborers she wanted. It was not a victory of which to be particularly proud—the Yankees had more to be proud of in losing—but how they did howl and speech-make and celebrate. As if they had defeated the mighty Northern industrial complex with its 20 million people and would be in Washington by May, which, indeed, Confederate Secretary of War Walker publicly predicted.

In Columbia, South Carolina, twelve-year-old Emma Florence Le Conte danced in the streets. Later, she recalled: "The joy—the excitement—how well I remember it. For weeks we had been in a fever of excitement. On the day news came of the Fall of Sumter we were all sitting in the library at Uncle John's. The bell commenced to ring. At the first tap we knew the joyful tidings had come. Father and Uncle John made a dash for their hats—Julie and Johnny followed. We women ran trembling to the veranda—to the front gate, eagerly asking the news of passersby. The whole town was in a joyful tumult."

On Surrender Sunday a newspaper dispatch from Charleston told of "bells chiming all day, guns firing, ladies waving handkerchiefs, people cheering, and citizens making themselves generally demonstrative. It is regarded as the greatest day in the history of South Carolina." Remarked a local newspaper: "This first fortress of despotic power fell prostrate to the cause of Southern Independence."

Throughout the South at least one hundred towns fired cannon salutes on the day the Yankees were to evacuate Sumter. In

221

Charleston there were celebrations in many churches and a Te Deum was chanted at the Cathedral of St. John in thanksgiving for the victory. "A shout of triumph rent the air from the thousands of spectators on the island and mainland," noted the fifteen-year-old Confederate soldier Augustus Dickert. "Flags and handkerchiefs waved from the hands of excited throngs in the city. Soldiers mounted the ramparts and shouted in exultation, throwing their caps in the air."

In the North *The New York Times* headlined "Fort Sumter Fallen," its long story describing the walls of Sumter honeycombed by Confederate guns, a breach "as big as a cart" on the side facing the Ironclad Battery, as well as news of the slight face wound Captain Crawford received and the jailing of the *Times*'s correspondent "Jasper" as a spy. "The Surrender of Fort Sumter—No One Killed—Several Wounded" blared the *Washington Star,* its story lamenting Sumter's "blackened mass of ruins" and describing Charleston's bells "ringing out a merry peal."

All but the mute in Charleston made speeches at the slightest provocation, The Citadel cadets gave a dress parade on the Battery, ferryboat captains charged fifty cents a head to transport gaily attired ladies and gentlemen out into the harbor crowded with craft of all descriptions, where they stared at the still smoking fort while the Yankee soldiers were packing. Again, about the only one in Charleston who didn't feel it was a joyous, gala occasion was crusty old Judge Petigru. "It is an odd feeling to be in the midst of joy and gratulations that one does not feel," the old Carolinian Unionist wrote in a letter. "The universal applause that waits on secessionists and secession has not the slightest tendency to shake my conviction that we are on the road to ruin."

Most, however, were jubilant; the South seemed at last as one, Jefferson Davis's primary reason for attacking Fort Sumter. The great majority agreed with Reverend J. H. Elliot of St. Michaels Church in Charleston, who ended his sermon that morning by saying that "the Lord's Providence is fast uniting the whole South in a common brotherhood of sympathy and action, and our first essay in arms has been crowned with perfect success."

Though there were reports of ladies and laborers in the North crying on learning that the flag had been hauled down at Sumter,

Northern reaction also showed a people at last completely united, President Lincoln's primary reason for *defending* Sumter. "Fort Sumter is lost, but freedom is saved," began one of Horace Greely's editorials. In another editorial Greeley, who had opposed the use of coercion against the South, wrote in a change of heart: "The echoes of the cannon fired at Sumter have barely rolled over the Western hills ere they are drowned in the shouts of indignant freemen, demanding to be led against the traitors who have plotted to divide and destroy the country.... We have a civil war on our hands—there is no looking away from the fact. For this year, the Chief business of the American people must be proving that they have a Government and that Freedom is not another name for Anarchy." Still another *Tribune* editorial had "Jeff Davis & Co.... swinging from the battlements at Washington at least by the 4th of July."

In Washington, amidst the prolific lilacs and Judas trees, Abraham Lincoln, who was framing a proclamation calling for 75,000 soldiers to suppress the Southern insurrection, listened to newsboys hawking extras about Sumter's surrender, yet he did not "fret at things that were," according to his secretaries Nicolay and Hay. All his "inner consciousness was abroad in the wide realm of possibilities, busily searching out the dim and difficult path towards things to be." But he knew deep down that the better angels of our nature had lost.

New York diarist George Templeton Strong also heard newsboys hawking extras on Sumter's surrender and wrote: "Civil War is inaugurated at last. God defend the Right." Northern backbones were "much stiffened already," he observed, and "the seventy" who fought "the seven thousand" would be as long remembered "as the four hundred of the Light Brigade at Balaklava... God Save The Union and Confound Its Enemies. Amen," he later printed in huge letters in his diary, and he described a Union rally in Union Square as "the greatest popular demonstration ever known in America."

Most Northerners were indeed "at the war point." Even Stephen Douglas joined forces with Lincoln now. Trumpeted the *New York Leader*: "When has the world witnessed a spectacle of nobler heroism.... We still have a flag for which heroes are proud to die." "There is but one feeling here now, and that is to sustain

223

our flag and our government at all hazards," a prominent New York merchant wrote to Navy Secretary Gideon Welles. Churches throughout the North were filled to overflowing and "ministers prayed that the foes of the nation might be smitten down." American flags were waving everywhere. Crowds in Newark, New Jersey, and Baltimore, Maryland, ripped palmetto flags from the masts of ships. While *The New York Times* observed that the curtain had risen on "the great tragedy of the age," another stirring Raymond editorial called "The Resurrection of Patriotism" declared: "The great heart of the American people beats with one high pulsation of courage, and of fervid love and devotion to the great Republic. . . . Nothing for years has brought the hearts of all the people so close together—or so inspired them all with common hopes, and common fears, and a common aim, as the bombardment and surrender of an American fortress. . . . The cannon which bombarded Sumter awoke strange echoes, and touched forgotten chords in the American heart. American loyalty leaped into instant life, and stood radiant and ready for the fierce encounter. From one end of the land to the other—in the crowded streets of cities, and in the solitude of the country—wherever the splendor of the Stars and Stripes, the glittering emblem of our country's glory, meets the eye, come forth shouts of devotion and pledges of aid, which give sure guarantees for the perpetuity of American Freedom."

The South thought it had that Freedom now. In Charleston Harbor ladies and gentlemen in rowboats and on yachts and ferries were joined by ships of war filled with Southern dignitaries who would enter Fort Sumter after Major Anderson saluted his flag and left. But it would be a full day before Charleston firemen could put out the fires completely. "The whole fort," wrote one observer, "wore an aspect as if the hand of the destroying angel had swept ruthlessly by, and left not a solitary object to relieve the general desolation." Another observer wrote of Sumter: "It was as if the Genius of Destruction had tasked its energies to make the thing complete, brooded over the desolation of ages. It could scarce have been developed to a more full maturity of ruin. The walls of the internal structure, roofless, bare, blackened and perforated by shot and shell, hung in fragments, and seemed in instant readiness to totter down."

Major Anderson told a Carolinian that "yesterday was one of the proudest days of his life, for while he had endeavored to do his duty as an officer, he had not taken the life of a fellow being." Most did agree that Sumter was a comparatively bloodless battle, Union casualties put at between four and six, including Hall's eyebrows, and Southern casualties put at five or six, including Pryor's stomachache. All of the casualties were said to be minor, and the only death officially reported during the entire battle was that of an old horse killed on Sullivan's Island by Union guns. A *New York Times* report had it that "quite a number [of Southerners] have been struck by spent pieces of shell, but none hurt seriously. . . . many fragments of these missiles [are] already circulating in the city" as souvenirs.

Yet Confederate losses may have been much greater and were possibly suppressed to keep Southern morale high. No one seems to have thoroughly investigated Doubleday's charges in his reminiscences that a large number of rebels were killed and wounded.

"I have reason to suspect, from several circumstances, that the contest was not as bloodless as it was represented to be at the time," Doubleday charged. "The coxswain of the boat that brought Beauregard emissary William Porcher Miles over heard him make the remark that no one was hurt on the Rebel side. The coxswain stared at him for a moment in undisguised amazement and then stepped aside behind an angle of the work, where he could indulge in a hearty fit of laughter. His whole action was that of one who thought his chief had been indulging in romance. . . . The fact is, Fort Moultrie was all slivered and knocked to pieces; and as I heard so much in reference to the narrow escapes of officers and soldiers there, I concluded that, if no one was hurt, a miracle must have taken place. The Rebel who carried dispatches between Fort Moultrie and Mount Pleasant in a small boat was in a position to know, and he told Peter Hart, some years after the war, that a schooner, to his certain knowledge, came from Charleston during the battle, and took off a number of killed from Fort Moultrie, who were taken to Potter's Field, on Cooper River and buried there on Sunday, at 4:30 A.M. I had previously seen the same story published as coming from Charleston. A similar statement was made on his arrival in New York, by the mate of the schooner *D. B. Pitts,* and it purported to be founded on his own observations."

Doubleday goes on to add that a Moultrie soldier named Galoway told a Sumter man that he "had seen with his own eyes a number of killed and wounded there." He also tells of hearing about a list of Confederate killed and wounded which had been posted on a bulletin board in Charleston and was "afterward torn down, for fear it might discourage the troops." And he mentions the "great many Irish laborers" in Fort Moultrie whose loss "would hardly have excited a remark in aristocratic Charleston." Nevertheless, in the official reports, in all the accounts of the Sumter battle, in letters, diaries, and books by Civil War participants and their survivors, no hard evidence of a Southern death at the battle of Sumter has yet been found.

There were deaths, however, *after* the surrender. Union deaths. Just before Major Anderson fired his farewell salute to the flag someone aboard the steamer *Isabel,* which was to transfer the Yankee troops out to the fleet that had failed them off the bar, asked him how many guns he would fire. It would not be the usual twenty-one-gun salute, nor thirty-four guns for the stars in the flag. "One hundred," the Major replied, choking up and suddenly sobbing, "and those are scarcely enough."

The first shot went off well enough, at 2:00 P.M., thousands of Charlestonians watching as the big barbette guns finally saw service, the entire garrison standing at attention, tears in the eyes of some, as the torn Stars and Stripes was lowered. Then, with the firing of the seventeenth gun, there was "the sound as of two reports," which proved to be an explosion. Most likely a gun exploded prematurely when Private Daniel Hough inserted a cartridge into the barrel, which was still flaming slightly because it hadn't been thoroughly swabbed out after the previous shot. The stiff sea breeze then blew some of the fire from the muzzle into a pile of cartridges below and exploded them, sending chunks of broken masonry flying like shell fragments across the parapet and doing much damage. In any case, Private Hough, "a good soldier," in Doubleday's words, was killed almost instantly, his right arm ripped off his body. Five were injured: Sergeant James Edward Galway, who later died in a Charleston hospital; George Fielding; John Irwin; George Pinchard; and James Hayes. The first Union dead of the war were not buried in Fort Sumter, as one persistent legend has it, but in Charleston.

Few would put it as cruelly as Colonel Wigfall, who later said of Anderson: "The only men of his killed, he killed himself, firing a salute to their old striped rag." Nevertheless, Major Anderson was badly shaken and despondent. He cut his hundred-gun salute to fifty guns. The torn Sumter flag folded neatly under his arm, he was finally ready to lead his men out of the fort at 4:00 P.M. It was the indomitable Doubleday's idea, despite the tragedy and personal threats against him from spectators in the harbor, to lead the troops out to the tune of "Yankee Doodle." As the band played, Sumter's defenders, in full uniform and wearing their arms, filed onto the *Isabel,* free from their prison at last, to be replaced almost at once by General Beauregard and other Confederate dignitaries who would make more speeches and raise both the palmetto flag and a silken Stars and Bars made by the ladies of Charleston. Edmund Ruffin wasn't first inside the fort with the Palmetto Guard, as tradition holds, but, canteen and blanket strapped on his shoulder, rifle in hand, he wasn't far behind. It was Mrs. Henry Bonnetheay, an artist and friend of Lieutenant Davis's sister, who had this distinction. Once inside, Ruffin soon began looking for souvenirs, becoming the first recorded souvenir hunter of the Civil War. Very popular was wood from the shattered flagpole, which he and others made into crosses.

Ironically, Major Anderson and his men were forced to watch the Confederate festivities, which Emma Holmes called "the universal rejoicing," because their ferryboat missed the tide and was unable to leave Sumter's wharf until the next morning. The enemy on Cummings Point "lined the beach silent, their heads uncovered" when the bone-weary troops finally passed by and transferred to the *Baltic.*

It was about 8:00 A.M. when the men of Sumter left the doomed fortress and began their voyage toward New York, where huge crowds celebrating their courage awaited them. They were to a man glad to go, but as the wounded Surgeon Crawford wrote, "many an eye turned toward the disappearing fort as it sank upon the horizon," the smoke-cloud of battle still "hanging heavily over its parapet." Major Anderson, never the same afterward, was perhaps framing the short formal statement he would dictate in New York—an awkward, hurried, one-sentence statement, the only statement he could ever bring himself to make about the battle, as if he wanted an end to it all: "Having defended Fort Sumter for thirty-four hours, until the quarters were entirely burned, the main gates destroyed by fire, the gorge walls seriously impaired, the magazine surrounded by flames, and its doors closed from the effects of the heat, four barrels and three cartridges of powder only being available, and no provisions remaining but pork, I accepted the terms of evacuation offered." He was a hero, but a broken man; brave, but at times more like a firm, kindly minister than a military man; devoted to peace, but also to honor, and torn apart by the two. His gentle voice and manner had been silenced completely, while for the moment the terrorists of the mind and mouth prevailed.

The war was on. Civil War, so long dreaded, had begun.

Brother against brother; the United States for the time being dead.

Each side united, the country asunder.

On board ship Yankees were telling tales of their heroism and still whistling "Yankee Doodle."

Back in Sumter rebels were telling tales of their heroism and whistling "The Bonnie Blue Flag."

The war was on, the ball continued.

"In eighteen hundred and sixty-one / The cruel war had just begun . . ."

Both sides were sure God was on their side.

The boys on each side were sure they were soon going to win.

14

After the Ball Was Over

My soul is sailing through the sea,
But the Past is heavy and hindereth me.
—Sidney Lanier,
"Barnacles"

THERE were victory balls in Charleston after Fort Sumter fell: green and glorious troops in splendid uniforms untouched yet with blood, waltzing with lovely ladies in crinoline. A popular dance was The Secession Two-step—written by a man down in Georgia.

On they danced in a fairyland of magnolia and jasmine and laurel and azalea and rhododendron, the scents sweet in the night, though the strong smell of gunpowder began to overwhelm the flowers.

"Did y' hear tell, Ashley," one belle asked her partner, "of that old nigra woman *Oola* down in Washington? A witch woman, they say, born in Africa. She saw a great 'war comet' comin' by. 'You see dat great fire sword blazin' in de sky,' she said. 'Dat's a great war comin' and de handle's to'rd the Norf and de point to'rd de Souf and de Norf's gwine take dat sword and cut de Souf's heart out. But dat Linkum man, chilluns, if he takes de sword, he's gwine perish by it.'"

"Don't you believe it. The war'll all be over in no more'n a few weeks, Melissa. We'll teach those Yankees a lesson."

In the intensely beautiful southern spring, around and around they whirled, glimpsing scores of trees and shrubs mangled by shells, thousands of blossoms too early fallen.

Plumed hats, silver swords, voluminous gowns . . .

To Judge Petigru it seemed like a ball in an insane asylum.

And a Northerner, anonymous to this day, was writing in his diary: "Is it possible there can be truth in the old notion that, in times of great national trial and excitement, so many men do go mad, so to speak . . . that madness becomes a sort of epidemic?"

But the waltzes and quadrilles continued after Bull Run or

231

First Manassas, different names, North and South, for the same slaughteryards . . .
Antietam . . .
Fredericksburg . . .
Chancellorsville . . .
The dancers always whispering to each other that it would all be over in a few days, a few weeks, a few months . . .
Shiloh . . .
Gettysburg . . .
Chickamauga . . .
The ball went on for four full years, the nation, the family, split in the bloodlust of monstrous hatred . . .
The Wilderness . . .
Petersburg . . .
Monacacy . . .
With each bloody battle there were fewer dancers . . .
Cedar Creek . . .
Atlanta . . .
Savannah . . .
Five Forks . . .
Until finally those left on the floor could dance no more, it was a ball of mutilés . . .
Out on the vast field from Sumter to Appomattox there were 700,000 dead, countless maimed and wounded in body, mind, and soul.
Finally, the ball was over.
Union dead numbered 360,000 or more, including over 38,000 of the 180,000 blacks who fought for the Union (a mortality rate 40 percent higher than that for white soldiers).
Southern dead numbered 258,000 or more, out of a population less than half the North's. The South itself, where most of the battles took place, was as ravaged as the Federal fort where it all began.
Casualties exceeded America's losses in all other wars up until today.
In contrast to Sumter, the three-day Battle of Gettysburg cost 51,000 casualties, including four thousand Confederate dead and three thousand Union.
Horace Greeley was right when he called Fort Sumter a com-

paratively bloodless first battle for one of the bloodiest wars in history. Would a bloodier prelude have been more of a deterrent . . .

Perhaps if Sumter hadn't been what Emma Holmes called "one of the most brilliant and bloodless victories in the records of the world . . ."

But we shall never know.

The war did free millions, though the hatreds and intolerances it nourished persisted another hundred years and still live . . .

It did help keep America out of anything resembling a major war for half a century . . .

Of the terrorists of mind and mouth, some were lucky, some not . . .

Old Edmund Ruffin wasn't.

Ruffin, who vowed he would never live under damn Yankee rule, kept true to his vow. During the war he put in brief appearances at Bull Run and other battles, doggedly shouldering his musket, his picture hawked back home as an inspiration to all Southerners. After Appomattox, his plantation was burned and looted by General Sherman's "Bummers," and graffiti, like "This House Belonged to a Ruffinly Son-of-a-Bitch," was scrawled on the walls. Ruffin ran and hid from the enemy for awhile; but, finally, he sat down to write a farewell as only he could: "And now with my latest writing, and utterance I here repeat my unmitigated hatred to Yankee rule and the prejudicious, malignant and vile Yankee race." Old Lochinvar then picked up his gun and blew out his brains. He had lived to the age of seventy-two. A long life, compared to that of his two hundred slaves, not one out of 25 of whom could expect to live beyond sixty, nor to that of so many of the boys on both sides who didn't come marching home.

Secretary of State Seward survived wounds inflicted by John Wilkes Booth's fellow conspirator, Louis Powell, at the same time Lincoln was assassinated. He remained as Andrew Johnson's secretary of state and is remembered today mostly for what was dubbed at the time Seward's Folly, or Seward's Icebox—the purchase of Alaska from Russia in 1867 for a mere $7,200,000.

They didn't hang old Jeff Davis from a sour-apple tree, but he did spend some time in jail.

General Beauregard was eclipsed by the rising star of Robert E.

Lee, who was always at least just a little better. Ill health plagued him, and while his strategy at Bull Run was admired and Southern ladies wrote poems and songs to him, he proved more of an engineer than a field commander.

Among Fort Sumter's stout defenders, five officers ended the war as Union generals: Doubleday, Crawford, Foster, Seymour, and even Jefferson Davis, despite his rebel name. But none ever achieved the fame he won at Sumter.

Young Lieutenant Hall made it to full colonel.

Lieutenant Meade went over to the South when his native Virginia seceded shortly after Sumter and became one of the few in the war who fought for both North and South.

Sergeant Chester came up through the ranks to captain.

Brave Peter Hart, celebrated throughout the North, lived to see Hart Island in New York City's East River named for him. But it would become New York's Potters Field, the municipal burial ground for unknown and unwanted dead.

Captain Gustavus Vasa Fox of the failed relief expedition became Union Assistant Secretary of the Navy.

Major Anderson himself was brevetted major general not long after Sumter as a reward for his valiant defense, although, permanently broken in health, a casualty of the battle, he was soon forced to retire from the service. His doctor forbade him even to write of Sumter. He died in 1871, only sixty-five, in Nice, France, and at his request was buried wrapped in his country's flag.

But Anderson did return once more to Sumter, on Good Friday, April 14, 1865, exactly four years after its surrender, for a ceremony commemorating the repossession of the fort by the Union. His comrade Peter Hart came with him to raise the U.S. flag at Sumter again. The fort was now little more than a huge gray pile of rubble. Yankee artillery had poured literally tons of shells into it over the years while the Confederates had valiantly held it to the very end. At the last they deserted it, but never surrendered Fort Sumter.

Hart fastened Anderson's tattered flag to the halyards "amidst joyous shouts and applause." Pale and silver-haired, still militarily erect, Anderson raised the same flag that had begun it all to the top of Sumter, along with a garland of roses. "I thank God that I have lived to see this day," he said, "and to be here to perform this, perhaps the last act of my life, of duty to my country."

234

Even as Anderson spoke President Lincoln was planning to attend Ford's Theatre that night, and John Wilkes Booth, the last of the fire-eaters, the first of the assassins, was plotting to meet him there . . .

Finally came the full one-hundred-gun salute. The shells could be seen by thousands on the Battery in Charleston. Unlike Sumter, the city had been spared destruction because Sherman's troops had swept past it along the Ashley River without bombarding it badly. Probably this had nothing to do with the fact that General Sherman had spent four years in Charleston before the war, later calling them the best years of his life. In any case, Charleston had already sunk from third in per capita wealth among U.S. cities to the bottom of the list. The rest of the state that had been so proud and joyous to be first to secede suffered far more. "In our march through South Carolina," wrote one of Sherman's harsh avenging soldiers in his diary, "every man seemed to think that he had a free hand to burn any kind of property he could put the torch to. South Carolina paid the dearest penalty of any state in the Confederacy, considering the short time the Union Army was in the state; and it was well that she should, for if South Carolina had not been so persistent in going to war, there would have been no war for years to come."

Charleston's Middleton Gardens, abandoned by its owner when the war began, overgrown with weeds, the main house burned by Union troops, did offer some hope in its flowering, though one visitor lamented "the camelia flowers in every hue . . . wasting their beauty on the desert scene."

Perhaps somewhere in the city, as Sumter's guns boomed for the last time, Henry Timrod, "the laureate of the Confederacy," was framing his touching romantic "Ode" to the Confederate war dead, first sung at Magnolia Cemetery in Charleston in 1867:

> Sleep sweetly in your humble graves
> Sleep, martyrs of a fallen cause;
> Though yet no marble column craves
> The pilgrims here to pause . . .

Walt Whitman, up North, was writing a draft of "When Lilacs Last in the Dooryard Bloomed . . ."

235

SUMTER

I saw battle corpses, myriads of them,
And the white skeletons of young men, I saw them,
I saw the debris and debris of all the slain soldiers of
    the war,
But I saw they were not as was thought.
They themselves were finally at rest, they suffered not,
The living remain'd and suffer'd, the mothers suffer'd
And the wife and the child and the musing comrade suffer'd . . .

Appendix I: Chronology of Causes Leading Up to the Battle of Fort Sumter and the Civil War

Prehistory—Slavery. In the era of hunters and gatherers, humankind usually killed (and possibly ate), rather than enslaved, war captives. The first slaves may have been women of a conquered tribe carried off as wives or servants. Some authorities consider the substitution of slavery for the killing of captives a great improvement, without considering that slavery can be worse than murder, in fact often involves the murder of future generations: murder in the future of the future. Slavery was not common until agricultural economies developed and made the practice profitable.

Classical Times—Enslavement of whites and blacks thrived among the ancient Greeks and Romans and was practiced all over the world, though there were many slave uprisings. In Africa there was an early slave trade conducted by the Arabs to supply slave markets in Mohammedan countries. Centuries later the famous missionary Dr. Livingston estimated that of every one hundred slaves captured by the Arabs and dominant tribes in the interior of Africa only *five* actually survived the terrible journey to market, all the rest dying en route.

Medieval Times—The word *slave* did not exist in Athens in the Periclean age, where there were twice as many slaves as freemen, nor in Rome, which was also a great slave empire. *Slave* derives from the name of a tribe that lived in what is now Poland and in other areas of eastern Europe. The name meant "glory" or "noble, illustrious" in the tribe's own tongue, but in about A.D. 6 this entire people was conquered by warlike German tribes from the west and either forced to serve their conquerors or sold into bondage to the Romans and Greeks. To the Romans their name was *Salavus*, which became the medieval Latin *sclavus*, a Slav captive, a term of contempt applied to any bondsman or servile person. *Sclavus* became *esclave* in French and came into English as *sclave*, retaining the *c* until about the sixteenth century, when *slave* was first used. The word *Slav*, for the race of people in eastern Europe, comes from the same source—the proud "noble" tribe whose name underwent a complete metamorphosis.

1494—Columbus sent home over five hundred American Indian prisoners captured in wars, with the suggestion that they be sold at auction in Seville. Queen Isabella instead directed that they be sent back to their native country.

1517—Bishop Bartolomé de las Casas, having seen how the American Indians suffered under the Spanish in Haiti and reasoning that blacks were stronger and would live longer in the mines, pleaded with King Charles that every Spanish resident there have the right to import a dozen African slaves. Charles agreed, selling the exclusive right to supply four thousand blacks annually to Haiti, Cuba, Jamiaca, and Puerto Rico. The patent wound up in the hands of Genoese merchants, who obtained the slaves from the Portuguese, thus beginning the first systematic slave trade between Africa and America—all as a result of Bishop de las Casas's "humanitarian action."

August 1619—The first slaves were brought to Jamestown, Virginia, by a Dutch ship from the coast of Guinea, which sold a part of its human cargo to the tobacco planters there. Although these particular black slaves were treated like white indentured servants and allowed to go free after a period of service, this trade is considered the beginning of slavery in British America. In the terrible slave trade to North America fully half of the African men, women, and children did not live to reach their destination —exclusive of slaves who died after capture but before being shipped. It has been estimated that over two million slaves reached all the British colonies of America and the West Indies between 1680 and 1786—which means that over four million others may have died.

1671—Quaker founder, George Fox, inveighed against the slave trade. Within less than a century after Fox's death the

Quakers in England and America constituted the first organized group to oppose the traffic in human lives, though of course individual voices had been raised against slavery long before this.

July 1776—The Declaration of Independence, signed by many slaveowners, called it "self-evident" that "all men are created equal." Of America's founding fathers, Franklin, Adams, Madison, Hamilton, and Patrick Henry all condemned the principle of slavery. George Washington's will provided for the emancipation of his slaves, and he remarked to Jefferson that it was "among his first wishes to see some plan adopted by which slavery in his country might be abolished by law," and that he would vote for such a plan. Declared Jefferson, regarding slavery: "I tremble for my country when I reflect that God is just."

July 1784—The Continental Congress passed the Northwest Ordinance, one of the clauses of which stated that there would be no slavery permitted in the area to become Ohio, Indiana, Illinois, Michigan, and Wisconsin, thus setting a precedent for no slavery in new territories.

September 1787—The U.S. Constitution outlawed the slave trade after 1808, but sanctioned the continuation of slavery. For the purpose of apportioning Congressional representatives on the basis of population, the Constitution counted each slave as three fifths of a white person. It also provided that fugitive slaves had to be returned to their owners. Slaves were already completely involved in the South's economy, but not in the North's, where slavery had been abolished or would soon be abolished in all states. Although South Carolina and Georgia had insisted on the recognition of slavery as a condition of their joining the Union, *slave* and *slavery* are never mentioned in the Constitution.

May 1792—Denmark became the first European country to abolish the slave trade.

October 1793—Northerner Eli Whitney's invention of the cotton gin resulted in the need for more slaves to pick more cotton in the South.

December 1798—The Virginia and Kentucky state legislatures declared that the Alien and Sedition Acts earlier passed by Congress were unconstitutional—one of the first expressions of states' rights. A year later, Kentucky declared that state "nullification" was the remedy for such acts.

March 1807—Great Britain abolished the slave trade.

January 1808—The Constitution forbid the importation of slaves from abroad after January 1, but slaves could still be bought and sold in the United States and continued to be smuggled into the country.

December 1814—New Englanders opposed the War of 1812 against England at the Hartford (Connecticut) Convention and considered seceding from the Union over their differences.

January–March 1820—Maine was admitted into the Union as a free state, but Congress also admitted Missouri as a state allowing slavery within its borders to preserve the balance between South and North. The Missouri Compromise was adopted as well, barring slavery in the territory of the Louisiana Purchase north of 36° 30' latitude.

May 1823—The British Anti-Slavery Society was established by William Willberforce and others to agitate for the end of slavery.

May 1824—A protective tariff law passed by Congress was strongly objected to by Southerners (who felt it discriminated against them) and led some of them to consider leaving the Union.

May 1828—What the South called the Tariff of Abominations was passed by Congress; this tariff, imposing high duties on raw materials, was protested throughout the region.

December 1828—South Carolina adopted resolutions protesting the Tariff of Abominations, attaching an essay by Vice-President John C. Calhoun, a South Carolinian, arguing that a state convention can nullify any Federal law it considers unconstitutional.

January 1830—In congressional debates on the sale of western lands, debates which centered upon Federal power versus states' rights, Senator Daniel Webster made his famous "Liberty and Union, now and forever, one and inseparable!" speech.

November 1832—A South Carolina state convention adopted an ordinance nullifying the tariff acts of 1828 and 1832. South Carolina readied itself to defend its position militarily and even to secede from the Union if necessary.

December 1832—President Andrew Jackson reinforced the Federal forts in Charleston Harbor and issued a warning to Carolinians that no state can secede from the Union.

March 1833—After South Carolina continued to defy King Jackson, Henry Clay, "The Great Compromiser," worked out a new tariff bill, including a gradual cutback in tariffs, that satisfied the Carolinians, who suspended their nullification ordinance.

December 1833—The American Anti-Slavery Society, which would have great influence in the abolitionist movement, was formed in the North ten years after its British counterpart. Within five years the Society had 250,000 members.

January 1834—Fiery radical William Lloyd Garrison published the first number of his influential abolitionist newspaper, *The Liberator.*

May 1836—A gag rule calling for no discussion of the issue of slavery was adopted by the House of Representatives and lasted until 1844, the House voting for the rule at the beginning of every session until then. The silence only exacerbated the situation.

January 1842—The Supreme Court ruled that a Pennsylvania state law forbidding the seizure of fugitive slaves was unconstitutional. *Prigg v. Commonwealth of Pennsylvania* also stated that the Federal government must enforce fugitive slave laws, which led many Northern states to pass personal liberty laws safeguarding slaves from slave owners in other states.

August 1846—As an amendment to an appropriations bill, the House of Representatives passed the Wilmot Proviso providing $2 million for President Polk to purchase territory from Mexico following the war with that country. The Wilmot Proviso, the same word for word as the 1787 Northwest Ordinance, stated that "neither slavery nor involuntary servitude shall ever exist" in any territories purchased from Mexico, but it was rejected by the Senate. In the debate South Carolina Senator John Calhoun argued that Congress cannot limit slavery in new territories and must protect slavery because slaves are private property.

December 1847—The doctrine of "popular sovereignty" was introduced by Michigan Senator Lewis Cass, who proposed in a letter that the decision of slavery or no slavery in a territory be left to the territorial government.

August 1848—A congressional bill organizing the Oregon Territory without slavery was passed and signed by President Polk.

October 1849—Californians adopted a constitution forbidding slavery and asked for admission to the Union. When Southerners objected to the admission of California and some threatened secession, Calhoun among them, President Zachary Taylor, a military hero, vowed that he would take the field once again to defeat any secessionist movement.

January 1850—Senator Henry Clay offered a compromise between North and South admitting California as a free state because its people wished it so; making no decision about slavery in the other territories won from Mexico; barring the slave trade; and proposing a stricter fugitive slave law.

March 1850—In the debates on Clay's compromise, Daniel

Webster, long an antislavery man, argued that the North must accept even slavery if it meant the preservation of the Union. Calhoun argued that the North must accept the extension of slavery and stop agitating about the institution. Moderates prevailed on both sides in the debate.

September 1850—Congress adopted Clay's proposals, which became known as the Compromise of 1850.

November-December 1850—At a convention in Nashville, extreme Southern leaders emphasized the South's right to secede from the Union. A month later, in December, a Georgia state convention declared that the state could secede if the Compromise of 1850 was violated.

March 1852—There were said to be 250,000 runaway or fugitive slaves in the North, and America's most popular novel was written about them. Harriet Beecher Stowe's immensely popular *Uncle Tom's Cabin* was published, selling 300,000 copies its first year and causing great controversy. In reality her work (later made into an immensely popular play without her permission) was a tract against the Fugitive Slave Law disguised as a novel, but Mrs. Stowe documented the book's accuracy the next year in *The Key to Uncle Tom's Cabin,* drawn from laws, court records, letters, and newspaper accounts. President Lincoln would later say to her: "So, you're the little woman who wrote the book that made this great war." One madman mailed her the ears of a slave.

May 1854—The Kansas-Nebraska Act, proposed by Senator Stephen Douglas of Illinois, was passed by Congress. The bill divided the Great Plains region in two: the Kansas Territory and the Nebraska Territory. Douglas, assuming that one of the regions would be settled by proslaveryites, let "popular sovereignty" decide which would prevail in each. This marked the beginning of great agitation by abolitionists and proslaveryites in the area.

May 1856—Senator Charles Sumner of Massachusetts, an outspoken antislaveryite, was brutally attacked with a stick as he sat at his Senate desk by South Carolina Representative Preston "Bully" Brooks. Sumner, incapacitated for over three years, became a Northern martyr.

November 1856—Democrat James Buchanan defeated Republican John Fremont for the presidency.

March 1857—The Supreme Court, in the Dred Scott case, declared the Missouri Compromise of 1820 unconstitutional. The decision said in effect that Congress has no right to deprive citizens of their property (slaves being considered property) anywhere in the country. Dred Scott, a slave, had sued for his freedom after his master had taken him from the slave state of Missouri into the free state of Illinois and then back to Missouri again.

June 1858—Abraham Lincoln was nominated by Illinois Republicans to run against the Democratic candidate, U.S. Senator Stephen A. Douglas. Lincoln lost the election but received national attention in the Lincoln-Douglas debates for his strong antislavery stand.

May 1859—At the Southern Commercial Convention delegates voted for the Federal government to reopen the African slave trade prohibited by the Constitution after 1808.

October 1859—Radical abolitionist John Brown seized the Federal arsenal at Harpers Ferry, Virginia, was captured within a day by U.S. forces, and was convicted of treason and hanged.

1860*

January 1—The 1860 census revealed that 22 million people lived in the free states and 9 million people lived in the slave states, about a third of the latter being slaves.

---

*The following chronology of events in 1860 and 1861 was revised and greatly expanded from the out of print *Battles and Leaders of the Civil War*, Vol. 1 (1884).

April 23—The National Convention of the Democratic party assembled at Charleston, South Carolina. Dissensions arising in regard to the question of congressional protection of slavery in the territories, the Southern delegates withdrew, organized another convention in Charleston, and adjourned on May 4, to meet in Richmond, Virginia, on June 11.

May 3—The Douglas, or Northern, wing of the National Convention adjourned, to reassemble at Baltimore, Maryland, on June 18.

May 9—The Convention of the Constitutional Union party (formerly the American, "Know-Nothing," party), held at Baltimore, Maryland, nominated John Bell of Tennessee for President and Edward Everett of Massachusetts for vice-president and adopted a platform evading the slavery issue.

May 18—The National Convention of the Republican party, held at Chicago, nominated Abraham Lincoln of Illinois for President and Hannibal Hamlin of Maine for vice-president and voted in favor of congressional prohibition of slavery in the territories.

June 23—The Northern Democratic National Convention, at Baltimore, nominated Stephen A. Douglas of Illinois for President and Benjamin Fitzpatrick for vice-president. (The latter declined and the national committee substituted Herchel V. Johnson, of Georgia.) The convention declared in favor of leaving the question of slavery in the territories to the people of the territories, or to the Supreme Court of the United States.

June 28—The Southern Democratic National Convention (adjourned from Richmond to Baltimore) nominated John C. Breckinridge of Kentucky for President and Joseph Lane of Oregon for vice-president. The convention declared that neither Congress nor a territorial legislature had the right to prohibit slavery in a territory, and that it was the duty of the Federal government in all its departments, to protect slavery in the territories when necessary.

November 6—U.S. presidential election results:

	States	Electoral Votes	Popular Votes
Lincoln	17	180	1,866,352
Breckinridge	11	72	845,763
Douglas	2	12	1,375,157
Bell	3	39	589,581

November 21—Major Robert Anderson took command of Federal troops in Charleston Harbor from Colonel John L. Gardner.

December 3—President Buchanan delivered a message to Congress that argued against the right of secession, but expressed doubt as to the constitutional power of Congress to make war upon a state.

December 6—Select Committee of Thirty-three was appointed to the House of Representatives to take measures for the perpetuity of the Union. (See February 28, 1861.)

December 10—Howell Cobb of Georgia, secretary of the treasury, a *Southerner* who didn't like Buchanan's action or inaction, resigned.

December 12—Chief of Staff General Winfield Scott arrived in Washington to confer with the President.

December 14—Lewis Cass of Michigan, secretary of state, a *Northerner* who didn't like Buchanan's action or inaction, resigned.

December 20—The Ordinance of Secession was adopted in South Carolina by a convention called by the state legislature, South Carolina thereby becoming the first state to secede from the Union.

December 26—United States troops commanded by Major Robert Anderson stole under cover of night from indefensible

Fort Moultrie to Fort Sumter, out in the harbor of Charleston, South Carolina.

December 27—Messrs. Barnwell, Orr, and Adams, commissioners from South Carolina, arrived in Washington to treat with the administration for the forts in the harbor.

Castle Pinckney and Fort Moultrie in Charleston Harbor were seized by the South Carolina authorities; no resistance was encountered.

The U.S. revenue cutter *William Aiken* was seized by the authorities of South Carolina.

December 29—John B. Floyd of Virginia, secretary of war, resigned at the request of President Buchanan because of the scandal surrounding him.

December 30—The U.S. Arsenal, Customhouse, and Post Office at Charleston, South Carolina, were seized by state authorities.

<hr>

1861

January 2—Fort Johnson, in Charleston Harbor, was seized by state authorities.

January 3—Fort Pulaski, Georgia, was seized by state authorities.

The War Department reversed former Secretary of War Floyd's orders to move big guns from Pittsburgh to forts in the South (which were likely to be seized by secessionists).

January 4—The U.S. Arsenal at Mt. Vernon, Alabama, was seized by state authorities.

January 5—Forts Morgan and Gaines, Mobile Bay, Alabama, were seized by state authorities.

The first expedition for relief of Fort Sumter, South Carolina, departed from New York City Harbor on the side-wheeler *Star of the West.* It had been authorized by Buchanan, who declared that he would defend Fort Sumter "against hostile attacks from whatever quarter."

January 6—The U.S. Arsenal at Apalachicola, Florida, was seized by state authorities.

January 7—Fort Marion, St. Augustine, Florida, was seized by state authorities.

January 8—Jacob Thompson of Mississippi, Buchanan's secretary of the interior, resigned.

A Federal guard at Fort Barrancas, in Pensacola, Florida, opened fire on twenty state troopers advancing toward him who were probably trying to determine if Barrancas had been abandoned. The troopers fled. Some historians hold that the sentry fired the first shots of the Civil War.

January 9—The *Star of the West,* conveying relief to Fort Sumter, was fired upon at the entrance to Charleston Harbor and driven back. These shots, too, have been described as the first of the Civil War.

Fort Caswell, North Carolina, was seized by citizens of Smithville and Wilmington.

January 10—An ordinance of secession was adopted in Florida.

U.S. troops under Lieutenant Adam J. Slemmer were transferred from Barrancas barracks to Fort Pickens, out in the harbor of Pensacola, Florida.

Reinforcements for the troops at Pensacola sailed from Boston, Massachusetts.

The U.S. Arsenal and barracks at Baton Rouge, Louisiana, were seized by state authorities.

January 11—The surrender of Fort Sumter was demanded by Governor Pickens of South Carolina and refused by Major Anderson.

Forts Jackson and St. Philip, in Louisiana, were seized by state authorities.

The U.S. marine hospital near New Orleans, Louisiana, was seized by state authorities.

January 12—The surrender of Fort Pickens, Florida, was demanded by the governors of Florida and Alabama and refused by Lieutenant Slemmer.

Barrancas barracks, forts Barrancas and McRee, and the U.S. navy yard at Pensacola, Florida, were seized by state authorities.

January 14—Fort Taylor, Key West, Florida, was garrisoned by U.S. troops in one of the few Federal government counter-moves against the secessionists; it became an important coaling station during the war.

Fort Pike, Louisiana, was seized by state authorities.

January 15—U.S. coast survey steamer *Dana* was seized at St. Augustine, Florida.

January 20—U.S. Fort Massachusetts on Ship Island, Mississippi, which controlled traffic on the Mississippi River, was seized by state authorities.

January 21—Abolitionist Wendell Phillips hailed the secession of slave states, saying in effect that the Union was better off without them.

January 24—Reinforcements for Fort Pickens, Florida, sailed from Fort Monroe, Virginia.

The U.S. Arsenal at Augusta, Georgia, was seized by state authorities.

January 26—Oglethorpe barracks and Fort Jackson, Georgia, were seized by state authorities.

An ordinance of secession was adopted in Louisiana.

January 28—Fort Macomb, Louisiana, was seized by state authorities.

U.S. property in the hands of army officers were seized at New Orleans, Louisiana.

February 1—An ordinance of secession was adopted in Texas. The U.S. Mint and Customhouse at New Orleans, Louisiana, were seized by state authorities.

February 4—A peace conference, representing thirteen free and seven border states, was called at Washington at the request of the Virginia legislature. (See February 28, 1861.)
A convention of the seceded states met at Montgomery, Alabama.

February 6—The *Brooklyn* arrived off Pensacola with reinforcements for Fort Pickens, Florida, but Pickens still wasn't reinforced mainly because Federal authorities did not want to disturb the balance of power.

February 7—The Choctaw nation of Indians declared its loyalty to the Southern states.

February 8—The U.S. Arsenal at Little Rock, Arkansas, was seized by state authorities.
A Constitution for the Provisional Government of the Confederate States of America was adopted at Montgomery, Alabama, by deputies from the state of Alabama, Florida, Georgia, Louisiana, Mississippi, and South Carolina.

February 9—Jefferson Davis of Mississippi was elected president and Alexander H. Stephens of Georgia vice-president of the Confederate States of America, by the Montgomery convention.

February 13—Abraham Lincoln and Hannibal Hamlin were officially declared the elected President and Vice-President of the United States.

February 15—The Confederate Congress passed a resolution for the appointment of commissioners to the government of the United States. Martin J. Crawford, John Forsyth, and A. B. Roman later left for Washington.

February 16—The U.S. Arsenal and barracks at San Antonio, Texas, were seized by state authorities.

February 18—Jefferson Davis and Alexander H. Stephens were inaugurated at Montgomery, Alabama.

February 21—Camp Cooper, Texas, was abandoned by U.S. troops. (During the next six months many other U.S. military posts in Texas and New Mexico were abandoned.)

February 23—Abraham Lincoln arrived in Washington. He was disguised as an invalid on his journey from New York.

February 26—The Confederate Congress passed an act to organize a general staff for the army.

February 28—The U.S. House of Representatives adopted a constitutional amendment offered by the Committee of Thirty-three forbidding any interference by Congress with slavery in the states. (This amendment was adopted by the Senate March 2, but never ratified by the necessary number of states.)

The Confederate Congress passed an act to raise provisional forces.

March 1—The president of the Confederate States assumed control of military affairs in the states of Alabama, Florida, Georgia, Louisiana, Mississippi, South Carolina, and Texas.

March 2—The U.S. revenue cutter *Dodge* was seized at Galveston, Texas, by state authorities.

Texas was admitted as a member of the Confederate States of America.

March 3—Brigadier General G. T. Beauregard, Confederate States Army, assumed command at Charleston, South Carolina.

March 4—Abraham Lincoln was inaugurated as President of the United States.

March 6—The Confederate Congress passed an act for the establishment of an army, not to exceed 100,000 men, for twelve months' service.

March 7—Ringgold barracks, Texas, was abandoned by Union troops.

Camp Verde, Texas, was abandoned by Union troops.

March 11—Brigadier General Braxton Bragg assumed command of Confederate forces in Florida.

The Constitution of the Confederate States of America was adopted at Montgomery, Alabama. It followed in general the Constitution of the United States, but prohibited the passage of any "law denying or impairing the right of property in negro slaves"; prohibited "the importation of negroes of the African race from any foreign country other than the slave-holding States and territories of the United States of America"; and gave to the Confederate Congress "power to prohibit the introduction of slaves from any State not a member of or territory not belonging to" the Confederacy. The preamble included a declaration of the "sovereign and independent character" of each state.

March 15—The Confederate Congress passed an act authorizing the construction or purchase of ten gunboats.

March 16—Arizona Territory voted to leave the Union and join the Confederacy. The Confederacy the same day appointed commissioners to Great Britain.

April 7—Reinforcements for Fort Pickens sailed from New York.

April 10—The second expedition for the relief of Fort Sumter sailed from New York.

April 11—The evacuation of Fort Sumter was demanded by General Beauregard.

April 12—Troops from Fort Monroe, Virginia, landed at Fort Pickens, Florida, and Fort Pickens was finally reinforced.

The bombardment of Fort Sumter commenced.

April 13—Fort Sumter surrendered.

April 14—Fort Sumter was evacuated by its garrison and occupied by the forces of the Confederate states.

April 15—President Lincoln issued a call for 75,000 militia for three months' service and a summons to Congress to assemble on July 4.

Appendix II: List of Union Officers, Enlisted Men, and Workmen Present at the Bombardment of Fort Sumter, April 12 and 13, 1861*

Commissioned Officers
Major Robert Anderson, First United States Artillery
Captain Abner Doubleday, First United States Artillery
Captain Truman Seymour, First United States Artillery
First Lieutenant Jefferson C. Davis, First United States Artillery
Second Lieutenant Norman J. Hall, First United States Artillery
Captain J. G. Foster, United States Engineers
Lieutenant G. W. Snyder, United States Engineers
Lieutenant R. K. Meade, United States Engineers
Assistant Surgeon S. W. Crawford, United States Army

Enlisted Men
Ordnance-sergeant James Kearney, United States Army
Quartermaster-sergeant William H. Hammer, First United States Artillery
Sergeant Peter Hart

Regimental Band, First Artillery
Sergeant James E. Galway   Private Peter Rice
Corporal Andrew Smith   Private Henry Schmidt
Private Andrew Murphy   Private John Urquhart
Private Fedeschi Onoratti   Private Andrew Wickstrom

---

*Adapted from Abner Doubleday's out of print *Reminiscences of Fort Sumter and Moultrie in 1860-61* (1876).

Company E, First Artillery
First Sergeant Eugene Scheibner
Sergeant James Chester
Sergeant William A. Harn
Sergeant Thomas Kirnan
Corporal Charles Bringhurst
Corporal Henry Ellerbrook
Corporal Owen M'Guire
Corporal Francis J. Oakes
Musician Charles Hall
Private Philip Anderman
Private Cornelius Baker
Private Thomas Carroll
Private Patrick Clancey
Private John Davis
Private James Digdam
Private George Fielding
Private Edward Gallway
Private James Gibbons
Private James Hays
Private Daniel Hough
Private John Irwin
Private James M'Donald
Private Samuel Miller
Private John Newport
Private John Emil Noack
Private George Pinchard
Private Frank Rivers
Private Lewis Schroeder
Private Carl A. Sellman
Private John Thompson
Private Charles H. Tozer
Private William Witzman

Company H, First Artillery
First Sergeant John Renehan
Sergeant James M'Mahon
Sergeant John Carmody
Sergeant John Otto
Corporal Christopher Costolan
Musician Robert Foster
Artificer Henry Strandt
Private Edward Brady
Private Barney Cain
Private John Doran
Private Dennis Johnson
Private John Kehoe
Private John Klein
Private John Lanagan
Private John Laroche
Private Frederick Lintner
Private John Magill
Private Frederick Meier
Private James Moore
Private William Morter
Private Patrick Neilan
Private John Nixon
Private Michael O'Donald
Private Robert Roe
Private William Walker
Private Joseph Wall
Private Edmond Walsh
Private Henry R. Walter
Private Herman Will
Private Thomas Wishnowski
Private Casper Wutterpel

Mechanics and Employees
George Coons, mason
John Schweirer, mason
John Buckley, smith

Wm. O. Lyman, overseer
John Lindsay, carpenter
John Saxton, rigger
James Tweedle, smith

Laborers
Michael Berne
John Branley
John Burns
Peter Caine
Patrick Conner
Michael Cummins
Edward Davis
Patrick Donahoe
Peter Donley
William Dorsey
William Eagen
Andrew Felton
Michael Goff
Patrick Heeney
James Howlett

Andrew Lindsey
Dennis Magrath
John M'Carty
James M'Mahon
Michael Meechins
Thomas Murphy
Thomas Myers
William Powers
Edward Quinn
Patrick Quinn
Martin Rafferty
John Riley
Michael Ryan
Jeremiah Ryan
James Ryan
James Shea

Cooks
Samuel Abraze

Patrick Walsh

Appendix III: Confederate Batteries at the Battle of Fort Sumter*

ON MORRIS ISLAND

Brigadier-general James W. Simons, commanding; Colonel Wilmot G. De Saussure, commanding Artillery Battalion; Lieutenant J. R. Macbeth, Captain J. Jones, and Lieutenant F. L. Childs, acting as aides to Colonel De Saussure.

STEVENS BATTERY
(fired 1,200 shots from three 8-inch Columbiads)

Garrisoned by the Palmetto Guard, Captain George B. Cuthbert, commanding; Lieutenant G. L. Buist. The ammunition was served out by Mr. Phillips and Mr. Campbell. One gun was disabled on Friday.

CUMMINGS POINT BATTERY
(two 42-pounders, three 10-inch mortars, one Blakely gun)

Garrisoned by a detachment of the Palmetto Guard and by cadets from The Citadel academy in Charleston. Captain J. P. Thomas of The Citadel, commanding Blakely gun; Lieutenant C. R. Holmes of The Citadel, commanding mortars; Lieutenant W. W. Armstrong of The Citadel, at the mortars; Second Lieutenant Thomas Sumter of the Palmetto Guard, in charge of the 42-pounders.

CHANNEL BATTERY (did not fire)

Captain Calhoun, commanding; First Lieutenant A. M. Wagner; Lieutenant _____ Sitgreaves; Second Lieutenant M. C. Preston.

---

*Adapted from Abner Doubleday's out of print *Reminiscences of Forts Sumter and Moultrie in 1860–61* (1876). The number of shots fired by Confederate batteries in this compilation far exceeds the 3,307-shot total given in the *Official Records of the Union and Confederate Armies in the War of the Rebellion.*

SUMTER

ON JAMES ISLAND
Major N. G. Evans, A. A. G., commanding.

BATTERY OF 24-POUNDERS
Captain George S. James, commanding.

MORTAR BATTERY
First Lieutenant W. H. Gibbes of the Artillery; Lieutenant H. S. Farley; Lieutenant J. E. M'Pherson, Washington; Lieutenant T. B. Hayne; Doctor Libby.

UPPER BATTERY (fired 2,425 shots from two 10-inch mortars) and LOWER BATTERY (two 10-inch mortars) Captain S. C. Thayer of the South Carolina Navy, commanding.

ON SULLIVAN'S ISLAND
Brigadier-general John Dunovant, commanding; Lieutenant-colonel Roswell S. Ripley, commanding the Artillery; Captain J. B. Burns, of General Dunovant's staff; Surgeons P. J. Robinson, R. F. Mitchell, and Arthur Lynch; Assistant-surgeons D. W. Taylor, Doctor F. F. Miles, Doctor F. L. Parker.

THE IRONCLAD FLOATING BATTERY (at the cove, fired 1,900 shots from two 42-pounders and two 32-pounders) Garrisoned by Company D, of the Artillery. Captain James Hamilton; First Lieutenant J. A. Yates; Second Lieutenant F. H. Harleston.

THE DAHLGREN BATTERY
(near the Floating Battery, with one 9-inch Dahlgren gun) Garrisoned by Company D, of the Artillery. Captain S. R. Hamilton; Mr. John Wells.

THE ENFILADE BATTERY (fired 1,825 shots)
Garrisoned by Company K, of the Artillery, Captain James H. Hallonquist, Company B of the Artillery, commanding; First Lieutenant J. Valentine; B. S. Burnett.

260

MORTAR BATTERY No. 1
(between Fort Moultrie and the cove)
Captain James H. Hallonquist, Company B of the Artillery, commanding; Lieutenant O. Blanding; Lieutenant Fleming.

FORT MOULTRIE (fired 1,825 shots from three 8-inch Columbiads, two 32-pounders, and four 24-pounders)
Garrisoned by the Artillery Battalion under Lieutenant-colonel Ripley. Captain W. R. Calhoun, Company A of the Artillery, executive officer.

SUMTER BATTERY (facing south-south-west)
Lieutenant Alfred Rhett, Company B, Artillery, commanding; Second Lieutenant John Mitchell, Jun.; Mr. F. D. Blake, Volunteer Engineer.

OBLIQUE BATTERY (on the west, with two 24-pounders)
Lieutenant C. W. Parker, Company D, of the Artillery.

MORTAR BATTERY No. 2
(east of Fort Moultrie with two 10-inch mortars)
Captain William Butler of the Infantry; Lieutenant J. A. Hugenin; E. Mowry, Mr. Blocker, Mr. Billings, and Mr. Rice assisted. This battery was joined to the Maffit Channel Battery.

TRAPIER BATTERY
(fired 1,300 shots from three 10-inch mortars)
Garrisoned by the Marion Artillery, J. Gadsden King, commanding. Lieutenant W. D. H. Kirkwood, J. P. Strohecker, A. M. Huger, E. L. Parker. The Marion Artillery was afterward relieved by the Sumter Guard, under Captain John Russell.

AT MOUNT PLEASANT BATTERY
(fired 2,925 shots from two 10-inch mortars)
Captain Robert Martin of the Infantry, commanding; Lieutenant G. N. Reynolds, Company B, of the Artillery; Lieutenant D. S. Calhoun of the Infantry.

Appendix IV: The South Carolina Declaration of Causes

The people of the State of South Carolina in Convention assembled, on the 2d day of April, A.D. 1852, declared that the frequent violations of the Constitution of the United States by the federal government, and its encroachments upon the reserved rights of the states, fully justified this state in their withdrawal from the federal Union; but, in deference to the opinions and wishes of the other slaveholding states, she forbore at that time to exercise this right. Since that time these encroachments have continued to increase, and farther forbearance ceases to be a virtue.

And now the State of South Carolina, having resumed her separate and equal place among nations, deems it due to herself, to the remaining United States of America, and to the nations of the world, that she should declare the immediate causes which have led to this act.

In the year 1765, that portion of the British Empire embracing Great Britain undertook to make laws for the government of that portion composed of the thirteen American colonies. A struggle for the right of self-government ensued, which resulted, on the 4th of July, 1776, in a declaration, by the colonies, "that they are, and of right ought to be, FREE AND INDEPENDENT STATES; and that, as free and independent states, they have full power to levy war, conclude peace, contract alliances, establish commerce, and to do all other acts and things which independent states may of right do."

They farther solemnly declared that whenever any "form of government becomes destructive of the ends for which it was established, it is the right of the people to alter or abolish it, and to institute a new government." Deeming the government of Great Britain to have become destructive of these ends, they declared that the colonies "are absolved from all allegiance to the British crown, and that all political connection between them and the state of Great Britain is, and ought to be, totally dissolved."

In pursuance of this Declaration of Independence, each of the thirteen states proceeded to exercise its separate sovereignty; adopted for itself a Constitution, and appointed officers for the administration of government in all its departments — legislative, executive, and judicial. For purposes of defense they united their arms and their counsels; and in 1778 they entered into a league known as the Articles of Confederation, whereby they agreed to intrust the administration of their external relations to a common agent, known as the Congress of the United States, expressly declaring, in the first article, "that each state retains its sovereignty, freedom, and independence, and every power, jurisdiction, and right which is not, by this Confederation, expressly delegated to the United States in Congress assembled."

Under this confederation the War of the Revolution was carried on; and on the 3d of September, 1783, the contest ended, and a definite treaty was signed by Great Britain, in which she acknowledged the independence of the colonies in the following terms:

"ARTICLE 1. His Britannic majesty acknowledges the said United States, viz.: New Hampshire, Massachusetts Bay, Rhode Island and Providence Plantations, Connecticut, New York, New Jersey, Pennsylvania, Delaware, Maryland, Virginia, North Carolina, South Carolina, and Georgia, to be FREE, SOVEREIGN, AND INDEPENDENT STATES; that he treats with them as such; and, for himself, his heirs and successors, relinquishes all claims to the government, propriety, and territorial rights of the same, and every part thereof."

Thus were established the two great principles asserted by the colonies, namely, the right of a state to govern itself, and the right of a people to abolish a government when it becomes destructive of the ends for which it was instituted. And concurrent with the establishment of these principles was the fact that each colony became and was recognized by the mother country as a FREE, SOVEREIGN, AND INDEPENDENT STATE.

In 1787, deputies were appointed by the states to revise the Articles of Confederation; and on the 17th of September, 1787, these deputies recommended, for the adoption of the states, the Articles of Union known as the Constitution of the United States.

The parties to whom this Constitution was submitted were the several sovereign states; they were to agree or disagree; and when nine of them agreed, the compact was to take effect among those concurring; and the general government, as the common agent, was then to be invested with their authority.

If only nine of the thirteen states had concurred, the other four would have remained as they then were—separate sovereign states, independent of any of the provisions of the Constitution. In fact, two of the states did not accede to the Constitution until long after it had gone into operation among the other eleven, and during that interval they each exercised the functions of an independent nation.

By this Constitution certain duties were imposed upon the several states, and the exercise of certain of their powers was restrained, which necessarily impelled their continued existence as sovereign states. But, to remove all doubt, an amendment was added, which declared that the powers not delegated to the United States by the Constitution, nor prohibited by it to the states, are reserved to the states respectively, or to the people. On the 23d of May, 1788, South Carolina, by a Convention of her people, passed an ordinance assenting to this Constitution, and afterward altered her own Constitution to conform herself to the obligations she had undertaken.

Thus was established, by compact between the states, a government with defined objects and powers, limited to the express words of the grant. This limitation left the whole remaining mass of power subject to the clause reserving it to the states or to the people, and rendered unnecessary any specification of reserved rights. We hold that the government thus established is subject to the two great principles asserted in the Declaration of Independence; and we hold farther, that the mode of its formation subjects it to a third fundamental principle, namely, the law of compact. We maintain that in every compact between two or more parties the obligation is mutual; that the failure of one of the contracting parties to perform a material part of the agreement entirely releases the obligation of the other; and that, where no arbiter is provided, each party is remitted to his own judgment to determine the fact of failure, with all its consequences.

In the present case that fact is established with certainty. We assert that fourteen of the states have deliberately refused for years past to fulfill their constitutional obligations, and we refer to their own statutes for the proof.

The Constitution of the United States, in its fourth article, provides as follows:

"No person held to service or labor in one state under the laws thereof, escaping into another, shall, in consequence of any law or regulation therein, be discharged from such service or labor, but shall be delivered up on claim of the party to whom such service or labor may be due."

This stipulation was so material to the compact that without it that compact would not have been made. The greater number of the contracting parties held slaves, and they had previously evinced their estimate of the value of such a stipulation by making it a condition in the ordinance for the government of the territory ceded by Virginia, which obligations, and the laws of the general government, have ceased to effect the objects of the Constitution. The states of Maine, New Hampshire, Vermont, Massachusetts, Connecticut, Rhode Island, New York, Pennsylvania, Illinois, Indiana, Michigan, Wisconsin, and Iowa have enacted laws which either nullify the acts of Congress, or render useless any attempt to execute them. In many of these states the fugitive is discharged from the service of labor claimed, and in none of them has the state government complied with the stipulation made in the Constitution. The State of New Jersey at an early day passed a law in conformity with her constitutional obligation; but the current of anti-slavery feeling has led her more recently to enact laws which render inoperative the remedies provided by her own laws and by the laws of Congress. In the State of New York even the right of transit for a slave has been denied by her tribunals; and the states of Ohio and Iowa have refused to surrender to justice fugitives charged with murder, and with inciting servile insurrection in the State of Virginia. Thus the constitutional compact has been deliberately broken and disregarded by the non-slaveholding states, and the consequence follows that South Carolina is released from her obligation.

The ends for which this Constitution was framed are declared by itself to be "to form a more perfect union, to establish justice, insure domestic tranquillity, provide for the common defense, promote the general welfare, and secure the blessings of liberty to ourselves and our posterity."

These ends it endeavored to accomplish by a federal government, in which each state was recognized as an equal, and had separate control over its own institutions. The right of property in slaves was recognized by giving to free persons distinct political rights; by giving them the right to represent, and burdening them with direct taxes for three fifths of their slaves; by authorizing the importation of slaves for twenty years; and by stipulating for the rendition of fugitives from labor.

We affirm that these ends for which this government was instituted have been defeated, and the government itself has been destructive of them by the action of the non-slaveholding states. Those states have assumed the right of deciding upon the propriety of our domestic institutions, and have denied the rights of property established in fifteen of the states and recognized by the Constitution; they have denounced as sinful the institution of slavery; they have permitted the open establishment among them of societies whose avowed object is to disturb the peace of and eloin the property of the citizens of other states. They have encouraged and assisted thousands of our slaves to leave their homes; and those who remain have been incited by emissaries, books, and pictures to servile insurrection.

For twenty-five years this agitation has been steadily increasing, until it has now secured to its aid the power of the common government. Observing the *forms* of the Constitution, a sectional party has found within that article establishing the Executive Department the means of subverting the Constitution itself. A geographical line has been drawn across the Union, and all the states north of that line have united in the election of a man to the high office of President of the United States whose opinions and purposes are hostile to slavery. He is to be intrusted with the administration of the common government because he has declared that that "government can not endure permanently half slave, half free," and that the public mind must rest in the belief that slavery is in the course of ultimate extinction.

This sectional combination for the subversion of the Constitution has been aided in some of the states by elevating to citizenship persons who, by the supreme law of the land, are incapable of becoming citizens; and their votes have been used to inaugurate a new policy, hostile to the South, and destructive of its peace and safety.

On the 4th of March next this party will take possession of the government. It has announced that the South shall be excluded from the common territory, that the judicial tribunal shall be made sectional, and that a war must be waged against slavery until it shall cease throughout the United States.

The guarantees of the Constitution will then no longer exist, the equal rights of the states will be lost. The slaveholding states will no longer have the power of self-government or self-protection, and the federal government will have become their enemy.

Sectional interest and animosity will deepen the irritation; and all hope of remedy is rendered vain by the fact that the public opinion at the North has invested a great political error with the sanctions of a more erroneous religious belief.

We, therefore, the people of South Carolina, by our delegates in Convention assembled, appealing to the Supreme Judge of the world for the rectitude of our intentions, have solemnly declared that the union heretofore existing between this state and the other states of North America is dissolved, and that the State of South Carolina has resumed her position among the nations of the world as a separate and independent state, with full power to levy war, conclude peace, contract alliances, establish commerce, and to do all other acts and things which independent states may of right do.

Appendix V: Southern Ordinances of Secession

SOUTH CAROLINA.

DECEMBER 20, 1860.

Vote of Convention—Unanimous.

---

*GOVERNOR FRANCIS W PICKENS.

At a convention of the people of the State of South Carolina, begun and holden at Columbia on the 17th day of December, in the year of our Lord one thousand eight hundred and sixty, and thence continued by adjournment to Charleston, and there, by divers adjournments, to the 20th of December in the same year:

An Ordinance to dissolve the Union between the State of South Carolina and other States united with her under the Compact entitled the Constitution of the United States of America.

We. the people of the State of South Carolina, in convention assembled, do declare and ordain, and it is hereby declared and ordained, that the ordinance adopted by us in convention on the 23d day of May, in the year of our Lord one thousand seven hundred and eighty-eight, whereby the Constitution of the United States of America was ratified, and also all acts and parts of acts of the General Assembly of this State ratifying amendments of said Constitution, are hereby repealed; and that the Union now subsisting between South Carolina and other States, under the name of The United States of America, is hereby dissolved.

Done at Charleston, the 20th day of December, in the year of our Lord one thousand eight hundred and sixty.

D. F. JAMISON,
*Delegate from Barnwell and President of the Convention,
and others.*
Attest: BENJAMIN F. ARTHUR, *Clerk of the Convention.*

MISSISSIPPI.

JANUARY 9, 1861.

Vote of Convention—84-15.

---

* GOVERNOR JOHN J. PETTUS.

The people of Mississippi, in convention assembled, do ordain and declare, and it is hereby ordained and declared, as follows, to-wit:

That all the laws and ordinances by which the said State of Mississippi became a member of the Federal Union of the United States of America be, and the same are hereby, repealed; and that all obligations on the part of said State, or the people thereof, to observe the same, be withdrawn; and that the said State shall hereby resume the rights, functions and powers which by any of said laws and ordinances were conveyed to the Government of the said United States, and is dissolved from all the obligations, restraints and duties incurred to the said Federal Union, and shall henceforth be a free, sovereign and independent State.

ALABAMA.

JANUARY 11, 1861.

Vote of Convention—61-39.

*GOVERNOR ANDREW D. MOORE.

An Ordinance to dissolve the Union between the State of Alabama and other States united under the Compact and style of the United States of America.

WHEREAS, The election of Abraham Lincoln and Hannibal Hamlin to tne offices of President and Vice-President of the United States of America by a sectional party, avowedly hostile to the domestic institutions and the peace and security of the people of the State of Alabama, following upon the heels of many and dangerous infractions of the Constitution of the United States by many of the States and people of the Northern section, is a political wrong of so insulting and menacing a character as to justify the people of the State of Alabama in the adoption of prompt and decided measures for their future peace and security.

Therefore, be it declared and ordained by the people of the State of Alabama, in convention assembled, that the State of Alabama now withdraws from the Union known as the United States of America, and henceforth ceases to be one of the said United States, and is, and of right ought to be, a sovereign independent State.

SECTION 2. And be it further declared and ordained by the people of the State of Alabama, in convention assembled, that all powers over the territories of said State and over the people thereof, heretofore delegated to the Government of the United States of America, be, and they are hereby, withdrawn from the said Government, and are hereby resumed and vested in the people of the State of Alabama.

And as it is the desire and purpose of the people of Alabama to meet the Slaveholding States of the South who approve of such a purpose, in order to frame a provisional or a permanent government, upon the principles of the Government of the United States, be it also

Resolved by the people of Alabama, in convention assembled, that the people of the States of Delaware, Maryland, Virginia, North Carolina, South Carolina, Florida, Georgia, Mississippi, Louisiana, Texas, Arkansas, Tennessee, Kentucky and Missouri be, and they are hereby, invited to meet the people of the State of Alabama, by their delegates, in convention, on the 4th day of February next, in Montgomery, in the State of Alabama, for the purpose of consultation with each other as to the most effectual mode of securing concerted, harmonious action in whatever measures may be deemed most desirable for the common peace and security. And be it

Further Resolved, That the president of this convention be, and he is hereby, instructed to transmit forthwith a copy of the foregoing preamble, ordinance and resolutions to the Governors of the several States named in the said resolutions.

Done by the people of Alabama, in convention assembled, at Montgomery, this 11th day of January, 1861.

271

FLORIDA.

JANUARY 11, 1861.

Vote of Convention—62-7.

---

* GOVERNOR M. S. PERRY.

An Ordinance to dissolve the Union now existing between the State of Florida and other States united with her under the Compact of Government, entitled the Constitution of the United States.

WHEREAS, All hope of preserving the Union upon terms consistent with the safety and honor of the Slaveholding States has been finally dissipated by the recent indications of the strength of the anti-slavery sentiment of the Free States ; therefore,

Be it resolved by the people of Florida, in convention assembled, That it is undoubtedly the right of the several States of the Union, at such time, and for such cause as in the opinion of the people of such State, acting in their sovereign capacity, may be just and proper ; and, in the opinion of this convention, the existing causes are such as to compel Florida to proceed to exercise that right.

We, the people of the State of Florida, in convention assembled, do solemnly ordain, publish and declare that the State of Florida hereby withdraws herself from the Confederacy of States existing under the name of the United States of America, and from the existing Government of the said States ; and that all political connection between her and the Government of said States ought to be, and the same is hereby, totally annulled, and said Union of States dissolved ; and the State of Florida is hereby declared a sovereign and independent nation ; and that all ordinances heretofore adopted, in so far as they create or recognize said Union, are rescinded ; and all laws, or parts of laws, in force in this State, in so far as they recognize or assent to said Union, be, and they are hereby, repealed.

272

GEORGIA.

JANUARY 19, 1861.

Vote of Convention—208-29.

*GOVERNOR JOSEPH E. BROWN.

An Ordinance to dissolve the Union between the State of Georgia and other States united with her under the Compact of Government entitled the Constitution of the United States.

We, the people of the State of Georgia, in convention assembled, do declare and ordain, and it is hereby declared and ordained, that the ordinances adopted by the people of the State of Georgia in convention in 1788, whereby the Constitution of the United States was assented to, ratified and adopted, and also all acts and parts of acts of the General Assembly ratifying and adopting amendments to the said Constitution, are hereby repealed, rescinded and abrogated.

And we do further declare and ordain that the Union now subsisting between the State of Georgia and other States, under the name of the United States, is hereby dissolved, and that the State of Georgia is in full possession and exercise of all those rights of sovereignty which belong and appertain to a free and independent State.

LOUISIANA.

JANUARY 26, 1861.

Vote of Convention—113-17.

---

* GOVERNOR THOMAS OVERTON MOORE.

---

*An ordinance to dissolve the Union between the State of Louis-
iana and the other States united with her under the Compact entitled the Constitution of the United States of
America.*

We, the people of the State of Louisiana, in convention assembled, do
declare and ordain, and it is hereby declared and ordained, that the ordinance passed by the State of Louisiana, on the 22d day of November, 1807,
whereby the Constitution of the United States of America and the amendments of said Constitution were adopted, and all the laws and ordinances
by which Louisana became a member of the Federal Union, be, and the
same are hereby, repealed and abrogated, and the Union now subsisting
between Louisiana and the other States, under the name of the United
States of America, is hereby dissolved.

We further declare and ordain that the State of Louisiana hereby
resumes the rights and powers heretofore delegated to the Government of
the United States of America, and its citizens are absolved from allegiance
to the said Government, and she is in full possession of all the rights and
sovereignty that appertain to a free and independent State.

We further declare and ordain that all rights acquired and vested
under the Constitution of the United States, or any act of Congress or
treaty, or under laws of this State, not incompatible with this ordinance,
shall remain in force and have the same effect as though this ordinance
had not passed.

We, the people of Louisiana, recognize the right of free navigation
of the Mississippi River and tributaries by all friendly States bordering
thereon : we also recognize the right of the ingress and egress of the
mouths of the Mississippi by all friendly States and powers, and hereby
declare our willingness to enter into stipulations to guarantee the exercise
of those rights.

TEXAS.

FEBRUARY 1, 1861.

Vote of Convention—166-7.

---

*GOVERNOR EDWARD CLARK.

An Ordinance to dissolve the Union between the State of Texas and the other States under the Compact styled the Constitution of the United States of America.

WHEREAS, The Federal Government has failed to accomplish the purposes of the compact of union between these States, in giving protection either to the persons of our people upon an exposed frontier, or to the property of our citizens, and

WHEREAS, The action of the Northern States is violative of the compact between the States and the guarantees of the Constitution ; and,

WHEREAS, The recent developments in Federal affairs make it evident that the power of the Federal Government is sought to be made a weapon with which to strike down the interests and property of the people of Texas, and her sister Slaveholding States, instead of permitting it to be, as was intended, our shield against outrage and aggression,

Therefore, We, the people of the State of Texas, by delegates in convention assembled, do declare and ordain that the ordinance adopted by our convention of delegates on the fourth (4th) day of July, A. D. 1845, and afterward ratified by us, under which the Republic of Texas was admitted into the Union with other States, and became a party to the compact styled " The Constitution of the United States of America," be, and is hereby, repealed and annulled.

That all the powers which, by the said compact, were delegated by Texas to the Federal Government are resumed. That Texas is of right absolved from all restraints and obligations incurred by said compact, and is a separate sovereign State, and that her citizens and people are absolved from all allegiance to the United States or the government thereof.

275

Bibliography

Sources I relied on most heavily, from the hundreds consulted, are listed here; some other books and pamphlets, however, are mentioned in the text, as are many newspapers and magazines of the time, North and South, that were used.

Anderson, Robert. *An Artillery Officer in the Mexican War: Letters of Anderson* . . . (1911).

Anonymous. *The Diary of a Public Man* (1946).

Bakeless, John. *Spies of the Confederacy* (1970).

Barnes, Frank. *Fort Sumter, National Park Service Historical Handbook Series No. 12* (1952).

Barton, E. Milby. *The Siege of Charleston* (1970).

Basler, Roy P., ed. *Abraham Lincoln: His Speeches and Writings* (1946).

Basso, Hamilton. *Beauregard, the Great Creole* (1933).

Blassingame, John W. *The Slave Community: Plantation Life in the Antebellum South* (1972).

Brogan, D. W. *American Aspects* (1964).

Buchanan, James. *The Administration on the Eve of the Rebellion* (1865).

Buel, Clarence C., and Johnson, Robert U., eds. *Battles and Leaders of the Civil War,* 4 Vols. (1884-87).

Carson, James Petigru, ed. *Life, Letters and Speeches of James Louis Petigru* (1920).

Catton, Bruce. *The Coming Fury* (The Centennial History of the Civil War, Vol. 1) (1963).

Cauthen, Charles E. *South Carolina Goes To War,* 1860-1865 (1950).

Chesnut, Mary Boykin. *A Diary from Dixie* (1905).

Commager, Henry Steele, ed. *Documents of American History* (1958).

Craven, Avery. *Edmund Ruffin, Southerner* (1932).

Crawford, Samuel W. *The Genesis of the Civil War: The Story of Fort Sumter, 1860-1861* (1887).

Current, Richard N. *John C. Calhoun* (1966).

Current, Richard N. *Lincoln and the First Shot* (1963).

Curtis, George Ticknor. *The Life of James Buchanan* (1883).

Davis, Jefferson. *The Rise and Fall of the Confederate Government* (1881).

Dickert, D. Augustus. *History of Kershaw's Brigade* (1899).

Dictionary of American Biography, 22 Vols. (1928-58).

Doubleday, Abner. *Reminiscences of Forts Sumter and Moultrie in 1860-1861* (1876).

Eaton, Clement. *Jefferson Davis* (1977).

Elliott, Charles Winslow. *Winfield Scott, the Soldier and the Man* (1937).

Evans, Clement A. *A Confederate Military History* (1899).

Fite, Emerson D. *The Presidential Campaign of 1860* (1911).

Fort Sumter, Battle of, and the First Victory of the Southern Troops Compiled chiefly from the detailed reports of the Charleston Press (1861).

Genovese, Eugene D. *The Political Economy of Slavery* (1961).

Halsey, Ashley. *Who Fired The First Shot?* (1963).

Hamilton, Holman. *Prologue to Conflict* (1964).

Harper's Pictorial History of The Civil War (1866).

Harris, W. A., comp. *The Record of Fort Sumter from Its Occupation by Major Anderson to Its Reduction by South Carolina Troops.* Pamphlet (1862).

Helper, Hinton R. *The Impending Crisis of the South. How to Meet It.* Ed. by George M. Frederickson (1968).

Hendrick, Burton. *Statesmen of the Lost Cause* (1939).

Holmes, Emma. *Diary of Miss Emma Holmes, 1861-1866.* Ed. by John F. Marszalek (1979).

Holzman, Robert S. *Adapt or Perish: The Life of General Roger A. Pryor, C.S.A.* (1976).

Journal of the Convention of the People of South Carolina (1862).

Ketchem, Richard, ed. *The American Heritage Picture History of the Civil War* (1960).

King, Alvy L. *Louis T. Wigfall, Southern Fire-eater* (1970).

Klein, Philip S. *President James Buchanan* (1962).

Lawton, Eba Anderson. *Major Robert Anderson and Fort Sumter* (1911).

Lebbey, Robert. "The First Shot On Fort Sumter," *South Carolina Historical and Genealogical Magazine* (July 1911).

Lewis, Emmanuel Raymond. *Seacoast Fortifications of the United States: An Introductory History* (1970).

Lossing, Benson. *Pictorial History of the Civil War* (1866).

Mitchell, Betty L. *Edmund Ruffin* (1981).

Moore, Frank, ed. *Anecdotes, Poetry and Incidents of the War, North and South* (1866).

Moore, Frank, ed. *The Rebellion Record* (1861-1868).

Nevins, Allan. *The Improvised War, 1861-1862 (The War for the Union, Vol. 1)* (1959).

Nicolay, John G., and Hay, John. *Abraham Lincoln, a History* (1890).

Official Records of the Union and Confederate Armies in the War of the Rebellion (1880-1901).

Official Records of the Union and Confederate Navies in the War of the Rebellion (1894-1917).

Phillips, Ulrich. *Life of Robert Toombs* (1913).

Population of the United States in 1860: The Eighth Census (1864).

Randall, J. G., and David Donald. *The Divided Union* (1961).

Ravenel, Henry William. *The Private Journal of Henry William Ravenel* (1947).

Ravenel, Mrs. St. Julien. *Charleston, the Place and the People* (1927).

Roman, Alfred. *The Military Operations of General Beauregard*, 2 vols. (1884).

Rosengarten, Theodore. *Tombee: Portrait of a Cotton Planter* (1986).

Russell, William Howard. *My Diary, North and South* (1863).

Sandburg, Carl. *Abraham Lincoln: The War Years* (1939).

Scarborough, William K., ed. *The Diary of Edmund Ruffin* (1972).

Schaff, Morris. *The Spirit of Old West Point, 1858-1862* (1907).

Scott, Winfield. *Memoirs of Lieutenant General Scott, LL.D. Written by Himself*, 2 vols. (1864).

Seward, Frederick W. *Seward at Washington* (1891).

Smith, Elbert. *Francis Preston Blair* (1980).

Stampp, Kenneth M. *And The War Came: The North and the Secession Crisis* (1980).

Stern, Philip Van Doren, ed. *Prologue to Sumter: The Beginnings of the Civil War from the John Brown Raid to the Surrender of*

SUMTER

Fort Sumter (1961)
Stern, Philip Van Doren. *When the Guns Roared* (1965).
Strode, Hudson. *Jefferson Davis, American Patriot* (1955).
Strong, George Templeton. *The Diary of George Templeton Strong*, Vol. 3. Ed. by Allan Nevins and Milton Halsey Thomas (1952).
Swanberg, W. A. *First Blood: The Story of Fort Sumter* (1957).
Thomas, E. M. *The Confederate Nation* (1979).
Thompson, Robert M., and Richard Wainwright, eds. *Confidential Correspondence of Gustavus Vasa Fox* (1918).
Thompson, William Y. *Robert Toombs of Georgia* (1966).
United States Congress, *Congressional Globe*, 36th Congress, 1st. session, Vol. 1.
Warner, Ezra J. *Generals in Gray* (1959).
Weitenkampf, Frank. *Political Caricature in the United States* (1953).
Welles, Gideon. *The Diary of Gideon Welles . . .* (1911).
White, Laura A. *Robert Barnwell Rhett, Father of Secession* (1931).
Williams, T. Harry. *P. G. T. Beauregard, Napoleon in Gray* (1954).
Wiltse, Charles M. *John C. Calhoun* (1949).
Within Fort Sumter, or a View of Major Anderson's Garrison Family for One Hundred and Ten Days, By one of the Company (1861).
Yearns, Wilfred Buck. *The Confederate Congress* (1960).

The Robert Anderson papers are in the Library of Congress, as are Samuel W. Crawford's diary and papers of Francis Pickens; the letters of Private John Thompson are in the Public Record Office, Belfast, Ireland; and the diary of merchant Jacob Schirmer is in the South Carolina Historical Society. Newspapers and magazines consulted include the *Charleston Mercury*, the *Charleston Courier*, *The New York Times*, the *New York Leader*, the *New York World*, the *New York Herald*, the *New York Illustrated News*, the *Washington Star*, the *Philadelphia Inquirer*, *Frank Leslie's Illustrated Newspaper*, *Harper's Weekly*, and the *Atlantic Monthly*. The South Caroliniana Library in Columbia has a good collection of state newspapers, small and large, of the time as well as a great number of pertinent letters, diaries, and memoirs, as does the Charleston Library Society and the South Carolina Historical Society.

Index